Preparing for the 2023 California Clinical Social Work Law & Ethics Exam

Preparing for the 2023 California Clinical Social Work Law & Ethics Exam

Benjamin E. Caldwell, PsyD

ISBN-13: 979-8-9864668-0-4

Ben Caldwell Labs
346 Kanan Rd, Suite 103
Oak Park, CA 91377

www.bencaldwelllabs.com

Ordering Information:

U.S. trade bookstores and wholesalers: Please contact Ben Caldwell Labs via email at support@bencaldwelllabs.com.

To you
You've got this
Pass

Contents

Acknowledgements

Profound thanks to Marcia Castro-Rohrer, who makes all our systems here at Ben Caldwell Labs work. Thanks as well to Emma Ekum and Jeff Liebert, my friends and former teammates here at Ben Caldwell Labs, without whom this book would not exist.

Thanks to my wife Angela and our two amazing daughters, who I am humbled to call my family, for their unwavering support and encouragement. Not just with this book, but with all my advocacy efforts on behalf of therapists across career stages.

My gratitude as well to all those associates, students, instructors, and supervisors who used and provided feedback on earlier generations of this book. Your feedback has likely had some influence here.

And most importantly to you, using this book to prepare for your exam: Thank you for the good and important work you do. The path to becoming a licensed clinical social worker is not easy, nor should it be. That you have chosen this path says a great deal about who you are, and how much you have to give to your community. I'm proud to be part of your journey.

About the author

Benjamin E. Caldwell, PsyD is an Adjunct Professor teaching Law and Ethics for California State University Northridge in Los Angeles. He routinely advocates for prelicensed therapists at licensing board meetings, and has been directly involved in several important pieces of legislation in the past 15 years. His research papers have been published in the *Journal of Marital and Family Therapy*, *American Journal of Family Therapy*, *Journal of Divorce and Remarriage*, *Journal of Systemic Therapy*, and elsewhere. He regularly gives presentations on legal and ethical issues impacting therapy work.

Other books by Benjamin Caldwell:

Basics of California Law for LCSWs, LPCCs, and LCSWs, 10th edition (2023)
Preparing for the 2023 California MFT Law and Ethics Exam
Saving Psychotherapy: How therapists can bring the talking cure back from the brink (2015)

Books and exam prep resources:

Visit bencaldwelllabs.com

Continuing education courses led by Benjamin Caldwell:

Visit bencaldwelllabs.com and simplepracticelearning.com

***Psychotherapy Notes* blog:**

Visit psychotherapynotes.com

Disclaimers

The information in this book is believed to be accurate at the time of publication. However, mistakes can happen, and legal and ethical standards can change quickly. It is the responsibility of each individual therapist to make sure they are remaining current with legal and ethical standards of practice.

Neither this book, nor *any* book or test preparation program, can guarantee success on the exam. While of course we do the best we can to assist, and we believe that our guidance here can be a critical element in a successful study plan, your success on the test depends on your ability to learn and recall key information and apply it in the test setting.

While this book discusses legal requirements for the practice of clinical social work, it is intended to be used exclusively in the study process for the California Clinical Social Work Law and Ethics exam administered by the Board of Behavioral Sciences. It is not intended as case-specific legal or ethical advice. **No part of this book should be construed as legal advice or as a substitute for consultation with a qualified attorney.** If you need legal guidance, your professional liability insurer and your professional association may provide legal resources to you at no cost.

Introduction

First thing's first:
You've got this.

The California Clinical Social Work Law and Ethics Exam is 75 questions over 90 minutes, and it is *absolutely* a test that you can pass. You've taken a graduate-level course in Law and Ethics that was probably pretty good, and probably not all that long ago. But even if it was a while back or a bit lacking in quality, you can catch up with the current standards quickly.

As licensing exams go, this exam is narrowly focused. Later, when it comes time to take the ASWB Clinical Exam, you'll need to know the theory and interventions involved in many different models of treatment; you'll need to know more about assessment and diagnosis; and you'll need to know a wide variety of additional information on effective clinical care *in addition to* knowing the legal and ethical rules governing the profession. But **this first test is just about those legal and ethical rules.** In that way, it's a better test all around: It's shorter, it's more clearly geared to public safety, and on your side, it's easier to prepare for.

You've got this.

About this book

This book is meant solely to help you prepare for the California Clinical Social Work Law and Ethics Exam. It aims to be as efficient as possible in providing the critical, current information you need to know to be successful on the test.

There are three main sources for the information covered in this book:

1) The *NASW Code of Ethics*, available at socialworkers.org
2) *Basics of California Law for LMFTs, LPCCs, and LCSWs, 10th edition*, available on amazon.com and at bencaldwelllabs.com
3) California statutes and regulations, a summary of which is available at bbs.ca.gov (complete California law is available at leginfo.legislature.ca.gov)

In addition to those sources, several other articles and books were used in the development of this book. This is similar to how the test itself is developed: Licensed Clinical Social Workers use source material common in the field, and they develop questions assessing an examinee's knowledge of 128 "knowledge statements" outlined in the BBS Exam Plan for this test.

That Exam Plan is a public document available on the BBS web site and in the Appendix here, where it also serves as an Index. Because it so clearly specifies the knowledge needed for the test, the exam plan was also key to the development of this book: **Next to each header in the study guide, you will see small numbers that start with the letter K. These numbers indicate the knowledge statements, in the BBS Exam Plan, that are addressed in that section of the book.** As you'll see, this book covers all 128 knowledge statements used in the development of the exam.

Of course, this book is not a substitute for a graduate-level Law and Ethics course, or for the textbooks used in such a course. For a deeper dive on California law for clinical practice, I would recommend my *Basics of California Law for LMFTs, LPCCs, and LCSWs*. For more detailed texts on ethical issues for clinical social workers, I would recommend the following:

- ***Ethics in Psychotherapy and Counseling*** by K. S. Pope, M. J. T. Vasquez, N. Y. Chavez-Dueñas, & H. Y. Adames (6th edition, Wiley, 2021)
- ***Issues and Ethics in the Helping Professions*** by G. Corey, M. S. Corey, & C. Corey (10th edition, Brooks/Cole, 2018; the 11th edition is scheduled to publish in March 2023)
- ***Social Work Values and Ethics*** by F. G. Reamer (5th edition, Columbia University Press, 2018)

All the information you need to know for the exam comes from sources in the field, including the NASW Code of Ethics, state law and regulation, and the same Law and Ethics textbooks (like my *Basics of California Law* text) commonly used in social work graduate courses in the state. What this book does is **organize and filter** that knowledge in ways that should be useful, and then give you practice **applying** that knowledge in vignettes that approximate the actual exam.

Throughout this book, clinical social worker is abbreviated as CSW and Licensed Clinical Social Worker is abbreviated as LCSW. You'll notice that in the Study Guide, we typically use "CSW," as the obligations presented in this section refer to both licensed and registered CSWs. However, practice questions generally refer to LCSWs, to be specific about licensure level. Unless otherwise specified, the terms "you," "social worker," "CSW," "LCSW," and "therapist" all refer to a clinical wocial worker who is practicing within the state of California.

About the Exam

Test basics

The California Clinical Social Work Law and Ethics Exam is a 75-item, 90-minute test. Of those 75 items, only 50 count toward your score. The other 25 items are being tested for possible inclusion as scored items in future test cycles. You have no way of knowing which 50 exam questions are scored and which are those 25 experimental items, so it is in your best interest to do the best you can on every item on the test. All questions are four-option, multiple choice questions, where you are tasked with choosing the *best* response from the available options.

The test is administered via computer at testing centers around the state, and it can be taken at some centers outside the state as well. You can see a complete list of test centers by going to home.pearsonvue.com/cabbs (Pearson VUE is an independent company the BBS contracts with for the administration of their exams) and selecting "Find a Test Center." No personal items are allowed into the test centers. They have strict rules about the clothing that examinees can wear, to ensure the security of testing. Some test centers have lockers where you can store personal items during your test, but some do not.

You will be seated at a workstation where your exam has been preloaded into the computer, and you may be offered a set of earplugs or noise-cancelling headphones to use during the test if you wish. (Some examinees find these very helpful for blocking out the sound of other computers in the room, while others simply find them uncomfortable.) The Pearson VUE testing centers administer a wide variety of tests for federal and state government agencies as well as private businesses, so it is likely that the other examinees in the testing room with you will be working on several different kinds of tests. Once you've had the opportunity to get settled in and familiarize yourself with the computer you will be using, you follow the on-screen instructions to begin your exam.

Content

Considered as a whole (but without considering the 25 experimental items), the test will break down into the following proportions:

Topic Area	% of scored items	# of scored items (out of 50)
Law	**40%**	**20**
Confidentiality, privilege, and consent	14%	7
Limits to confidentiality, including mandated reporting	16%	8
Legal standards for professional practice	10%	5
Ethics	**60%**	**30**
Professional competence and preventing harm	18%	9
Therapeutic relationship	27%	13-14
Business practices and policies	15%	7-8

The exam is not separated into these sections; you will get questions from various categories in random order. These are merely overall proportions. Still, they can be helpful to know. For example, knowing that ethical issues surrounding the therapeutic relationship make up more than a quarter of the test, you may place an emphasis in your studying on this area.

These percentages also are helpful to keep in mind if you hear from other examinees that they had a surprising amount of questions on a particular topic area on their test. You shouldn't adjust your studying on the basis of such reports. Surprises like that usually result from *experimental* (that is, non-scored) items having emphasis in a particular content area on *that specific version* of the exam. Multiple versions can be in use at the same time, so another person's version of the test may not match yours. *Scored* items for all versions of the test will break down to the percentages above.

Scoring

Your score is based on the total number of non-experimental items that you answered correctly, out of 50 total. Every item is worth one point – there is no weighting of items based on difficulty, complexity, topic (legal versus ethical), or any other factor. There is also no penalty for an incorrect response; it is counted as 0 points, just the same as if the item were left blank.

The minimum passing score on the test (sometimes referred to as the passing score cutoff) varies from one test cycle to the next, and sometimes among different versions of the test being given within the same test cycle. Some versions of the test are more challenging than others, so the BBS conducts careful statistical analysis of each test -- and of every *item* on each test -- to make sure they set the passing score appropriately. While the BBS no longer publicly announces the passing score, they used to. During that time, the minimum passing score was consistently *around* 35 out of 50 scored items (70%). It would be unusual for the minimum passing score to be above 38 or below 33 for any specific test cycle.

Accommodations

Accommodations are available for examinees with recognized disabilities. If you need accommodations, you will need to arrange for a letter to be sent from your health care provider documenting your disability. Common accommodations include a quiet room for testing, or additional time to complete the exam. It is Pearson VUE, and not the BBS, who determines accommodations for examinees with documented disabilities. More information about the process of applying for accommodations, as well as the forms that must be completed, are at home.pearsonvue.com/Test-takers/Accommodations.aspx

As a separate process, the BBS will also allow additional testing time for those who do not speak English as their native language. There are strict requirements to qualify for this additional time, however. The form to apply for this additional time is at www.bbs.ca.gov/pdf/forms/esl_specaccom.pdf

If you are considering applying for exam accommodations, it's important to plan ahead. All requests for accommodation should be received at least 90 days prior to scheduling your exam. Actual processing time varies based on time of year, application volume, staffing, and other variables.

While many examinees with disabilities report that it is beneficial to receive accommodations, I have also sometimes observed those who do *not* have recognized disabilities trying to receive accommodations to get extra time on the exam. You should note here that 1) test anxiety, in and of itself, is not a recognized disability; and 2) unless you have a history of benefiting from disability accommodations, you probably don't need accommodations for this exam. Remember that the majority of those who attempt this exam pass on their first try, and among those who don't, rarely does inadequate time come up as an issue.

Test-Taking Strategy

There are many different test-taking strategies that can help you perform well on the exam. Of course, no test-taking strategy will substitute for having detailed knowledge of the material you're being tested on and being able to apply that knowledge across a wide variety of clinical situations. But strategies can help maximize your score by helping with items you don't know the answer to, and strategies can also help with time and anxiety management.

In general, I defer here to your knowledge of your own strengths and challenges. You probably already know how good of a test-taker you are, and what strategies work best for you. (If you don't, it may be worth it to you to try the practice exams here in a couple of different ways, to see what strategies help you the most.) Just like for studying, the only bad strategy for test-taking is one that doesn't work for you.

If you're already clear on the strategies that help you the most on exams, you can safely ignore the rest of this section. If you're interested, here are some strategies specific to this exam that may help you. Note that these strategies are not mutually exclusive, and you can use as many as you like at the same time.

Timing

- **Take the easy ones first.** You can go forward and backward on the test as much as you like. Remember that you have a time limit and that items are not weighted, so a good way to start the exam (and possibly build some confidence) is to go through the whole test, marking the responses you are sure of. Then you can go back and spend more time on those items that you need more time to consider. You may find that in a very short time period, you already have half or more of the test completed – and that almost all of those answers are likely correct.

- **Don't get stuck in a rabbit hole.** You have 90 minutes to respond to 75 questions. That gives you a little more than 70 seconds per question. If you find yourself getting hung up on a difficult question, move on. Make a mental note (or, if you're using the blank paper provided at the test center, an actual note) of the question you're struggling with and any responses you have ruled out, and then go on to other questions you may be able to answer more quickly.

Content

- **Pay close attention to what each item is actually asking for.** One way of eliminating wrong answers is to notice when a question is asking specifically for a *legal* response or specifically for an *ethical* one – that will allow you to eliminate any response choices that would fall into the other category. Similarly, when a question asks what action you would take *first* or *next* in a given situation, there may be multiple answers that reflect things you would do. The question is demanding that you *prioritize* those actions to focus on the most urgent, which often means action to protect the physical safety of clients or those around them.

  The line between legal concerns and ethical concerns isn't as clear in real practice as it is on the test. Several standards in the NASW Codes of Ethics include compliance with relevant laws, and the (legal) unprofessional conduct category known as "general unprofessional conduct" can make ethical violations into legal ones as well. But for the purposes of the test, the two are clearly distinguished – in ways that can help you succeed on the test, if you understand which issues fall into which category. The table on page 27 addresses where several common concerns ***generally*** lie: Legal, ethical, or both. There may be exceptions within each.

- **Use the process of elimination.** Even when you aren't certain of the *right* response on a particular question, there is a good chance you will be able to identify one or more of the response choices as obviously *wrong*. Eliminating wrong options greatly increases your chance of getting the question right, even if you're not ultimately sure what the best answer would be.

- **Don't overthink.** In my experience, when people struggle with the law and ethics exam, it's often not a knowledge issue. Quite the opposite. It's because they spend *too much* time pondering all of the possibilities hinted at by each question, rather than focusing only on the information included in the question itself. As a general rule, you should not assume any "facts not in evidence," as a lawyer might say. Focus solely on the information presented in the question itself. If your initial response to a question is "it depends," that's a cue to refocus *just on what is presented in the question*.

- **Go ahead and guess.** Because there is no penalty for an incorrect response, if there are items you are truly unsure about, it is in your best interest to go ahead and mark your best guess. **Use the last few minutes of your test to mark your best guess on all remaining items you haven't already answered.** The worst thing you can do is leave an item blank, since that gives you a 0% chance of getting the point for it. Even if you're not able to eliminate *any* of the response choices from consideration, guessing at it gives you at least a 25% chance of getting it right.

Mindset

- **Stay confident.** You're likely to encounter some weird questions on the test – either things that just don't make sense to you, or items that are strangely worded. You may even see bad grammar, spelling, and sentence structure. Don't panic. These kinds of items may be the non-scored, experimental items being tested for possible inclusion as scored items on future tests. This is precisely why the BBS does that kind of experimentation: They need to weed out bad items. It's still worth it to answer them as best you can, but if you can't figure some items out, don't let that shake your confidence in your overall knowledge. If a question is confusing, it's probably *a problem with the question,* not a problem with you.

- **It doesn't matter.** If you believe that the test is a meaningful indicator of your value – as a clinician, or as a person – then you're at risk of sending yourself into an anxiety spiral, especially if you run into a few difficult questions in a row. This test *is not* a meaningful indicator of your clinical skills or your value of a person, and it should not be thought of as such. It's simply a step on the path to licensure. You will probably pass, but even in the unlikely event that you don't, you just wait 90 days and try again. If you find anxiety creeping up on you, remember that this exam is very small in the grand scheme of things. Your clients, friends, and family will all think of you the same way after the exam as they do before it.

Primarily legal, ethical, or both?

Legal	Both	Ethical
	Informed consent for telehealth	Informed consent for therapy or research
Privilege	Confidentiality	
Scope of practice		Scope of competence
Retaining records 7 years	Maintaining adequate records; Client access to records	Storage and destruction of records
Professional titles	Truth in advertising	Testimonials
Telehealth regulations; HIPAA compliance	Telehealth competence	
		Personal values, attitudes and beliefs
		Countertransference
Ownership of records	Client autonomy	
	Non-discrimination	Cultural competence
	Fees for referrals Fee disclosures	Bartering; Termination for overdue balance
Abuse reporting	Minors' consent for therapy	
Involuntary hospitalization	Crisis management	
Insurance parity	Accurate info to payors	Advocacy with payors
		Termination and non-abandonment
Providing *Therapy Never Includes Sexual Behavior* brochure	Sexual relationships	Multiple relationships
	Monitoring self for impairment	Assisting impaired colleagues
Licensure requirements	Supervision	

See the important cautionary notes about this chart on the previous pages. In real life, the categories aren't as cleanly divided as they are here. Also, a quick reminder: Stuff like this takes a long time to put together. **Please don't share this or other content from this guide online.** Doing so violates our copyright (there would be some irony in breaking the law while preparing for a law and ethics test), and ultimately drives up prices for everyone. Thanks for being awesome and not doing that. ☺

Before the test

Weeks and months before

The material on which you will be tested is largely consistent with what you would have learned in graduate school, particularly what you learned in your Law and Ethics class. So, a lot of your preparation will simply be re-familiarizing yourself with that material and making sure you're caught up on any recent changes that have taken place in the legal and ethical rules governing the profession.

There are, of course, lots of ways to **study the material for the exam.** Do what you know works for you. The law and ethics exam does not contain trick questions, and there is no "secret" way to study. The only wrong way to study is a way that doesn't work for you. If you work well with flash cards, make them. If you're someone who does better with reading and rereading, well, hopefully this book is helpful! The point is, trust your instincts and experience when deciding how to study, and how much. Some will find that an hour a night is all they can handle, while others will want to take several-hour-long blocks of time to study. Similarly, some find it more useful to study with friends or colleagues who are also about to test, while others prefer to study on their own.

The most important thing to do several weeks before the test is to **schedule your exam.** Review the list of test centers on the Pearson VUE website and choose the one that is most convenient to you. While all of the test centers are designed to have ample parking and similar testing conditions, you might want to consult with others who have recently taken exams at locations close to you. They can prepare you for things like the friendliness (or lack thereof) of test center staff, which can make a big difference in your testing experience. Note that the center you choose to schedule might not be the one that is geographically closest to you; you might find there's one farther away that is easier to schedule on your preferred day and time, or in a neighborhood that you like to visit.

One thing you may find helpful once you have your test scheduled is to **clear your test day of other obligations.** Arrange to take the day off from work, and don't put any other appointments on your schedule. You will want to focus squarely on the test. And once it's over, you will not want to go back to work right away. If you pass, you'll want (and deserve!) a bit of celebration, and if you don't pass, you'll want some time to shake it off.

Another thing to address once your test is scheduled: **tell employers, supervisors, and loved ones about your upcoming test.** Part of this is simply pragmatic: They will need to know that you will be entirely unreachable, even in the event of an emergency, during the time you are taking the test. (Cell phones are, of course, not allowed in the testing room.) But part of it is also to shore up social support: It's good to go into a test knowing that a lot of people are cheering for you, and that they will be ready to celebrate with you once you pass.

The week before

Since you schedule your exam by phone or online, you may not be familiar with the specific location of the test center where you will take the exam. It can reduce anxiety on your test day if you actually **visit the test center** during the week before the test. Try to go to the center in advance around the same time of day that you'll be going for the actual test. This can help you get a feel for traffic, parking, and the like. Based on how long it takes you to get there, you can better plan your actual test day, making sure to give yourself ample time for unexpected delays.

The week before the test is also the time to **wrap up studying**. Hopefully by this time you're feeling confident and ready. If not, it's worth taking an honest look at *why* you're not feeling that way. Is it simple anxiety about the test, or is it a recognition that you don't know the material as well as you should? Anxiety can be managed through relaxation techniques, time with friends, and perhaps a visit to your own therapist. If there are parts of the material you are struggling with, you still have time to shore up your weak points before going into the exam.

The wrap-up process does involve studying, of course, but **take care of yourself** during this time. There is indeed such thing as too much studying: if it is interfering with sleep, your ability to care for your clients, or your relationships with loved ones, you may find that simply adding on more study time this late in the process will do you more harm than good.

Part of taking care of yourself can be to **adopt a mantra**, or a brief statement you can use repetitively to center yourself and calm your nerves. A mantra can be part of a larger spiritual or meditation practice, but it doesn't have to be. Here are a few you can choose from, or create one that is a good fit for you:

It's just a test. It doesn't define me as a person or as a social worker.
I am ready.
I've had good education, good supervision, and good preparation.
I will be the same therapist after the test that I am before it.
This is a milestone, just one checkpoint on a larger journey.
I will pass.
My friends and family will love me the same no matter what happens.
I know the things I need to know.

Occasionally, people find that they are really not ready for the test at this point, and they may consider rescheduling it for a later date. That's fine, but before taking this step, consider whether it is truly about your readiness, or whether it simply reflects anxiety creeping up on you. If it's anxiety, putting off the test may just mean you repeat the experience a few weeks later.

The day before

The day before the test, spend time reviewing what you know and making sure you have everything ready for the next day. You may want to prepare a checklist of things to do and things to bring to the test with you, such as photo ID, paperwork confirming the test time and location, and the like. (Remember that test centers will not allow you to bring personal items into the exam room. Some test centers have lockers you can use to store personal items during the test, but not all do.) Make sure you eat well and get a good night's sleep the night before the exam.

The day of the test

Different people have different ideas about whether it is helpful to do some last-minute studying on the actual day of the test. Again, do what works best for you. Some find that reviewing material one last time increases their confidence, as they recognize material, get practice questions right, and generally go into the test feeling good about how much they know. Others find that continuing to review at the last minute only increases their anxiety.

The most important thing you can do on the day of the test is to keep your anxiety in check. Have a normal, healthy breakfast. (Food and drinks are not allowed in the testing room, so don't go in on an empty stomach.) Get a pep talk from your partner or a close friend. If you've chosen a mantra, spend time repeating it to yourself.

Before you leave home or work for the test, make sure you have the documents you will need to get in: your photo ID and the confirmation from Pearson VUE that includes the date, time, and location of your test. Without these materials, you may not be allowed to take the exam.

After the test

Unless you have a disability accommodation that requires paper-and-pencil testing, or there is some other unusual circumstance, you will find out immediately whether you passed the exam. As of late 2022, some examinees were receiving their score notifications by email within 24 hours of their exams, but the norm is to receive a printout with your results at the test center.

If you pass, congratulations! You will not need to go through another test until you complete your 3,000 hours of supervised experience for licensure and are sitting for the Clinical Exam. Spread the word about your success to friends, family, colleagues, supervisors, social media, or anyplace else you want to announce it so that people can join in celebrating your accomplishment. **Please also let us know:** An email to **support@bencaldwelllabs.com** to share your success story gives me the chance to provide a personal congratulations!

If you do *not* pass on your first try, don't worry. You can take the test again after a 90-day waiting period, and pass on that attempt. You need to *attempt* the exam at least once during each one-year associate registration period, until you pass it.

The BBS will not allow anyone to register with a second associate number, or to sit for the Clinical Exam, until they have passed the Law and Ethics Exam.

2023 key changes in California law

There were a handful of changes in California law affecting social workers and other psychotherapists in 2022. While I would not describe these changes as major, you are likely to be directly impacted by at least some of them:

- Video-based supervision is now legal across all work settings. Supervisors providing supervision via video now must assess each supervisee's appropriateness for video-based supervision at the beginning of the supervision process.
- All Associate Clinical Social Workers now must take a 3-hour CE course in law and ethics for each registration renewal, regardless of whether you have already passed your Law & Ethics Exam. I have this course available at **bencaldwelllabs.com/associates** and plan to update it annually.
- All applicants for licensure as of July 1, 2023 must have completed at least 3 hours of training in telehealth, including specific content. The training can be from a CE course or have been included in your graduate degree.
- There are other new rules surrounding continuing education, including expanding the activities that can result in CE credit. Serving on an ethics committee, serving as a subject matter expert in a BBS disciplinary process, or completing an occupational analysis survey all can now result in CE credit.

As is usual, there were also several additional technical changes in law, though these are largely not substantive changes. Where the changes above (and other changes from 2022) link to topics in the Exam Plan, they have been included in the study guide portion of this book.

Here we go!

The next section is a summary of information likely to be included on the exam. The BBS uses 128 "knowledge statements" outlining what they believe you need to know in order to practice therapy within your legal and ethical boundaries. They've been organized here in such a way that should make them easier to study and retain. I've kept the descriptions as brief and simple as possible.

This study guide is divided into subsections that correspond with the knowledge categories on the exam plan:

- Law: Confidentiality, privilege, and consent
- Law: Limits to confidentiality, including mandated reporting
- Law: Legal standards for professional practice
- Ethics: Professional competence and preventing harm
- Ethics: Therapeutic relationship
- Ethics: Business practices and policies

At the beginning of each subsection, you'll see the number of questions from that section you are likely to encounter on your actual exam, out of 50 total scored items. This should help you determine how much emphasis to give each section.

If you have questions about any of the explanations here, or want to dive deeper on any of the subjects covered in this book, you best first stop is the primary source material used in the development of this book.

You've got this.

Good luck!

Study Guide

LAW

Confidentiality, Privilege, and Consent

Scored exam questions (approximate): **7**

Understanding confidentiality K1-2

Laws about confidentiality. Unless a specific exception to confidentiality applies, CSWs are legally required to keep the content of therapy confidential. This means that they do not share any information about clients, including even the existence of a therapeutic relationship, with outsiders.

Maintaining confidentiality means more than simply not sharing a client's identity. All information gained in a confidential context is deemed confidential under state law, unless the client has given permission to share that information or a legal exception to confidentiality applies.

Laws about disclosure. While confidentiality is the default state, several legal exceptions to confidentiality exist. In fact, there are more than 20 instances in state law where confidentiality either *can* or *must* be broken, and information shared with outside persons or agencies.

The times when a CSW is legally *required* to break confidentiality can be generally broken down into five categories:

- Suspected child abuse
- Suspected elder or dependent adult abuse
- Danger to self or others
- Legal authorization, such as a court order or client release
- Other, less common instances where disclosure is required

The first four categories will be discussed in greater detail within this study guide. As a CSW, you need to be keenly aware of each of them.

The fifth category – those less-common instances where disclosure is required – includes an investigation by a board, commission, or administrative agency; a lawful request from an arbitrator or arbitration panel; a coroner's investigation of client's death; and a national security investigation. These instances rarely come up in therapy, but they may be the focus of exam questions. In the event of a national security investigation, CSWs not only are required to turn over client records, but they are legally prohibited from informing the client that they have done so.

Those instances where confidentiality *can* be broken present more opportunity for professional judgment. Social workers will typically err on the side of confidentiality in such instances. However, there may be instances where a social worker breaks confidentiality because they legally *can* do so, and they believe it is in the best interest of the client to do so.

For example, the law allows but does not require disclosure of confidential information to the person or entity paying for services, to the extent necessary to determine who is responsible for payment and payment to be made. As another example that has become especially relevant during the pandemic, confidential information can be disclosed to public health authorities for the purpose of public health surveillance and intervention (in other words, to control disease spread).

Understanding privilege K3-6

Privilege refers to information that can be excluded from court proceedings. Normally, all communications between a therapist and their client are considered privileged communications, meaning that they cannot be used in court. Other examples of communication that is usually privileged include communication between spouses, and communication between an attorney and their client.

This is particularly important in therapy. Clients need to be able to trust that information they have shared with their therapist about mental health symptoms or other emotional problems will not be used against them in court; if that risk exists, clients will understandably be less open with their therapists about struggles in the clients' lives.

Clients generally hold their own privilege. In other words, only the client can waive their own right to privileged communication in most instances. Even when the client is a minor, the client is usually considered the holder of their own privilege, although the minor may not be allowed to *waive* privilege on their own. A judge may block a minor (or an adult, for that matter) from waiving privilege if the judge believes that waiving privilege is not in the person's best interest. In any case, it is never up to the therapist to determine whether privilege should be waived. That is up to the client, the client's guardian, another court appointee, or a judge.

Release of privileged information. By definition, privileged information cannot be used in a court proceeding. Privileged information may only be released in court if the client has waived privilege, or if a judge has determined that privilege does not apply, based on one or more of the exceptions spelled out in state law (more on that in the next section).

Responding to a subpoena or court order. If a CSW receives a subpoena (a legal document requesting that the therapist produce records, appear in court, or both), the CSW is commonly advised to take these steps:

1. **Contact an attorney as soon as possible.** The CSW will benefit from legal guidance throughout this process.
2. **Assess the subpoena for its source and validity.** A subpoena *from a judge* is a court order – the CSW must obey it. A subpoena from a *private attorney*, on the other hand, may be fought if the client wishes. Occasionally, an attorney may advise the CSW to object to the subpoena, though this is less common.
3. **Contact the client to determine their wishes.** Often, the client will freely authorize the CSW to release the records or appear in court. Sometimes, the client will prefer that the CSW assert privilege on the client's behalf, asking that the therapist's records or testimony not be made part of the court proceeding.
4. Unless the client has specifically waived privilege or a judge has determined that privilege does not apply, **assert privilege on behalf of the client.** This is generally considered the best default position for a therapist to take in the absence of other guidance from the client or the court.

If the client does waive privilege, or if a court determines that privilege does not apply, the CSW must comply with the subpoena. And regardless of what path the CSW and the client choose, the CSW always must respond to the subpoena in some form, even if to assert privilege. Simply failing to respond to a subpoena can result in sanctions from the court.

Treatment of minors K7

Treatment of minors. In most cases, parents provide consent for the treatment of their child. Anyone under age 18 is a minor under state law, and parents can consent for treatment on their child's behalf. If a minor has two legal parents (either because the parents are married, or because they never were married and both have retained parental rights), then typically either parent can provide consent on their own for therapy for the minor.

If the minor's parents are divorced, consent becomes more complicated. The CSW can request a copy of the custody order to determine which parent's consent is necessary for treatment of the minor. In joint custody, typically either parent can provide consent on their own. If one parent has sole custody, typically only that parent can provide consent for the minor's treatment. If that parent refuses or withdraws their consent, the CSW should not treat the minor.

Other caregivers may sometimes bring a minor in for therapy. Another relative who lives in the same home as the minor may provide consent for the minor's treatment if they sign a "Caregiver's Authorization Affidavit." The necessary language of this document is specified in state law.

Minors as young as 12 can consent to mental health care on their own if the minor is mature enough to participate intelligently in treatment. That determination is made by the therapist. In these cases, the therapist still must either try to contact the child's parents to involve them in treatment, or document why they believe doing so would be harmful. Parents do not have a right to access records of their child's treatment if the child consented independently, and parents cannot be forced to pay for services provided without the parents' consent.

Documentation K8-11

Documentation of services. Documentation of therapy is both a legal and ethical requirement. Neither state law nor professional ethical codes define the specific *content* that needs to be in treatment records, and there are many formats for things like assessments and progress notes. However, all CSWs are legally required to keep records that are consistent with "sound clinical judgment, the standards of the profession, and the nature of the services being rendered" (CA BPC 4992.3(w)). As we will see, there are some specific things that legally must be documented when they occur, such as client releases of information and specific consent for telehealth services.

If a client wishes, they have the right to include a statement in their treatment record of up to 250 words. Clients sometimes ask to do so when they disagree with some element of their clinical record, and want their disagreement included in case their file is ever released to a court or to another provider.

Maintenance and disposal of records. Under state law, records must be maintained for at least 7 years following the last professional contact. If you are working with a minor, records must be maintained for at least 7 years after the minor turns 18.

During the time you are maintaining records, you must take reasonable steps to ensure they are secure and confidential. When the time comes to dispose of old client records, this disposal must also be done in a manner that protects security and confidentiality (and, if you're a HIPAA-covered entity, is HIPAA compliant). You should never just throw old files in the trash.

Client access to records. Clients generally have a legal right to access their records, though there are some limitations on this. Unless you believe that the release of records to the client would be harmful, you must comply with their request in a timely manner: Within 5 days if the client simply wants to inspect their records, and within 15 days if the client wants a copy of their record. You cannot refuse a client's request for records simply because they owe you money. You can, however, charge for reasonable costs associated with accessing and copying the client's file, and you can provide a summary of the file rather than the full record if you prefer (this typically must be within 10 days of the client's request). Any client who inspects their record and believes some part of it to be incomplete or incorrect can submit a brief statement to be included in the client file.

If you believe that releasing records to a client would be harmful to them, you may refuse to do so. If you refuse, you need to document the request and your reason for refusal. The client may then request that a third-party professional review the records to see whether that third party agrees with you that the record should not be released.

In the case of couple or family treatment, CSWs get consent from all members of the treatment unit prior to releasing records.

Release of records to others. Records of treatment can be released to third parties if the client requests it or if there is some other appropriate legal authorization. Most commonly, clients request that their records be forwarded to another therapist or health care provider for continuity of care, or they request that records be provided to their insurance company for the purpose of receiving reimbursement.

When a client requests that their records be released to a third party, this request typically must be in writing, and it must be signed and dated by the client or their legal representative.

There are some instances when a specific authorization to release information is *not* required by law, such as when the information is needed by another active health care provider or health care facility to for the purposes of diagnosis or treatment (in an emergency, for example, there may not be time to gather written authorization), or when the information is required as part of a billing process.

As discussed previously, records are also sometimes released by court order, which is its own form of legal authorization.

On occasion, clients may ask CSWs to provide letters on the client's behalf. For example, a CSW may write a letter to a client's employer in support of the client's request for time off to address mental health needs. Such letters are typically legal so long as they are accurate and are released with the client's written permission. In 2022, California enacted specific rules around therapists writing letters in support of a client's request for an Emotional Support Dog. For the therapist to write such a letter, they must have had at least a 30-day clinical relationship with the client, and in that time the therapist must have completed a clinical assessment. The therapist must include their licensure information in the letter. The therapist also must inform the client that falsely presenting an ESD as a service animal is a crime.

Telehealth laws K12-13

Telehealth consent. Under California law, therapists who offer services via telemedicine are legally required to first obtain specific consent for telemedicine (the consent can be verbal or in writing) and document this in the client's file. Failure to do so is considered unprofessional conduct. While purely administrative contacts, such as contacting clients by phone or email to schedule in-person sessions, would likely not qualify as telehealth, actually providing therapy by phone, videoconference, or other technology certainly would.

Telehealth delivery. California and federal laws govern the delivery of services by telehealth. When delivering services by telehealth, all the laws regarding scope of practice, client confidentiality, and client rights to information and records continue to apply. CSWs must be particularly cautious when considering using telemedicine to treat clients located outside of California, as a California CSW license only governs services provided to clients who are physically located within the state at the time of service.

Starting in July 2023, all California CSWs applying for licensure must have completed at least 3 hours of telehealth training, either through a continuing education course or as part of their graduate degree program.

By regulation, California social workers wishing to conduct therapy via telehealth need to take several specific steps. *At the start* of engaging a client in telehealth, the social worker must:

- Get specific telehealth consent (as noted above)
- Inform clients of the risks and limitations of telehealth services
- Provide the social worker's licensure/registration information
- Document reasonable efforts to locate crisis resources local to the client

Regarding that last point: A low-risk client wouldn't require the same effort to locate crisis resources local to them as a high-risk client would. So based on your assessment of client risk, you may locate crisis resources local to them just in case they're needed. Whatever you do in this area, it should be documented.

In addition to the steps above, the social worker must do the following *at each instance* of telehealth:

- Obtain and document the client's full name and current location (this should be a specific location such as an address, to confirm that you are qualified to provide services where they are and to allow you to send help to the client if needed in an emergency)
- Assess whether the client is appropriate for telehealth (this may be based on their symptoms as well as the technology and privacy available to the client at that time, among other factors)
- Use best practices for security and confidentiality

HIPAA. Under the Health Insurance Portability and Accountability Act (HIPAA), CSWs covered by the act have specific additional responsibilities to protect the privacy of client records. However, not all CSWs are considered "covered entities" and bound to HIPAA's requirements. HIPAA applies to those providers who digitally transmit a client's protected health information as part of a health care transaction. Put plainly, this means that HIPAA applies to therapists who submit billing documents electronically, to insurers or other payors. Among the requirements for covered entities:

- Designating a privacy official
- Informing clients and staff of privacy policy and procedures
- Disciplining staff members who violate privacy or security rules
- Repairing harmful effects of privacy violations
- Maintaining safeguards against the release of private information
- Having complaint procedures for violations of privacy
- Ensuring confidentiality of electronic health information
- Protecting against threats to information security
- Notifying the department of Health and Human Services of breaches of unsecured health information
- Getting client permission before using unsecured email

Rather than memorizing that list, it may work best to simply recall that under HIPAA, CSWs need to have and enforce specific policies to protect the security and confidentiality of health information, and that clients are to be informed of the relevant policies. Therapists covered under HIPAA provide clients with a Notice of Privacy Policies that outlines how private information is gathered and used.

There is a specific category of documentation that HIPAA calls "psychotherapy notes," which are different from typical progress notes. "Psychotherapy notes" are a therapist's notes documenting or analyzing conversation with a client that happens in a private psychotherapy session. Within this definition, psychotherapy notes cannot include information like session start and stop times, diagnosis, progress, treatment plans, symptoms, interventions, or prognosis. Psychotherapy notes, as defined under HIPAA, must be kept separate from the rest of the client file and are not considered part of the client record. However, under California law, these records may still be subject to subpoena.

Sample Questions

See the next page for answers and rationales

1. A former client calls the LCSW who had treated her two years earlier. The former client verbally requests that the LCSW forward her file to her new therapist in a different state. The former client confirms her identity using her social security number and is able to identify specific topics of the prior therapy, leaving the LCSW confident in the identity of the caller. The LCSW should:

   a. Take down the information for the new therapist and forward the file as the client requested
   b. Take down the information for the new therapist, contact that therapist, and have that therapist complete a written records request
   c. Take down the information for the new therapist, and inform the former client that she will need to request that the records be released directly to her. She can then forward the file to the new therapist if she so chooses
   d. Take down the information for the new therapist, and send the former client appropriate paperwork to request in writing that her file be released

2. A potential client with partial paralysis contacts an LCSW and asks whether he may receive therapy by phone for his symptoms of depression. The LCSW assesses the potential client by phone and determines he is appropriate for phone-based services. Legally, the LCSW must:

   a. Obtain consent for phone-based services and inform the potential client of the possible risks and benefits
   b. Obtain consent in writing for phone-based services and inform the potential client that such services are currently considered experimental in nature
   c. Assess the client in person at least once before moving to phone-based services
   d. Assess the client in person and identify the closest hospital emergency room to the client, in case of emergency

Sample Questions: Answers and Rationales

1. A former client calls the LCSW who had treated her two years earlier. The former client verbally requests that the LCSW forward her file to her new therapist in a different state. The former client confirms her identity using her social security number and is able to identify specific topics of the prior therapy, leaving the LCSW confident in the identity of the caller. The LCSW should:

a. **Incorrect.** Take down the information for the new therapist and forward the file as the client requested. *The client should provide permission in writing for the release of their records. This option does not leave the therapist with adequate documentation of the request.*
b. **Incorrect.** Take down the information for the new therapist, contact that therapist, and have that therapist complete a written records request. *The request for records should come from the client, not from the new treatment provider.*
c. **Incorrect.** Take down the information for the new therapist, and inform the former client that she will need to request that the records be released directly to her. She can then forward the file to the new therapist if she so chooses. *With the client's permission, records can be transferred directly to the new treatment provider. They do not need to first go through the client.*
d. **CORRECT.** Take down the information for the new therapist, and send the former client appropriate paperwork to request in writing that her file be released. *The client should provide permission in writing for the release of their records.*

2. A potential client with partial paralysis contacts an LCSW and asks whether he may receive therapy by phone for his symptoms of depression. The LCSW assesses the potential client by phone and determines he is appropriate for phone-based services. Legally, the LCSW must:

a. **CORRECT.** Obtain consent for phone-based services and inform the potential client of the possible risks and benefits. *These are current legal requirements.*
b. **Incorrect.** Obtain consent in writing for phone-based services and inform the potential client that such services are currently considered experimental in nature. *Consent for telehealth can be provided verbally under state law, and does not need to be in writing.*
c. **Incorrect.** Assess the client in person at least once before moving to phone-based services. *While assessing the client in person first may be helpful, it is not currently a legal or ethical requirement.*
d. **Incorrect.** Assess the client in person and identify the closest hospital emergency room to the client, in case of emergency. *While assessing the client in person first may be helpful, it is not currently a legal or ethical requirement.*

LAW

Limits of Confidentiality

Scored exam questions (approximate):	8

Exceptions to confidentiality: Child abuse K18-19

Laws about reporting child abuse. California therapists are **mandated reporters** of suspected child abuse when serving in their professional roles. In other words, CSWs are required to report abuse you observe or suspect while in the office, but not what you observe or suspect at the grocery store, at home, or in other non-professional settings.

Your mandated reporting responsibilities are triggered when, in your professional role, you develop **reasonable suspicion** that a minor has been abused or neglected. ("A minor" is important here. The victim does not need to have been your client, it can be any minor whose abuse you learn about in your professional role.)

Reasonable suspicion is a specific term with a specific meaning. As the law is written, if another therapist with similar training and experience, when presented with the same information, would reasonably suspect that abuse had taken place, then so should you. You do not need to be certain that the abuse happened to reasonably suspect it. For example, you do not need to have personally observed injuries to suspect physical abuse.

There are five categories of abuse that *must* be reported:

- **Physical abuse.** Anyone who willfully causes an injury to a child or engages in cruel or unusual corporal punishment is committing physical abuse. Key terms there include "willfully" and "injury" – accidental contact is not abusive, and the child must have suffered an injury (such as a scratch, bruise, or other observable impact) for an event to qualify as physical abuse.

The law makes an exception to the reporting requirement for physical abuse when the injury occurred in the context of a "mutual affray among minors." This is meant to exclude common schoolyard fights from being mandated abuse reports. However, it is possible for a minor to physically abuse another minor if the events in question do not qualify as mutual.

- **Sexual abuse.** This category includes sexual assault, sexual exploitation, and what the law calls "lewd and lascivious acts." When minors engage in consensual, **heterosexual intercourse,** the therapist must consider their ages, using these two rules:

  The 14th birthday rule:
  If one partner is 14 years old or older, and the other is under 14, the therapist must report.

  The 21/16 rule:
  This rule can be thought of as the "drinking and driving" age rule: If one sexual partner is old enough to drink (at least 21), the other partner needs to be old enough to drive (at least 16). To put this another way, if one partner is *under* 16 and the other is 21 or older, the therapist must report.

  For any other age combinations, the therapist should consider the age and maturational levels of the partners in assessing their capacity to consent and the nature of the relationship (i.e., is it exploitive or otherwise abusive) when deciding whether to report.

  Notably, the law specifically states that the pregnancy of a minor, in and of itself, is *not* sufficient grounds to suspect abuse. This remains true regardless of the age of the minor.

  When minors consensually engage in **oral sex, anal sex, or object penetration,** the 21/16 rule applies, but the 14th birthday rule does not. Of course, any non-consensual oral sex, anal, object penetration, or intercourse will always be reportable when a minor is involved.

"Lewd and lascivious acts" may include non-penetrative sexual behaviors like mutual masturbation. These acts are a mandated report if performed on a minor under age 14, regardless of the age of the partner. If the act is performed on a minor age 14 or 15, it is a mandated report if the partner is 10 or more years older than the minor. If the minor is 16 or older, these acts are not a mandated report.

The law specifically defines both the **distribution and the intentional downloading of child porn** as child abuse.

- **Willful harm or endangerment.** Any person causing a child "unjustifiable physical pain or mental suffering," or any caregiver who allows it to happen, is committing child abuse.

- **Neglect.** Even if it happens by accident, children are being neglected if their basic needs for adequate food, clothing, shelter, medical care, or supervision are not being met. A child does not need to have suffered actual harm for a report of neglect to be made.

  Note that a parent's "informed and appropriate" medical choices, including choices to refuse medical treatment for their child based on religious belief, are not neglect. However, this only applies if the parents have taken the child to a physician for assessment. Otherwise, the parent's medical choices may not be considered "informed and appropriate."

- **Abuse in out-of-home care.** This is given its own category for reporting purposes. It applies to kids who are physically injured or killed in child-care or school settings.

In addition to those types of abuse, **emotional abuse** operates on a *permissive* reporting standard, which means that you can report this if you choose to, but you are not required to. Emotional abuse is defined in law as "serious emotional damage or [...] substantial risk of suffering serious emotional damage." Children who witness domestic violence are sometimes reported as victims of emotional abuse.

Once you have developed reasonable suspicion, there are specific **timeframes for abuse reporting** that must be followed. You must make a report by phone to your local child protective agency immediately and follow up with a written report within 36 hours. This timeframe does not change for nights, weekends, or holidays.

Indicators of child abuse. Since the reasonable suspicion standard relies on therapists having a shared understanding of the times when abuse should be reported, it is critical that social workers are aware of common physical and behavioral indicators of abuse, neglect, and exploitation. The National Children's Advocacy Center has compiled the following lists of indicators. While none of these indicators by themselves would lead to a conclusion of abuse, they should lead a therapist to *consider* whether abuse or neglect may be taking place. Common physical indicators include:

- Unexplained bruises
- Unexplained burns
- Unexplained fractures or cuts
- Evidence of delayed or inappropriate treatment for injuries
- Multiple injuries in various stages of healing
- Injury or trauma to genital area
- Sexually transmitted disease
- Pain, swelling, itching, bruising, or bleeding in genital area
- Unattended medical needs
- Consistent hunger or poor hygiene
- Consistent lack of supervision

Common behavioral indicators of abuse and neglect include the following. As with all child and adolescent behaviors, a therapist must be especially cautious not to reach premature conclusions on the basis of behavioral indicators alone, as there are a number of potential causes for each of these that would *not* indicate abuse. However, these behaviors should get a therapist's attention:

- Sudden withdrawn behavior
- Self-destructive behavior
- Bizarre explanations for injuries
- Shying away from contact with familiar adults
- Sleep disturbances, including nightmares or flashbacks
- Substance use
- Anger and rage
- Aggressive, disruptive, or illegal behavior
- Frequent absence or tardiness from school or other activities
- Consistent fatigue or listlessness
- Stealing food
- Extreme need for affection
- Extreme loneliness

Exceptions to confidentiality: Elder and dependent adult abuse K14-17

Laws about reporting elder and dependent adult abuse. Under California law, you must report any time you observe, suspect, or have knowledge of elder or dependent adult abuse. For mandated reporting purposes, **an elder is anyone age 65 or older who resides in California.** (A 2022 change in state law impacted the definition of an elder for other purposes related to Adult Protective Service agency functions, but it did not change how an elder is defined for mandated reporting purposes.) **A dependent adult is anyone age 18 to 64 who resides in California and has physical or mental limitations** that restrict their ability to carry out normal activities or protect their own rights. Anyone admitted as an inpatient in a hospital or other 24-hour health care facility is, by definition, a dependent adult. Reportable types of abuse include:

- **Physical abuse, which includes willful over- or under-medication.** Be careful with this, though – an elder reporting that they are in pain does not mean they are being abused. As long as they are being given the correct amount of medication prescribed by their doctor, it would simply call for a referral back to the client's physician to make any necessary adjustments in medication dosage or type. Various forms of sexual abuse are also included here as physical abuse.

- **Financial abuse.** This category is not a form of child abuse but does apply to elders and dependent adults.
- **Abduction.** Specifically, the law refers to an elder or dependent adult being taken *outside of California*, or prevented from returning, against their will.
- **Isolation.** Elders who are physically restrained from seeing visitors, or who are being prevented from receiving mail, phone calls, or visitors (when the elder wants to see the visitor), are being isolated. In rare instances, a health condition may make limitations on mail and phone calls clinically appropriate, but there should be good medical documentation for such a decision, and other normal contact should not be restricted.
- **Abandonment.** Caretakers accept responsibility for the adults in their care. Abandonment occurs when a caretaker deserts their patient or gives up on their caretaking responsibilities when a reasonable person would not have done so.
- **Neglect, including self-neglect.** This is reportable not so that the elder or dependent adult will be punished, but so that they can be moved to a higher level of care if it is appropriate to do so.

Unlike child abuse laws, elder and dependent adult abuse reporting laws allow for permissive reporting of any other form of abuse not otherwise defined in the law. This gives a CSW broad latitude to report behaviors that the CSW considers to be abusive or exploitive, even if those behaviors do not fit neatly into any of the categories listed.

As with child abuse reporting, you do not need to have heard a direct report of abuse from the victim in order to develop suspicion that abuse has taken place. However, unlike child abuse reporting laws, the laws on reporting elder and dependent adult abuse say that **if you do hear of abuse directly from the victim, you *must* report it.** There is only a very narrow exception, for when the person has been diagnosed with mental illness, there is no other evidence of the abuse, and the therapist does not reasonably believe the abuse occurred.

The **timeframes for reporting** elder or dependent adult abuse are complex. If the abuse did *not* take place in a long-term care facility, then a phone report of the abuse must be made immediately to Adult Protective Services or another local agency authorized to receive adult abuse reports. You then must follow up with a written report within two working days. Recent state law allows for elder and dependent adult abuse reports to be made via Internet, in which case the Internet report should be done immediately, and it replaces both the phone *and* written reports.

If the abuse happened within a long-term care facility, the rules are more complicated. For example, physical abuse in a long-term care facility that results in serious bodily injury to the victim must be reported to law enforcement immediately, with written reports sent to law enforcement, the local ombudsperson, and the facility's licensing agency all within two hours.

Indicators of elder and dependent adult abuse. Common indicators of elder abuse include the following. As is the case with child abuse, it may be inappropriate to conclude that abuse has occurred based solely on an indicator here, as each of these can be caused by incidents that would not qualify as abuse. However, they can raise a therapist's suspicion, and suspicion is the standard for reporting:

- Physical or sexual abuse
    - Unexplained bruises, welts, or scars
    - Broken bones, sprains, dislocations
    - Restraint injuries (marks on wrists)
    - Unexplained bleeding or injury to genitals
    - Sexually transmitted disease
    - Medication over- or under-dosing relative to prescribed amounts
- Abandonment or neglect
    - Unusual weight loss
    - Poor nutrition or dehydration
    - Poor hygiene
    - Unsanitary or unsafe living environment
    - Inappropriate clothing (inadequate for cold weather)
    - Lack of needed medical aids, such as glasses

- Financial abuse
  - Sudden changes in financial status
  - Valuable items or cash missing from residence
  - Unpaid bills when the person has money to pay them
  - Unusual financial activity, or activity the person could not have done (e.g., large withdrawals, ATM withdrawal by hospital inpatient)
  - Sudden appearance of unnecessary goods or services
  - Signatures on checks do not match the person's
- Unusual caregiver behavior (can indicate risk any type of abuse)
  - Threatening, belittling, or controlling behavior
  - Deserting
  - Burnout (can be evidenced by mental health symptoms, substance use, poor resilience, irritability, or resentment toward the person being cared for, as examples)

It is important for CSWs to be aware that stress and burnout are common among caregivers, and these indicate a risk of abuse, but may also simply mean that the caregiver needs some time away from their responsibilities. Caregiving is difficult, particularly if the person being cared for has severe illness or dementia, is socially isolated, is physically aggressive, or has a history of domestic violence. These factors place the person at greater risk of abuse.

Exceptions to confidentiality: Danger to self or others K20-25

Identifying need for hospitalization. Under state law, an individual can be hospitalized against their will if, because of a mental health condition, they are a danger to others, are a danger to themselves, or are gravely disabled. In such instances, the person is taken to a hospital or other county-designated facility for assessment for up to 72 hours, which you may know as a "72-hour hold" or a "5150."

While dangerousness to self and others is explained in additional detail below, the term "gravely disabled" has a specific meaning in law. It refers to instances where, because of a mental condition, the individual is unable to meet their most basic survival needs for food, shelter, and clothing. Especially as California has dealt with a rising homeless population, many of whom struggle with mental health conditions, determining whether someone is gravely disabled has gotten more complex. A severe mental illness in and of itself is not enough grounds for such a determination, but if the illness causes the person to be unable to meet those survival needs, then they may be considered gravely disabled.

Legal requirements for initiating involuntary hospitalization. When a CSW believes hospitalization is necessary, having a client go voluntarily is usually preferable to the process of involuntary hospitalization. However, if the CSW believes the client has a mental disorder that is causing them to be a danger to themselves or others or is gravely disabled, and the client refuses voluntary treatment, the CSW can begin the process of involuntary hospitalization.

For a client to be hospitalized against their will, a therapist must be able to cite specific facts (client words, appearance or behaviors) supporting the dangerousness of the client, and the conclusions the therapist drew from those facts. The therapist must then find what the county considers an "eligible professional" to actually write the 5150 application. (Usually a police officer or other person designated by the county serves this role. LCSWs can serve in this role, but may need to first go through additional training and certification.)

Ultimately, it is up to a professional at the facility designated by the county to receive involuntary holds to determine whether the client is to be involuntarily hospitalized. If that professional agrees, the client can be initially held for up to 72 hours. If the client remains dangerous to themselves or others, or gravely disabled, at the end of the 72 hours, they can be certified for an additional hold of up to 14 days for intensive treatment.

Laws about confidentiality in situations of client danger to self or others. Danger to self or others is commonly understood as an exception to confidentiality under the law. The *Tarasoff v. California Board of Regents* case established that danger to a reasonably identifiable victim outweighs client confidentiality. A social worker dealing with a client who poses an imminent danger of serious bodily harm to reasonably identifiable victims must take reasonable steps to resolve the threat, which typically include breaking confidentiality (see “Duty to protect law” below). When a client is suicidal, the *Bellah v. Greenson* case established that therapists have a responsibility to act to protect the client’s safety, and this can involve breaking confidentiality if needed. If a client poses a general danger to others because of a mental health condition, *Tarasoff* does not apply, but the therapist still can move to have the client involuntarily hospitalized if necessary.

In each of these instances, the CSW can break confidentiality. The CSW shares information about therapy with others who are involved in resolving the immediate danger. Even in these situations, though, the CSW should share *only* the information necessary to resolve the immediate threat. Sharing unrelated information about the client’s therapy may still be seen as a violation of confidentiality rules.

Sometimes, law enforcement and therapists work together in mental health crisis response teams. These teams must be supervised by mental health professionals. The therapists and law enforcement officers responding to mental health crises on these teams are not doing therapy, but they may benefit from knowing some information about the potentially dangerous person. If you are providing information about your client to emergency responders, it is up to your judgment to determine what information is appropriate to share to resolve the threat, and not to share more than necessary.

If a *Tarasoff* situation arises where the therapist resolves the immediate danger *without* notifying law enforcement, the CSW still must inform law enforcement of the threat within 24 hours. This law was enacted to help law enforcement put potentially dangerous individuals into a database that prevents them from buying guns.

Methods and criteria to identify when a client poses danger to self or others. There are good, brief ways of assessing clients who may pose a danger to themselves or others, including screening instruments and structured interviews. Assessments for suicide and violence to others tend to focus on the following factors:

- **Ideation (thoughts).** Is the person actively considering harming themselves or someone else? If suicidal, are they romanticizing what their death would be like, for them or others around them?

- **Planning.** Do they have a specific plan for how they would hurt themselves or someone else? Is it immediate?
- **Intent.** Does the person intend to commit violence? How sure are they? Some clients will fantasize about violence or death without any intent to ever act on these fantasies.
- **Access to means.** How easy would it be to carry out the plan? If they are considering suicide or homicide by gun, is there a gun in the house?
- **Past experience.** Have they attempted suicide or been violent with others before? How? Note that *previous suicide attempts* is the strongest risk factor for future attempts.
- **Protective factors.** What are the reasons the person has not hurt themselves or someone else so far? What would prevent them from suicide or violence in the future?

Demographic factors are also important to keep in mind, though these are not predictive of violence. While suicide is a leading cause of death among adolescents (because other causes of death are not common at this age), statistically, the highest risk for suicide is among the elderly (85+) and the middle-aged (45-64). Men are at higher risk than women. Whites and Native Americans have the highest suicide rates among racial groups. Military veterans and those who identify as LGBTQIA+ have heightened risk.

Duty to protect law. You are probably familiar with *Tarasoff v. California Board of Regents*, the court case that established a therapist's responsibility to act when a client poses an imminent danger of serious bodily harm to a reasonably identifiable victim or victims. In such instances, CSWs have a legal obligation known as "duty to protect." While this is not technically a duty to *warn* (and in rare instances, it might be inappropriate to warn the intended victim, such as times when doing so might trigger the victim to commit a violent act), the most common methods of protecting potential victims are to notify the victims and law enforcement of the threat. You also have additional protection from liability when you make reasonable efforts to notify both the victim and law enforcement.

The law does *not* require you to report or otherwise act on threats to property, so such threats typically must remain confidential. Animals are considered property under state law, so threats against animals do not provoke any obligations or opportunities for the therapist to break confidentiality. However, threats to property are not considered privileged communication under the law (more on Privilege is below), so they could be disclosed in the context of a court proceeding.

Indicators of intent to harm. Obviously, the strongest indicator of a client's intent to harm someone is when they tell you directly that they intend to harm someone. However, this is not the only indicator a therapist should be aware of. Third-party reports of a client intending to harm another person may be treated similarly to direct reports, if the therapist believes that the third party is a trustworthy reporter. Threats made in writing or by other means may be considered evidence of intent to harm. Indirect statements such as "after today, she won't be around any more" may also be reasonable indicators, based on the CSW's knowledge of the client. Threatening behaviors may also qualify. Clients who are actively using drugs or alcohol may present heightened danger to potential victims.

Exceptions to privilege K26-31

As noted earlier, privilege refers to information that can be excluded from court proceedings. Normally, all communications between a therapist and their client are considered *privileged communications*, meaning that they cannot be used in court. However, there are several exceptions to this rule defined in law. Normally privileged information may be used in court if:

1) The client makes their mental or emotional condition an issue in a lawsuit.
2) The client alleges breach of duty by the therapist.
3) Evaluation or therapy is taking place by court order.
4) A defendant in a criminal case requested the evaluation or therapy to determine their sanity.
5) The client is under age 16 and is the victim of a crime, and the therapist believes that disclosing that information is in the child's best interests.
6) The therapist was sought out for the purpose of committing a crime or avoiding detection after the fact.

This list is worth memorizing. Each one of these exceptions gets its own Knowledge Statement in the BBS Exam Plan, so there is a strong likelihood you will be specifically asked to apply your knowledge of one or more of these on your exam.

Recall here that while clients can waive privilege, only a judge can determine whether an exception to privilege applies to a specific situation. That's never your determination to make. Even in situations where you believe a judge is likely to ultimately determine that an exception applies, if your client is asserting privilege, you should also assert privilege on the client's behalf until the judge makes that determination.

Sample Questions

See the next page for answers and rationales

1. An elder client tells an LCSW working in hospice care that the client was recently taken to a local religious gathering against her will by her 50-year-old daughter. The daughter is a member of the religious group. By the client's report, the daughter told her mother that "this might be good for you, being around people with good values" and did not bring the mother home when the mother said she was uncomfortable there. Furthermore, the daughter donated the cash in the client's purse to the religious group, despite the client's repeated statements to her daughter that the client did not support the group. How should the LCSW respond to their legal obligations in this case?

   a. Report suspected elder abuse (specifically, abduction)
   b. Report suspected elder abuse (specifically, financial abuse)
   c. Report suspected elder abuse (specifically, emotional abuse)
   d. Report suspected elder abuse (specifically, isolation)

2. An LCSW's client confesses to her that he is struggling with guilt over his involvement in three recent gang-related murders. Two adults were killed: one was a rival gang member, the other was an innocent bystander. The third victim was also a rival gang member, and was just 17 years old. The client tells the LCSW that he does not believe he or the others in his gang will be caught, but this is only worsening his guilt. How should the LCSW handle her legal obligations surrounding confidentiality?

   a. Break confidentiality for the three murders and work with law enforcement to warn other members of the rival gang
   b. Break confidentiality for the murder of the bystander and work with law enforcement to warn other members of the rival gang
   c. Break confidentiality for the murder of the 17-year-old, and otherwise maintain confidentiality
   d. Maintain the client's confidentiality for all past acts, and encourage him to consider self-reporting to law enforcement if necessary to resolve his guilt

Sample Questions: Answers and Rationales

1. An elder client tells an LCSW working in hospice care that the client was recently taken to a local religious gathering against her will by her 50-year-old daughter. The daughter is a member of the religious group. By the client's report, the daughter told her mother that "this might be good for you, being around people with good values" and did not bring the mother home when the mother said she was uncomfortable there. Furthermore, the daughter donated the cash in the client's purse to the religious group, despite the client's repeated statements to her daughter that the client did not support the group. How should the LCSW respond to their legal obligations in this case?

a. **Incorrect.** Report suspected elder abuse (specifically, abduction)
b. **CORRECT.** Report suspected elder abuse (specifically, financial abuse)
c. **Incorrect.** Report suspected elder abuse (specifically, emotional abuse)
d. **Incorrect.** Report suspected elder abuse (specifically, isolation)

All four options share reporting, so it is safe to presume that reporting is a requirement here. The differences relate to the *type* of abuse being reported. The law surrounding abduction (a) requires that the elder have been taken across state lines, which is not stated in the question. Emotional abuse (c) is not a specific category of elder abuse in statute, though the elder abuse rules do provide wide latitude for therapists to report anything they find to be abusive to an elder. Isolation (d) is perhaps most clearly not appropriate here, as the daughter took the client to a social event. Financial abuse (b) is most appropriate here, given that the client states her daughter took her money against her will and spent it on a cause she would not have supported on her own.

2. An LCSW's client confesses to her that he is struggling with guilt over his involvement in three recent gang-related murders. Two adults were killed: one was a rival gang member, the other was an innocent bystander. The third victim was also a rival gang member, and was just 17 years old. The client tells the LCSW that he does not believe he or the others in his gang will be caught, but this is only worsening his guilt. How should the LCSW handle her legal obligations surrounding confidentiality?

a. **Incorrect.** Break confidentiality for the three murders and work with law enforcement to warn other members of the rival gang. *When the crime is not child, elder, or dependent adult abuse, LCSWs have no obligation to report past crimes, and doing so could be considered a breach of confidentiality.*
b. **Incorrect.** Break confidentiality for the murder of the bystander and work with law enforcement to warn other members of the rival gang. *When the crime is not child, elder, or dependent adult abuse, LCSWs generally have no obligation to report past crimes, and doing so could be considered a breach of confidentiality.*
c. **CORRECT.** Break confidentiality for the murder of the 17-year-old, and otherwise maintain confidentiality. *Child abuse must be reported, and in this case the murder of the 17-year-old qualifies as child abuse. Child abuse must be reported even when it resulted in the death of the victim.*
d. **Incorrect.** Maintain the client's confidentiality for all past acts, and encourage him to consider self-reporting to law enforcement if necessary to resolve his guilt. *The murder of the 17-year-old qualifies as child abuse. It must be reported, so the LCSW cannot legally maintain confidentiality for "all past acts."*

LAW

Standards for Professional Practice

Scored exam questions (approximate): **5**

Sexual relationships K32-33

Sexual conduct between therapist and client. Sexual behavior between therapist and client is specifically prohibited under California law. (Such contact is also specifically prohibited by the NASW Code of Ethics, which we will discuss in the Ethics section.) "Behavior" here is a broader term than intercourse, and it applies to a wide range of sexual activities.

Intimacy between therapist and *former* client. For former clients, state law prohibits sexual behavior for two years after the last professional contact. Sexual relationships with former clients after this time may still be problematic and are further discouraged in the NASW ethics code. But they are not legally *prohibited* so long as two years have gone by since the last professional contact.

The *Therapy Never Includes Sexual Behavior* brochure. If your client informs you that they have had a sexual relationship with another therapist, you are required by law to provide for them the state-authored brochure *Therapy Never Includes Sexual Behavior*. (This was previously called *Professional Therapy Never Includes Sex*, which may be how your supervisor refers to it.) Failure to provide the brochure is considered unprofessional conduct. Many therapists keep a copy or two of the brochure readily available in their offices; it also can be downloaded and printed when you need it.

Scope of practice K34

Your scope of practice is set in state law. It specifies what someone with an LCSW license can legally do.

The CSW scope of practice allows you to work with individuals, couples, families, and groups. (The word "client" may refer to an individual, couple, or family.) The CSW scope of practice specifically allows you to use "counseling and [...] applied psychotherapy," making you a psychotherapist. And it allows you to use the training you received in your required coursework – which is key to understanding that CSWs can independently diagnose mental illness.

One of the most important pieces in understanding scope of practice is understanding its limits. **CSWs *cannot* provide legal advice, medical advice, or other forms of guidance that are outside the CSW scope of practice.** Referring a client to a doctor, lawyer, or other professional is fine, and it's good to recognize when clients have these needs. But recommending that a client take a certain medication, for example, or change their medication dosage, would be outside of the CSW scope of practice. Social workers should refer to physicians to make determinations about medication use and dosage.

It is helpful here to understand the difference between scope of *practice* – which is set in state law and is the same for every CSW in the state – and scope of *competence*, which is based on your specific education, training, and experience. Scope of competence varies by individual CSW and is primarily an ethical issue. It is discussed later.

Unprofessional conduct laws K35

When a therapist violates professional standards, they are said to have committed unprofessional conduct. The BBS exists to protect the public, not the professionals, and will investigate and (if appropriate) punish unprofessional conduct when it is reported.

State law defines 28 specific categories of unprofessional conduct. For our purposes, it's most important to know what unprofessional conduct *means*: It refers to **actions taken in a professional role that are below**

minimum professional standards. Unlike criminal cases (where you could go to jail) or civil cases (where you might have to pay damages to someone you have wronged), unprofessional conduct rules apply to your professional role. Unprofessional conduct can result in action being taken against your license or registration.

The types of conduct defined in state law as unprofessional conduct include the following. The language here is lightly edited from state law, and grouped into categories:

Sexual misconduct

Sexual contact with a client or former client
Committing a sex crime with a minor
Committing a sex crime
Sexual misconduct
Failure to provide *Professional Therapy Never Includes Sex*

Scope of practice and competence

Performing or offering services outside of scope

Impairment

Impairment due to mental or physical illness or drug dependence
Drug dependence or use with a client while providing services

Confidentiality

Failure to maintain confidentiality

Crimes and bad acts

Conviction of a crime
Committing a dishonest, corrupt, or fraudulent act
Discipline by another board or by another state

Fraud

Getting or attempting to get a license by fraud
Misrepresenting your license or qualifications
Impersonating a licensee
Aiding someone else's unlicensed activity

Testing

Violating exam security or integrity

Supervision

Improper supervision of a trainee or associate
Violations during or involving required hours of experience

Fees and advertising

Failure to disclose fees in advance
False, misleading, deceptive, or improper advertising
Paying, accepting, or soliciting a fee for referrals

Record-keeping

Failure to keep records consistent with sound clinical judgment
Failure to comply with client requests for access to records

Telemedicine

Violating state telehealth standards

General misconduct

General unprofessional conduct
Gross negligence or incompetence
Intentionally or recklessly causing physical or emotional harm

The category simply called "general unprofessional conduct" allows the BBS to act against you if you violate other law, professional ethical codes, or the professional standard of care while in your professional role. In this way, behaviors that are unethical can also be considered illegal, even if they aren't specifically designated as such in the law.

You do not need to memorize the entire list above. Most of it is simply what you would expect (and what is covered in this book). Knowing all of the categories will not be nearly as helpful to you as being able to determine whether a *particular behavior* qualifies as unprofessional conduct under the law.

When a therapist engages in unprofessional conduct with a client, the client may submit a complaint to the BBS. The BBS then has an investigations unit that assesses the complaint, determines whether it is actionable, and investigates if appropriate. During this time, the CSW has the opportunity to defend themselves. If the CSW is found to have committed unprofessional conduct, the BBS can levy fines, place the CSW's license (or registration, in cases involving CSW associates) on suspension or probation, restrict their practice, and in severe cases, revoke the CSW's license or registration. They also may require other actions, such as regular drug testing, while the CSW is on probation or in order to resolve the disciplinary issue. The disciplinary process is meaningfully different from a criminal trial or a civil lawsuit; the BBS only needs to find *clear and convincing evidence* that a violation occurred to issue a penalty.

Disclosing fees K36

Required disclosures. Under state law, you must inform clients before treatment begins of (1) the fee they will be charged and (2) the basis upon which that fee was computed. If you're confused about that second part, think about the sliding-fee scales used at many training clinics: *Client income* is the basis on which the fee is computed. As another example, some CSWs charge more for couple and family sessions than they do for individual sessions. That's fine, but clients need to know about this before treatment starts. Failure to disclose fees and their basis prior to starting treatment is considered unprofessional conduct.

Every new client also must be informed of the process of filing a board complaint, should the client choose to file a complaint in the future.

Starting in 2022, federal law requires therapists and other health care professionals to provide a Good Faith Estimate of a new client's treatment costs, if the client is not planning to use their insurance to cover those costs. The GFE provides more information about the anticipated treatment, including estimated costs over the next 12 months. There are specific legal requirements for the content of a GFE and the time by which it must be provided to the client.

Third-party reimbursement K37-38

Third-party reimbursement rules. Health insurance coverage has expanded significantly since the passage of the Affordable Care Act. Of course, insurance is not the only form of third-party payment; employers, courts, nonprofit organizations, family members, and others may be the ones who are actually paying for client care. CSWs need to be aware of the rules surrounding third-party payment, including the limits on information that can be shared with third-party payers.

Some of the key legal rules regarding third-party payment include:

- **Freedom of choice.** Insurance companies typically must reimburse CSWs alongside other mental health providers. Associates do not have to be reimbursed, though some plans will pay for services provided by associates.
- **Mental disorder only.** Most insurers will only reimburse when there is a diagnosed mental disorder. Some will cover services when there is no mental health diagnosis, but plans are not legally required to do so.
- **Protests and complaints.** Providers can (and generally should) appeal denials of reimbursement. Consumers and providers both can complain to the state about insurance company practices. Depending on the plan, it may be governed by the state Department of Insurance or the Department of Managed Health Care.

One of the most important legal rules regarding third-party reimbursement is the prohibition against insurance fraud, which can draw criminal and civil penalties in addition to action against your license. Any falsification of diagnosis, procedure code, amount paid, or any other information for the purpose of receiving insurance payment is insurance fraud.

Parity laws. State and federal law require parity in insurance coverage for mental health. What this means is that insurers cannot use a different deductible or other forms of treatment limitations for mental health that they do not apply to other medical coverage. Co-payments, deductibles, and treatment limitations (like caps on visits or days of coverage) for mental health must be equal to or better than the limits placed on other medical coverage. Under a new law for 2021, any plan language aiming to give the insurer "discretionary authority" to refuse coverage for medically necessary mental health or substance abuse treatment is invalid.

Advertising laws K39

Advertising laws. Essentially any public statement where you suggest that you offer therapy or counseling services to the public would be considered an advertisement – the law is purposefully broad on that. The only exception in the law is for bulletins within a religious setting, published only to members of that religious group.

State law is highly specific on the **licensure status** disclosures that need to be included in *any* advertisement of a CSW's services. A licensed CSW needs to include their name, their license number, and their title ("licensed clinical social worker") or an acceptable abbreviation ("LCSW"). An associate needs to include their name, their registration number, their employer's name, an indication that they are under licensed supervision, and their title ("Registered Associate Clinical Social Worker"). That title can be abbreviated "Registered Associate CSW."

LCSWs and associates can advertise themselves as **psychotherapists** and say that they perform psychotherapy, as long as they clearly list their licensure type, something the law already requires anyway.

LCSWs can advertise using **fictitious business names**, so long as those names are not misleading and clients are informed of the business owners' names and licensure status before treatment begins.

Ads making any kind of **scientific claims** must be backed by published, peer-reviewed research literature.

Any **fees** included in an advertisement must be exact; you cannot advertise fees in ways like "$95 and up." For this reason, many LCSWs and clinics choose not to list their fees in their advertising.

It would be unprofessional conduct for any CSW to advertise in a manner that is **false, misleading, or deceptive**. Any claims that would be likely to create unjustified expectations of treatment success are also prohibited by law.

Payment for referrals K40

Clinical social workers are legally prohibited from giving or receiving any form of payment for referrals. (There is a parallel ethical prohibition.) This includes payments to or from clients, payments to or from the professional you referred the clients to (sometimes called "kickbacks"), or payments to or from third parties. The idea here is that referrals should be made *solely* based on what is in the best interests of the client. If you are getting paid for referrals, there is at least the *appearance* of a conflict of interests, as you might make a referral based more on what will financially benefit you than what will clinically benefit the client.

This issue has become more complex in recent years. Some CSWs participate in "networking groups," which are organizations of professionals who sell a wide variety of goods and services. Members join the networking group for the specific purpose of referring potential customers to one another. However, because these groups often operate in a structure where members are rewarded for the referrals they generate (the reward might be the *absence* of a fee that they would otherwise have to pay to participate), CSWs in such groups risk being disciplined for violating the standards against receiving payment for referrals.

Sample Questions

See the next page for answers and rationales

1. To show support for the local high school basketball team, an LCSW plans to offer new clients their first six sessions at a per-session fee equal to the number of points scored by the basketball team's opponent in their most recent game. So, if the team plays great defense, new clients receive lower fees. After six sessions, clients who wish to continue therapy would do so at the LCSW's standard rate of $120 per session. Which best reflects the LCSW's legal obligations related to this offer?

   a. The LCSW must put in their advertising how many points the team's opponent scored in their last game, so that clients will know precisely what the promotional rate would be
   b. The LCSW must include both the promotional rate and the standard rate in all advertisements
   c. The LCSW must inform each new client, prior to the beginning of services, what their specific rate would be and why
   d. The LCSW must set a minimum and maximum rate to protect both clients and the therapist from potential exploitation if basketball scores are unusually high or low

Sample question #2 is on the next page.

2. An LCSW has been learning about herbal medicine and its connections with overall health and wellness. The LCSW mentions this to some clients, and the clients respond with interest in learning how herbal medicine might be incorporated into their therapy processes. Some clients report difficulty with sleep and anxiety, and are hopeful that herbal remedies could work alongside talk therapy. How can the LCSW respond to the clients' inquiries?

a. Refer interested clients to external books, videos, or herbal medicine practitioners
b. Provide recommendations for herbal remedies only to target those issues also being addressed in therapy
c. Provide herbal teas, lotions, and other potential remedies specific to clients' presenting issues, noting that clients may use or apply those remedies themselves during sessions
d. Seek certification as an herbal wellness practitioner, and integrate herbal remedies into therapy only after receiving the appropriate certification

Sample Questions: Answers and Rationales

1. To show support for the local high school basketball team, an LCSW plans to offer new clients their first six sessions at a per-session fee equal to the number of points scored by the basketball team's opponent in their most recent game. So, if the team plays great defense, new clients receive lower fees. After six sessions, clients who wish to continue therapy would do so at the LCSW's standard rate of $120 per session. Which best reflects the LCSW's legal obligations related to this offer?

a. **Incorrect.** The LCSW must put in their advertising how many points the team's opponent scored in their last game, so that clients will know precisely what the promotional rate would be
b. **Incorrect.** The LCSW must include both the promotional rate and the standard rate in all advertisements
c. **CORRECT.** The LCSW must inform each new client, prior to the beginning of services, what their specific rate would be and why
d. **Incorrect.** The LCSW must set a minimum and maximum rate to protect both clients and the therapist from potential exploitation if basketball scores are unusually high or low

LCSWs are not required to disclose fees in their advertising (A and B). However, if they choose to include mentions of fees in their advertising, the listed fees must be exact. Simply setting a range (D) is not required and does not resolve any obligations. LCSWs are legally required to inform each client what their specific fee will be, and the basis for how it was computed, before beginning services. In this case, the promotion may explain the basis for the fee, but not all new clients may have seen the advertisement.

2. An LCSW has been learning about herbal medicine and its connections with overall health and wellness. The LCSW mentions this to some clients, and the clients respond with interest in learning how herbal medicine might be incorporated into their therapy processes. Some clients report difficulty with sleep and anxiety, and are hopeful that herbal remedies could work alongside talk therapy. How can the LCSW respond to the clients' inquiries?

a. **CORRECT.** Refer interested clients to external books, videos, or herbal medicine practitioners
b. **Incorrect.** Provide recommendations for herbal remedies only to target those issues also being addressed in therapy
c. **Incorrect.** Provide herbal teas, lotions, and other potential remedies specific to clients' presenting issues, noting that clients may use or apply those remedies themselves during sessions
d. **Incorrect.** Seek certification as an herbal wellness practitioner, and integrate herbal remedies into therapy only after receiving the appropriate certification

While they can have tremendous value, herbal remedies are not a psychotherapeutic technique. As such, they fall outside of the LCSW scope of practice, regardless of how much knowledge or training the LCSW may have on the subject. The LCSW can refer to external resources, but should not offer any remedies or specific recommendations for herbal remedies themselves.

ETHICS

Competence and Preventing Harm

Scored exam questions (approximate): **9**

Scope of competence K41-45, K49

Understanding scope of competence. Your scope of competence is defined by your education, training, and professional experience. Your scope of competence is unique to you and can change over time. Scope of competence is primarily an *ethical* issue, though practicing outside of one's scope of competence is also considered unprofessional conduct in state law.

Knowing your own limitations. Just as it is important to be able to identify actions that would be out of the CSW scope of practice, it is also critical to understand when issues come before you that are outside your scope of competence. You can't possibly have training and experience for every possible situation you will encounter in your practice, so acknowledging limitations in your scope of competence is not a weakness. It is good professional behavior.

Need for consultation. When a situation comes up in therapy that is outside of a CSW's scope of competence, a responsible CSW will consult with a supervisor, treatment team, or others to determine what appropriate next steps would be. However, a need for consultation is not the same as a need to refer the client out. In many cases, the therapist will work to expand their competence while continuing to work with the client.

Collaborating to determine need for referrals. It is up to the CSW to monitor their own scope of competence. However, the assessment of client needs, and determinations of whether referrals are clinically indicated, should be a collaborative process with the client. There is little point in providing clients with referrals or resources they do not believe will benefit them. Social workers commonly collaborate with clients to determine what the clients' needs and expectations are, and to provide referrals (where appropriate) that are relevant to those needs.

Protecting client rights in consultations. Of course, CSWs are encouraged to regularly consult with other professionals and community resources to promote quality client care. It is common for CSWs to collaborate and consult with physicians, teachers, social service providers, and other important persons in a client's life, on issues that are outside the CSW's scope of competence.

CSWs are expected to be aware of colleagues' competence and expertise, so that when consulting is appropriate, the CSW can easily find a knowledgeable person. Ethically, the CSW should only seek consult from someone with appropriate knowledge or competence.

When doing such consultations, CSWs respect the confidentiality of their clients. Each member of the treatment unit (individual, couple, or family) must give their permission for clinical information to be shared with any outsider, unless an exception to confidentiality applies. Even when client permission or an exception to confidentiality is present, the CSW should only provide the information necessary for the consultation.

Expanding competence. If one's scope of competence is determined by education, training, and experience, then it makes sense that CSWs can expand into new areas of practice, or improve their competence in existing ones, by getting additional education, training, and experience. One's competence in working with a particular population can be improved through exposure to that population, including visiting or interacting with members of that population. In many cases it also is appropriate for a CSW to seek out new knowledge through books, videos, and other research about a topic or population that is new to the CSW.

Responsibility to remain current. The social work field is constantly growing and changing, with new treatment models and new scientific developments occurring on a regular basis. The training and experience that make you competent to work with a certain problem today may be considered outdated and inaccurate 10 years from now. CSWs have an ethical responsibility to remain current with new developments in the profession, through education, training, and supervised experience. This is part of the reason why LCSWs are required to get continuing education hours in each license renewal cycle.

Self-awareness K46-48, 50-51

Impairments. Good social workers are keenly aware of their own limitations. Social workers are expected to continually monitor themselves for potential impairment, and to engage in appropriate self-care. If you are struggling with a serious emotional problem, mental or physical illness, major life stressors, or substance use, it can interfere with your ability to provide effective services to clients. In addition, if you have a strong emotional reaction to a particular client – perhaps because their struggle mirrors one you have gone through, or because there is something in the client's behavior that you strongly dislike – you may not be able to provide effective services.

Impairment tends to show up as difficulty with clinical judgment. The therapist becomes more friendly, or harsher and more judgmental, toward clients than they typically would be. Sometimes impairment becomes visible through changes in a therapist's ability to complete routine tasks like documentation or follow-up contacts with clients and others. Sometimes impairment is most clear when reviewing client outcome data.

Responding to impairments. CSWs need to know the referrals and resources available if the therapist is struggling with an impairment and needs to step away from client care, either temporarily or on a longer-term basis. (Knowledge of appropriate referrals and resources comes up multiple times in the BBS Exam Plan, as it is important in many different sets of circumstances. Obviously, the test will not ask what the closest hospital is, since the same test is being given across the state. But you may be asked about the *kinds* of referrals and resources that would be most appropriate to a given situation. Referrals should always be appropriate to the level and type of client need.)

For the social worker, seeking treatment is appropriate when the problem is a serious emotional problem, mental or physical illness, or substance use. For these and other forms of impairment, the CSW could also seek supervision and consultation, engage in self-care, and consider going to therapy. In whatever time it takes for the CSW to resolve their impairment, protecting the welfare of the client is the highest priority.

Referrals and resources. Speaking of clinician awareness, CSWs are expected to have a strong working awareness of referrals and resources to assist clients in meeting their needs. CSWs should be prepared to connect clients with resources related to health and well-being, social services, housing, legal needs, and the like. When clients present needs that CSWs do not have resources to help clients meet, the CSW should assist the client in researching what resources may be available.

Methods to facilitate transfer. In some cases, the impairment of a CSW will lead to their needing to transfer clients to other therapists. If it is possible and appropriate, the CSW may have a termination session with the client, focused on transitioning them to a new provider. The CSW should provide appropriate referrals based on client need. The CSW and client should consider a Release of Information authorizing the transfer of client records to the new provider, and authorizing the old and new providers to communicate to ensure continuity of care. The CSW should follow up with the new provider to transfer the records and coordinate care appropriately.

Personal values, attitudes, and beliefs. CSWs are ethically prohibited from influencing client decisions on preferred treatment or outcomes based on personal values, attitudes, and beliefs. (Going forward, I'll just say "attitudes" to refer collectively to "values, attitudes, and beliefs.") Obviously, it is important for CSWs to be aware of their own attitudes and how they might impact the therapy process. Social workers allowing for their attitudes to influence them might pathologize the behavior of clients the social worker doesn't like, leading to incorrect diagnoses and poor treatment decisions. They might show bias toward one or more family members, impacting the effectiveness of couple or family work. They might become overly friendly (or overly hostile) with a client. They might place their own belief about a particular problem above current scientific knowledge in the field. Ultimately, the social worker is likely to miss or misinterpret important clinical information, decreasing the likelihood of effective therapy.

Managing the impact of therapist attitudes. So what happens, then, when a CSW becomes aware that they have personal attitudes that are entering into the therapy room? It depends on the nature of what is arising. You are of course allowed to hold whatever attitudes you hold, and subject to your employer's policies, you are ethically allowed even to discuss those attitudes in therapy when it is clinically appropriate to do so. What you cannot do is *impose* those attitudes on the client or the therapeutic process.

If the therapist is experiencing judgment or bias toward the client based on personal attitudes, the therapist should carefully consider how those attitudes are impacting treatment. The therapist may seek out supervision or consultation to ensure quality of care, and may go to their own therapy to identify the source of the attitude, working to change it if appropriate. If the therapist attitude is likely to continue interfering in the therapeutic relationship, the therapist may consider referring the client to another therapist – but must be cautious to avoid client abandonment, and to ensure that the referral is not discriminatory in nature. If the therapist refers clients out based on personal attitudes about race, gender, or other protected characteristics, the therapist may be engaging in discrimination.

Multiple Relationships K52-56

A multiple relationship (or "dual relationship" -- the terms are used here interchangeably) occurs any time a CSW has a relationship with a client that is separate from being their therapist. Not all multiple relationships are unethical, and some can't be avoided, especially in rural areas or in work with more tight-knit communities. The NASW Code of Ethics clarifies that multiple relationships do not have to be simultaneous – a multiple relationship can still occur (and can still be problematic) when one type of relationship begins after the other has concluded.

Assessing multiple relationships. Not all multiple relationships can be avoided, especially if you are working in a rural area or with a highly-specific population. It is also true that not all multiple relationships are problematic. If a colleague tells you that you can't see a client because "that would be a dual relationship," they haven't adequately made their case.

Potential multiple relationships must be carefully examined to see whether they would **impair clinical judgment** or create **risk of client exploitation**. These two considerations are critical to determining whether a multiple relationship can be allowed. If you know and like someone in your community and they ask to see you in therapy, your liking of them would probably influence how you observe them clinically -- in other words, your pre-existing view of them would impair your clinical judgment. (Impairment can mean positive bias as well as negative.) Having a client who coaches your daughter's soccer team could create risk of exploitation, as you could use your knowledge of the client's personal secrets to push for more playing time for your daughter. The fact that you wouldn't actually do this does not eliminate the risk of it, nor does it take away your responsibility to protect clients from that risk.

Even when such risks exist, though, in some cases it may be appropriate to continue with the therapy. If you are the only provider in a rural area, for example, or if you are the only local provider who speaks the same language as the client, the best interests of the client might be better served by going ahead with therapy. You would then need to take specific actions to reduce the risk of impaired judgment or exploitation.

Prohibited multiple relationships. Sexual relationships with clients and those close to the client are expressly prohibited, and discussed in greater detail below. Social workers are also ethically prohibited from taking advantage of any professional relationship to further the social worker's personal, religious, political, or business interests.

Managing boundaries. CSWs commonly take steps to ensure the integrity and boundaries of the therapy relationship. This can be especially important when it appears that a client is becoming confused about the nature of the relationship, or is wanting more of a personal or social relationship than what therapy allows. Examples of clients testing boundaries include inappropriate questions about a therapist's personal life, seeking to start sessions early or extend them past the scheduled end time, attempting to connect with the therapist's personal social media accounts, or contacting the therapist between sessions for reasons unrelated to the therapy.

Examples of methods for managing boundaries include having a conversation with the client to remind them of the boundaries of therapy; maintaining a clear treatment plan with identified therapy goals; making sure all contact between client and therapist stays focused on therapeutic issues; starting and ending sessions on time; and, when clinically appropriate, limiting contact by phone or other means between scheduled session times.

Potential conflicts of interest. CSWs are ethically obligated to be alert to potential conflicts of interest as they arise. A potential conflict emerges any time a therapist engages in a non-therapist role, such as consultation, coaching, or behavior analysis, with people who are or have been clients in therapy. A potential conflict also emerges any time an outside interest may interfere with the CSW's ability to exercise impartial professional judgment.

In any instance of potential conflict of interests, CSWs have an obligation to clarify their roles, and to distinguish how any applicable non-therapist role is different from therapy. In order to avoid any risk to clients, it may be preferable to refer out for additional services that are different from those for which the CSW was initially hired.

One common example of a conflict of interests emerges when a CSW who has been serving as a *therapist* is then asked to also serve as an *evaluator* for the same client. The phrase "conflict of interests" can be quite literal here: If a CSW is asked to provide a recommendation in a custody case where they have been serving as a therapist, then the interests of the client (in maintaining a trusting bond with their therapist, and pursuing their goals related to custody or whatever else) *conflict* with the interests of the court (which would want as much information about the client, positive and negative, as they could obtain, in the interests of making an objective determination). CSWs can serve as clinicians or evaluators, but unless compelled by a court, typically should not serve in both roles at once.

The NASW code of ethics includes discussion of conflicts of interest that can emerge when social workers share personal information online. Such sharing is allowed, but social workers must understand the potential for boundary confusion and inappropriate dual relationships to result.

When a conflict of interests arises, social workers should seek to resolve the conflict in ways that place the best interests of the client as the highest priority. As the code notes, protecting client interests may require terminating the therapeutic relationship and making proper referrals.

Potentially damaging relationships. Sexual relationships, which are discussed at greater length below, are the best example of a relationship that can be damaging to the client. However, they are not the only example. Other forms of multiple relationships can harm clients directly, through poor care or exploitation, or they may harm clients more indirectly, by reducing their overall confidence in therapy as an effective and worthwhile treatment. Social relationships between CSWs and clients can create confusion about the therapist's role, for example, and can hinder success in therapy by clouding the CSW's clinical judgment.

Social workers are ethically prohibited from terminating clinical services in order to pursue a social, financial, or sexual relationship with a client.

When multiple relationships can't be avoided. Some multiple relationships are unavoidable. For example, some level of multiple relationship is created any time a CSW gets a new client through a referral from an existing client. Another example occurs in a rural area, where a CSW may have regular interaction with many clients at community gatherings. In these and similar situations, the NASW Code of Ethics (standard 1.06(c)) requires CSWs to "take steps to protect clients and [be] responsible for setting clear, appropriate, and culturally sensitive boundaries."

In some cases, the precautions may be as simple as having a conversation with the client to reassure them of confidentiality and to clearly separate roles. In other cases, more stringent precautions may be appropriate, like the CSW regularly consulting on the case with a colleague.

Sexual relationships K57-59

Risk of exploitation. The rules prohibiting sexual contact between therapists and their clients come from a fundamental understanding that because the therapist has power in the therapy relationship, because clients are often emotionally vulnerable, and because the therapy process happens behind closed doors, sexual relationships between therapists and clients are likely to be exploitive and ultimately harmful to clients.

This exploitation does not require sexual *intercourse*, and the ethical standards around sexual relationships are worded in such a way as to include sexual behavior generally, even if there has not been intercourse. The NASW code even includes "inappropriate sexual communications," either in person or via technology, as an ethical violation. (If you're working with a couple on sexual issues, that might require candid conversation about their sexual behavior; that's appropriate, as it is clinically relevant.)

Intimacy between therapist and client. As noted in the legal section, sexual conduct -- again, a purposefully broader term than intercourse -- between therapist and client is specifically prohibited under California law. Such contact is also specifically prohibited by the NASW code of ethics.

Intimacy between therapist and *former* client. The NASW Code of Ethics *forever* discourages sexual relationships or sexual contact with former clients, due to the risk that such contacts will be exploitive and harmful to the former client. While state law has a prohibition against such contact that lasts for two years beyond the last professional contact, the NASW ethical standard has no time limit attached.

The NASW standard is not a prohibition – discouraging a behavior is different from disallowing it – but it makes clear that if a social worker engages in sexual contact with a former client, the burden of proof would be on the social worker to demonstrate that the former client had *not* been exploited, coerced, or manipulated, even if unintentionally.

Intimacy between therapist and client's spouse, partner, or family member. State laws about sexual relationships with clients and former clients apply only to the clients themselves. Under ethical guidelines, the prohibition is broader: Social workers *also* may not enter into sexually intimate relationships with clients' spouses or partners, other family members, or anyone else with whom the client maintains a personal relationship, if there is risk of exploitation or harm to the client (and there typically is such risk). The NASW code makes no direct mention of sexual relationships with the partners, family members, or friends of *former* clients.

Therapy with former romantic partners. Just as it would typically be unethical to start having sex with a former client (subject to the rules noted above), it would also be unethical to accept a client in therapy who was a former sexual partner. This is expressly prohibited by the NASW Code of Ethics, considering the potential for harm to the individual and the likelihood that the prior relationship would make it difficult to maintain professional boundaries.

Sample Questions

See the next page for answers and rationales

1. An experienced LCSW working with clients from a variety of backgrounds is gently questioned by a supervisor after making comments that clients perceived as offensive and unwelcoming. The LCSW argues that she has completed more than 30 hours of training in working with different racial groups over the course of their career, and even gave talks on working with Black clients in the mid-1980s, shortly after she was first licensed. Considering her ethical responsibilities, the LCSW should:

a. Update her knowledge on diversity and inclusion
b. Apologize to the clients who were offended, and ask them to help her become more knowledgeable about their backgrounds
c. Provide the supervisor a list of the diversity-related coursework she has taken throughout her career
d. Avoid discussing client race or other demographics in future sessions

2. An LCSW begins a therapeutic relationship with a local schoolteacher. Several months later, the LCSW's daughter starts 3rd grade, and the daughter's class is taught by the client. There is only one teacher for the grade level at that school. How can the LCSW best address their obligations in this situation?

a. Clarify therapeutic boundaries and transfer the daughter to a different school for the year
b. Acknowledge the risk of exploitation, clarify therapeutic boundaries, and seek regular consultation
c. Clarify therapeutic boundaries and request that the client carefully document conversations outside of therapy about the daughter, to ensure that no abuse of power is occurring
d. Assess the client's comfort level, and do not attend any school events for the year

Sample Questions: Answers and Rationales

1. An experienced LCSW working with clients from a variety of backgrounds is gently questioned by a supervisor after making comments that clients perceived as offensive and unwelcoming. The LCSW argues that she has completed more than 30 hours of training in working with different racial groups over the course of their career, and even gave talks on working with Black clients in the mid-1980s, shortly after she was first licensed. Considering her ethical responsibilities, the LCSW should:

a. **CORRECT.** Update her knowledge on diversity and inclusion
b. **Incorrect.** Apologize to the clients who were offended, and ask them to help her become more knowledgeable about their backgrounds
c. **Incorrect.** Provide the supervisor a list of the diversity-related coursework she has taken throughout her career
d. **Incorrect.** Avoid discussing client race or other demographics in future sessions

Race and other demographic factors are key elements of client identity and experience, and should not simply be ignored. Here, the LCSW has taken some diversity training, but more than 30 hours of such training amounts to very little over what appears to be a 30-plus-year career, and the clients' complaints suggest that the LCSW's knowledge may be out of date. While apologies to the clients may be appropriate, it is not appropriate to ask clients to do the emotional labor of providing the LCSW with training on how to work effectively with diverse groups. It's the LCSW's job to get training on her own, and then to bring that knowledge and skill into session.

2. An LCSW begins a therapeutic relationship with a local schoolteacher. Several months later, the LCSW's daughter starts 3rd grade, and the daughter's class is taught by the client. There is only one teacher for the grade level at that school. How can the LCSW best address their obligations in this situation?

a. **Incorrect.** Clarify therapeutic boundaries and transfer the daughter to a different school for the year
b. **CORRECT.** Acknowledge the risk of exploitation, clarify therapeutic boundaries, and seek regular consultation
c. **Incorrect.** Clarify therapeutic boundaries and request that the client carefully document conversations outside of therapy about the daughter, to ensure that no abuse of power is occurring
d. **Incorrect.** Assess the client's comfort level, and do not attend any school events for the year

With any dual relationship, social workers are required to assess the risk of exploitation and the potential for impaired clinical judgment. Both are present here, but not to high degrees. The risk of exploitation comes from the possibility that the social worker could use what she learns in therapy about the teacher to push for special treatment for the social worker's daughter. The potential impairment of clinical judgment stems from the possibility that their interactions surrounding the daughter's behavior in school will influence how the social worker treats the client in session. All of that said, monitoring this situation and seeking consultation are better than the other options here. Transferring the daughter or refusing to attend school events may raise questions for the daughter and others, and might even reveal the therapeutic relationship. Asking the client to document conversations about the daughter is improper as it makes the client responsible for the social worker's ethical compliance.

ETHICS

Therapeutic Relationship

Scored exam questions (approximate): **13-14**

Informed Consent K60-65

Informed consent. For a client to offer consent that is truly *informed*, they need a reasonable amount of *information* about the treatment process. CSWs have an ethical responsibility to provide clients with appropriate information about the treatment process, so that the client can make an informed decision about whether they want to participate. Because treatment plans and methods can change during therapy, informed consent for treatment is best understood not as a single event but as an ongoing process.

Facilitating client decisions about treatment. Professional ethics require CSWs to provide enough information to clients that the clients can make meaningful choices about whether to start therapy. The nature of this information may vary by therapist and by treatment type, but CSWs are specifically required to inform clients of:

- The purpose for all services provided
- Risks associated with those services
- Limits to services imposed by third parties
- Limits to confidentiality, and potential consequences of disclosure
- Uses of technology in service delivery
- Service costs
- Alternative services
- Clients' right to refuse or withdraw consent
- How long their consent is considered valid if not withdrawn

Couple, family, and group clients should be specifically informed of how the CSW handles confidentiality among members of the treatment unit – and that the CSW cannot guarantee that other members of that treatment unit will maintain confidentiality.

Social workers should obtain specific consent before creating audio or video recordings of sessions, or conducting a digital search related to the client (except in cases of "compelling professional reasons," such as in an emergency).

All this information is intended to help clients make well-informed decisions about their participation in treatment. Clients should always be given the opportunity to ask questions related to informed consent (this, too, is an ethical requirement), and if a client has doubts or hesitancies about treatment as a result of what is presented to them in the informed consent process, the CSW should focus on providing the client with any additional information that may help their decision-making, and not on simply trying to "sell" the client on the services the CSW provides.

Client autonomy in treatment decisions. Clients have the fundamental right to choose for themselves what kinds of mental health treatment they will participate in. While there are exceptions to this, such as for clients who present an imminent danger to themselves or others and thus can be involuntarily hospitalized, most clients can choose their treatment type, treatment provider, and treatment goals as they see fit. (Some goals would be considered inappropriate for therapy, such as a parent bringing their child into therapy in hopes of changing the child's sexual orientation. While a parent is certainly free to pursue this goal, it would not be appropriate for a therapist to attempt to offer this treatment.) Consistent with this principle, clients can also discontinue treatment or change treatment provider at any time. Even when treatment is taking place by court order, clients can typically choose their provider. CSWs respect clients' rights to choose whether to start therapy and whether to leave it at any time. Of course, therapists can and should discuss such decisions with clients, but CSWs cannot require a client to remain in therapy, or to remain in therapy with the specific clinician, if the client does not wish to do so.

Culturally and developmentally appropriate methods. CSWs should gain consent for treatment in a manner that is culturally and developmentally appropriate. If a client is illiterate, does not read English, comes from a culture that promotes deference, or is otherwise unable to make sense of the informed consent document, their signature on it may not truly reflect informed consent. The informed consent process would be better served with a verbal discussion in language that the client can understand. CSWs also should be aware of the possibility that clients may be attending therapy against their wishes, at the demand of a family member or someone else; in such instances, it is important for the CSW to determine whether the client is truly providing voluntary consent for treatment.

Guardians and representatives. When clients are unable to make informed decisions on their own, their guardians and legal representatives have the right and responsibility to make choices on the client's behalf. Most commonly, this happens when a parent or legal guardian consents to the treatment of a minor. However, it can also apply when a client under conservatorship is put into treatment by their conservator, or when a court-appointed *guardian ad litem* seeks treatment for minors involved in a custody dispute. In these and other instances, guardians and legal representatives are responsible for making informed decisions about treatment that will be in the best interest of the client.

Clients who can't provide voluntary consent. When a client is unable to provide voluntary consent for treatment, the CSW remains responsible for protecting client welfare. Clients may be unable to voluntarily consent for treatment if they are under the influence of drugs or alcohol, if they have been involuntarily hospitalized as a danger to themselves or others, or if they are a child brought to treatment by their parents, as a few examples.

In these instances, the CSW would still take steps to promote client welfare and facilitate the client's ability to make decisions about treatment to the degree possible. In the case of a client under the influence of drugs or alcohol, the CSW may simply take steps to keep the client safe until the influence of the drug has worn off and the client can voluntarily consent to further treatment. A more thorough informed consent process may take place at that point. If a client has been involuntarily hospitalized, the CSW may remind them of their remaining rights. In the case of a minor, a CSW may utilize an assent agreement, which spells out the purpose, risks, and benefits of therapy in a way that is developmentally appropriate to the child, and allows them to ask questions about the therapy.

Clients mandated to treatment by a court or other outside entity typically retain their right to choose their treatment provider and voluntarily consent to therapy. They may be required by a court to be in therapy, but typically, they don't have to be in therapy *with you*. CSWs working with mandated clients are ethically required to clarify the CSW's role and the limits of confidentiality that will apply to the mandated services. This clarification helps protect client rights, as they can choose whether to go forward in treatment under those rules.

Concurrent services K66-68

Effects of concurrent treatment. When done well, concurrent treatment can maximize therapeutic gains. Coordinated care among multiple therapists can mean that family members receive individual therapy to work on their individual concerns at the same time they are receiving family therapy to address relational issues. This may speed improvement by addressing multiple levels of concern at once, and by reducing the homeostatic processes in family systems that can keep individual symptoms locked in place.

Concurrent treatment can also cause problems, however, especially when the multiple therapists involved are not in communication with one another. It is not in the best interests of clients to go to one therapist who encourages the client to create distance from the client's mother, and then to go to another therapist who is working to develop a closer relationship between mother and client. When multiple service providers are working with the same client and not coordinating their care, the different services may confuse the client or even actively work against one another.

Collaborating with other professionals. Social workers are not just encouraged but *expected* to participate in interdisciplinary teams and to establish collaborative professional relationships with others who are involved in the client's treatment. These steps support the welfare of the client. Establishing collegial relationships can be as simple as friendly outreach. Sometimes it requires multiple efforts, or proof that your client has authorized you to discuss their case.

These principles apply regardless of the role or location of the other service provider. CSWs successfully collaborate with physicians, schools, social services, nutritionists, alternative medicine practitioners, other therapists, and many others both inside and outside of the world of mental health care. If the client is working with another professional of any kind, and there is potential benefit from the CSW and the other professional coordinating their efforts, the CSW should be proactive in seeking to do so, obtaining releases from the client for such collaboration when appropriate.

In a treatment team context, CSWs are expected to help clearly establish the professional and ethical obligations of each individual member of the team. Once your role on a treatment team has been established, you are expected to contribute to the team's work in order to support the client. CSWs are ethically expected to "participate in and contribute to decisions that affect the well-being of clients by drawing on the perspectives, values, and experiences of the social work profession" (standard 2.03(a)). This, of course, requires that the CSW be familiar with those current professional perspectives, values, and experiences.

Occasionally, a decision made by a treatment team will raise ethical concerns for a CSW. In those instances, the CSW should first try to resolve the issue through appropriate channels. If that fails, the CSW should seek out additional means of addressing their concerns to support the client as well as possible.

Protecting client rights in consultation and collaboration. Of course, CSWs are encouraged to regularly consult with other professionals and community resources to promote quality client care. It is common for CSWs to collaborate and consult with physicians, teachers, social service providers, and other important persons in a client's life. CSWs are expected to be aware of colleagues' competence and expertise, so that when consulting is appropriate, the CSW can easily find a knowledgeable person. Ethically, the CSW should only seek consult from someone with appropriate knowledge or competence.

When doing such consultations, CSWs respect the confidentiality of their clients. Each member of the treatment unit must give their permission for clinical information to be shared with any outsider, unless an exception to confidentiality applies. Even where permission has been given, the CSW should disclose the minimum amount of confidential information necessary to fulfill the purpose of the consultation.

Involvement of multiple clients or third parties K69-73

Identifying the "client." CSWs are ethically obligated to clarify at the beginning of therapy which person or persons are considered clients, and the nature of the relationship the therapist will have with each person involved in treatment. There is a meaningful difference between a partner or family member *visiting* treatment, where they might offer input or moral support to a client's problem, and being a *client*, where they may be directly involved in therapeutic interventions. Whether someone is a client or not will impact the social worker's responsibilities to that person. If work with a family creates the potential for a conflict of interests, the CSW should take steps to minimize that conflict.

Confidentiality. When working with couples or families, confidentiality becomes a key concern. If a client calls between sessions and informs the therapist of a secret, does the therapist have the right to bring that information up in a couple or family session?

The NASW Code of Ethics requires that CSWs inform clients of applicable policies regarding the handling of individual confidences. Some CSWs and agencies support a no-secrets policy, where individual confidences will *not* be upheld. Others prefer a limited-secrets policy, believing this is better for accurate assessment of the couple or family. In either case, the CSW should ensure that all individuals in the couple or family being treated are aware of the policy, and the CSW should then stick to that policy.

In couple, family, or group therapy, CSWs should seek agreement among participants as to their responsibilities to each other. Such clients should be warned that others participating in treatment with them may not honor those agreements. Some CSWs ask group members to sign an agreement that they will respect the privacy of the group.

Preserving the therapeutic relationship. Of course, it would not be possible to list all the factors that can influence the therapeutic relationship. Nor is that necessary for an exam about legal and ethical practice. Lots of things can influence the relationship, not all of which are foreseeable. If the

CSW keeps client welfare and the preservation of the therapeutic relationship paramount, the CSW will be able to manage most of these factors easily.

Consider two examples: In the first example, a CSW doing couple therapy begins to feel hostility from one of the partners and is not sure why. The CSW asks the other partner whether it would be ok to meet alone with the hostile partner for a few minutes, and the other partner agrees. During this time, the hostile partner reveals that she is concerned the therapist is siding with her spouse over her. While this was not the CSW's intent, the CSW is able to change behavior moving forward, and offers an apology to the hostile partner.

In the second example, a CSW doing family therapy with a mother, father, and their two adolescent girls assesses that the girls' acting out behavior appears to be related to conflict in the parental subsystem. The CSW discusses with the family the possibility of changing the treatment modality to focus on couple work. While the CSW reminds the family that he enjoys having them all come in, he believes the girls have done their job, and now it is time for him to do his in treating the family's core issue.

In each of these cases, the therapist took steps to support client welfare and the therapeutic relationship, when it would have easily been possible for therapy to go down an unproductive path. A CSW should be able to address therapeutic issues related to their role, the modality of treatment, and the involvement of outsiders openly with clients.

Potential conflicts in concurrent treatment. When a CSW is providing concurrent therapy to multiple people in the same family system – for example, when the CSW is seeing members of a couple both individually and as a couple – conflicts can quickly emerge. Individuals in the same couple or family may have competing and even incompatible needs. An individual may want to talk with the CSW privately about something they don't want their family to know. More practically, scheduling and costs can become difficult in these situations. While this kind of concurrent treatment is not prohibited, CSWs are ethically obligated to carefully consider potential conflicts in these situations, and to take steps to avoid or minimize those conflicts. Good ways to do so include having a clearly identified "client," maintaining a clear policy on individual secrets, regularly addressing confidentiality issues, and following a clear treatment plan.

Treatment involving multiple systems or third parties. The NASW Code of Ethics encourages CSWs to revisit discussions of confidentiality with clients when appropriate. This is especially important when treatment involves multiple systems or third parties. In some cases, providing services to an adolescent may mean involving their teacher, their religious leader, their doctor, and others. Everyone involved should be clear about what the CSW's role is and what the third parties' roles are in the treatment, and how information may be shared among treatment providers and others. Managing privacy and confidentiality in these situations can be a complex task. Of course, clients should give permission before third parties are brought in to treatment, and should be made aware that they can revoke this permission at any time.

Managing confidentiality K74-75

Ethical standards. The NASW Code of Ethics requires social workers to specifically inform clients of the limits of confidentiality at the beginning of treatment. Of course, this is not the only time when it may be relevant to discuss confidentiality. The code notes that therapy may require multiple discussions of confidentiality and its limits.

In addition, throughout the course of therapy there are multiple standards that relate to social workers' responsibility to keep information from therapy private. Consultations, recordkeeping, telemedicine, supervision, teaching/presentation, and preparation for moving or closing a practice are *all* to be done in ways that protect client confidentiality, unless a specific exception applies or the client has granted permission for their information to be shared.

Managing the impact of confidentiality issues. When it is possible and appropriate to do so, CSWs are expected to discuss disclosures of confidential information with clients *before* the disclosure is made. This discussion should include considerations of the potential consequences of that disclosure.

Particularly if a social worker has been required to share information from therapy, a discussion with the client about what information was shared, with whom, and why can help minimize negative impacts on the therapeutic relationship. Such a discussion can also serve to remind the client of the limits of confidentiality, and of the therapist's commitment to protecting the safety of any others involved. For example, if a report of suspected child abuse has been made, the CSW may want to discuss the role that the CSW plays in larger society in protecting vulnerable populations from suspected abuse. Ultimately, a conversation like this can refocus client and therapist on the therapeutic process and may help repair any harm done to the therapeutic relationship.

Such discussions are not always appropriate or even possible. But they can often be helpful if the CSW has been required to share information from the therapy without a specific authorization from the client to do so.

Managing crises K76-78

Methods for assessing risk. There are good, brief ways of assessing clients who may pose a danger to themselves or someone else. Assessments for suicide and violence to others tend to focus on the factors listed previously (in the Law section). Direct client expressions of intent to harm should of course be taken seriously. More often, clients present with some combination of risk and protective factors, which must be weighed to determine risk. All sources of information that the CSW deems trustworthy can be used in making this determination: Screening instruments; direct observation of client behavior; client statements; information from family members, friends, and others, when available; consultation with colleagues, supervisors, or others involved in the client's care; and client history, especially when that history suggests a pattern of risky behavior.

Ethical obligations for protecting safety. The first standard in the NASW Code of Ethics defines social workers' primary responsibility as promoting the well-being of clients. Many other ethical standards logically stem from this responsibility. For example, CSWs normally recognize and respect a client's right to self-determination. However, the CSW may limit clients' right to self-determination if the CSW believes that the client poses a risk to themselves or others. As another example, confidentiality is not to be protected when disclosure would prevent a serious and foreseeable harm.

In addition to this responsibility to individual clients, social workers also have a responsibility to the larger community and society. CSWs are expected to provide appropriate professional services in public emergencies, and to actively work for the general well-being of society.

Procedures for managing safety needs. Safety needs should be addressed through the *least intrusive means* necessary to resolve the concern. You wouldn't hospitalize a mildly depressed patient, after all. Here are a few procedures for managing safety needs, ranging from the least to the most intrusive. This is not a complete list, and the options here are not mutually exclusive; it may be appropriate to develop a safety plan *and* increase the frequency of contact with a client, for example.

- **Continue to assess.** In the absence of any specific safety concerns, the therapist would simply continue assessing for safety in future interactions with the client, documenting the process.
- **Consult with the treatment team.** If you are participating on a treatment team and have appropriate authorization to share information, it may be helpful to consult the team for their assessment of risk and to collaborate on methods for continued assessment and intervention.
- **Conduct more detailed assessment.** If a client suggests that their depression is deepening or that their hostility to others is increasing, but does not discuss any specific danger or threat, the therapist should assess the area of concern in more detail.
- **Develop a safety plan.** If a client has a history of safety issues or is currently showing non-specific safety concerns (for example, a client with mild passive suicidality, but no plan or intent to harm themselves), a therapist may work with the client to develop a safety plan. This plan lays out specific steps the client can take if their symptoms worsen. Steps usually follow a progression if early steps are unavailable or do not solve the problem. Steps may include contacting loved ones, contacting the therapist, contacting another on-duty therapist, and if these steps are unsuccessful, contacting a 24-hour crisis hotline or calling 988 or 911.
- **Increase frequency of contact.** If you have been seeing a client weekly and you begin to have concerns about their safety, but those concerns do not rise to the level where more immediate intervention is needed, you may ask to see them more often, or

for the client to check in by phone more regularly. You may also choose to increase the frequency of collateral contacts (with probation officers, family members, or others who see the client regularly).

- **Refer to a higher level of care.** Clients whose symptoms get worse or who become dangerous during outpatient psychotherapy may be better served through inpatient treatment.
- **Use voluntary hospitalization.** Clients who pose an imminent danger to themselves or others and are willing to be assessed and treated voluntarily at a hospital will not be held there against their will. When a therapist is firm with a client that hospitalization is necessary, most clients will choose voluntary hospitalization over involuntary hospitalization.
- **Use involuntary hospitalization.** If a client presents a major safety risk and is not willing to be hospitalized, a CSW may initiate the process of involuntary hospitalization. While most CSWs cannot invoke involuntary hospitalization, they can demand that a client be evaluated for a possible 72-hour hold.

Of course, if the safety concern is that the client poses an immediate danger of severe bodily harm to a reasonably identifiable victim, the appropriate procedure would be to notify the victim and law enforcement.

Best interests of the client K79-81

How legal and ethical obligations impact therapy. The legal and ethical obligations of CSWs exist primarily to protect the best interests of clients. Those obligations can have the side effect of protecting therapists, by setting clear standards of professional behavior, and thus protecting CSWs from accusations of being unprofessional when the CSW is not. But the obligations fundamentally exist to protect clients *from* social workers.

Sometimes, those legal and ethical obligations can create an inconvenience for therapist and client alike. Clients may not read every word of a long informed consent document, and therapists may not want to spend time in therapy discussing the limits of confidentiality. However, a social worker failing to meet obligations can place clients at risk in a variety of ways. Social workers fulfill these obligations because it is good for clients, even when it isn't convenient.

Social workers are instructed in multiple ways through the NASW Code of Ethics to inform clients when legal and ethical standards of the profession will limit the client's rights or change the therapist's role. For example, the ethics code requires that CSWs advise clients of those instances (such as child abuse reporting) where the therapist's responsibility to the larger society supersedes the therapist's responsibility to the client.

Conflicts between legal and ethical obligations. There are many times when there is not a direct conflict between law and ethics, but they set different standards. For example, the law may offer a stricter standard than the ethics code, or vice versa. In these instances, a CSW should follow the stricter standard, regardless of which set of rules it comes from.

If there is a direct conflict between the code of ethics and the law – that is, if the law says that you *must* do one thing, while the code of ethics says that you *must* do something that is different from and incompatible with what the law requires – the law wins. CSWs should follow the law, and practice in accordance with the code of ethics to the greatest extent possible.

Conflicts between agency and ethical obligations. It is also common for CSWs to work in settings where ethics codes conflict with workplace policy. The NASW code requires CSWs to make their commitment to ethical standards known to the organization, and to take reasonable steps to resolve the issue in a way that allows the social worker to practice in keeping with their ethical responsibilities. Social work administrators have an additional ethical responsibility to work within their roles to change any policies that might conflict with, or otherwise discourage compliance with, the ethics code. The overriding principle is clear: Agency policy does not provide an excuse for CSWs to ignore their ethical duties.

Diversity and nondiscrimination K82-85

Ethical standards for non-discrimination. The NASW code of ethics states that social workers shall not "practice, condone, facilitate, or collaborate with any form of discrimination" in professional services based on the following factors:

- Race
- Ethnicity
- National origin
- Color
- Sex
- Sexual orientation
- Gender identity or expression
- Age
- Marital status
- Political belief
- Religion
- Immigration status
- Mental or physical ability

In addition, social workers are expected to hold institutions accountable for cultural competence, and to "take action against oppression, racism, discrimination, and inequities, and acknowledge personal privilege." Among major mental health professions, social workers have the greatest ethical duty to actively work toward social justice, in the therapy room and beyond.

Diversity factors in therapy. Social workers are specifically called upon to recognize the strengths that exist in all cultures, and to work toward reducing discrimination and exploitation on societal levels. CSWs understand the impact of culture on human behavior. This can mean, for example, recognizing when a behavior is culturally appropriate and thus should not be diagnosed as a mental illness, even if it otherwise meets diagnostic criteria.

Virtually any area of difference between client and therapist has the potential to impact the therapy process. While discussions of diversity in the US tend to center on issues of race, ethnicity, sexual orientation, and gender identity, a wide variety of other factors can impact a client's identity and cultural norms. Diversity factors impact how clients experience and express the distress that led them into therapy, and impact how the client relates to the therapist. In addition to all of the factors listed in the non-discrimination standards above, therapy can be impacted by differences between client and therapist in urban versus rural setting, educational level, regional identity, and many more.

Ethical standards for providing services to diverse groups. Social workers are ethically obligated to be mindful of all forms of historical and social prejudice, as this prejudice can lead to misdiagnosing clients or pathologizing culturally-accepted behavior. In addition, CSWs "obtain education about and demonstrate understanding of the nature of social diversity and oppression with respect to" all of the factors listed in the non-discrimination standard. Social workers should be able to demonstrate competence in providing services that are sensitive to client culture and to cultural differences. The services social workers provide should be "culturally informed services that empower marginalized individuals and groups."

Improving knowledge, skills, awareness, and sensitivity. So what can a CSW do when approached by a client who is different from the therapist in ways that impact the therapy process? While postmodern models of therapy encourage CSWs to allow clients to inform the therapist about the client's life and circumstances, it is likely to be inadequate for a CSW to take no other action to improve their knowledge and skills around the relevant diversity issues. The social worker could:

- Attend a training on working with the client's population
- Seek consultation or supervision from other therapists who identify as part of, or regularly work with, the client's population
- Seek out greater exposure to the client's population
- Read articles and other literature on the client's population
- Attend their own therapy to address issues of bias

Client self-determination K86-88

Role of the therapist. Clients have a fundamental right to self-determination (also commonly referred to as autonomy). As discussed in the context of informed consent, this means that they alone can choose whether to participate in treatment, what the goals of treatment should be, and what provider to use.

This same principle applies to making major life decisions. Clients are free to determine for themselves what goals to pursue and how to best pursue them. Social workers may collaborate with clients in the process of determining those goals, but should not impose their own ideas about what may be best for the client. Treatment should be a collaborative process to the degree possible. Social workers only limit clients' right to self-determination in situations of "serious, foreseeable, and imminent risk" to the client or others.

Facilitating client decisions about treatment. As discussed in the section on informed consent, the NASW code of ethics requires CSWs to provide enough information to clients that the clients can make meaningful choices about whether to start therapy. The nature of this information may vary by therapist and by treatment type. Clients should be given the opportunity to ask questions about their treatment. If the client is receiving services involuntarily (as happens with court-mandated clients, as one example), they still should be informed about the relevant consent issues, and the extent of their right to refuse service. Specific consent should be obtained for any third-party observation or for any audio or video recording of services. All of this information must be given in clear and understandable language.

When clients are wrestling with decisions about treatment, including whether to engage in treatment (either starting or terminating), social workers should provide whatever information may be necessary and helpful in the client reaching an informed and appropriate decision. It may also be useful to discuss alternatives to treatment, and the potential risks, benefits, and other consequences of various treatment options available to the client.

Methods to assist clients in making decisions and clarifying goals. Moving beyond the immediate treatment context to consider client decisions more broadly, there are many ways a social worker can assist a client in decision-making without interfering with the client's autonomy in making those decisions. The social worker can help the client list various courses of action they could take in a difficult time, often expanding the possibilities beyond those the client may see on their own. The social worker can help the client foresee possible consequences of each of the possible courses of action, using current research as well as the social worker's knowledge of the client's specific context. The social worker can assess the client's readiness to act. The social worker can reflect and validate the client's excitement about some possibilities and anxiety about others. Each of these tasks facilitates the client making an important decision on their own, with the social worker's guidance and support.

Multidisciplinary teams K89-90

Methods for establishing collaborative relationships. Just as social workers should engage in outreach to develop collaborative relationships with outside professionals serving the same client, social workers should also be proactive in developing collaborative relationships on a multidisciplinary team. They should treat colleagues with respect and actively participate in team discussion and decision-making. Clear guidelines for the treatment team should be established, including defining the obligations of the team as a whole and each of its members individually.

Additional ethical standards. Treating colleagues with respect includes representing colleagues' opinions, qualifications, and responsibilities fairly and accurately.

CSWs should avoid unwarranted criticism of colleagues, especially criticism on the basis of demographic factors such as race, age, gender identity, immigration status, or disability. This does not mean that CSWs are prohibited from ever criticizing colleagues, just that such criticism should be focused on the topic at hand, and should seek to represent the colleagues' views fairly. It should not include personal criticism or attacks.

CSWs should draw on the values, experiences, and perspectives of the profession when contributing to team decisions that impact client well-being.

When a treatment team makes a decision that raises ethical concerns for the social worker, the social worker should seek to resolve the dispute through appropriate channels. If that is ineffective at resolving the issue, the social worker should seek other ways to resolve their concern, placing the well-being of client(s) as the highest priority.

Improving access to care K91-94

Evaluating client ability to advocate for themselves. Many clients can effectively advocate for themselves with third-party payors and with others involved in their care, but some clients struggle to do so. A key component of removing barriers to care is determine when clients can advocate on their own behalf, and when they need assistance.

Social workers should assess clients' ability to advocate for themselves. This can include examining their advocacy efforts to date, and seeing what has been effective compared to what has not; considering their current mental and emotional state (obviously, clients who are overwhelmed or in crisis may have more difficulty advocating on their own behalf than clients who are more stable); and broadly assessing their resource needs. This evaluation process can also help the social worker assess the client's overall level of need for the social worker's services.

Interaction with third-party payors. CSWs are ethically obligated to be truthful and accurate in documentation submitted to third-party payers. Additional ethical rules that can be applied to CSWs' interactions with third-party payers include:

- Do not "participate in, condone, or be associated with dishonesty, fraud, or deception"
- Ensure that billing practices accurately reflect the services provided, including the identity of service providers
- Do not disclose confidential information to payers without a specific release to do so
- Inform clients of limits to services imposed by third-party payers

Interaction with other service delivery systems. Standards applying to interactions with other service delivery systems include:

- Protect confidentiality unless authorized to share information
- Do not give or receive payment for referrals
- Ensure an orderly transfer of responsibility for the client
- Discuss whether consultation with prior providers is warranted

Enhancing clients' abilities to meet their own needs. Where it is possible to do so, teaching clients to advocate on their own behalf can have broader and more lasting positive impacts than simply advocating on behalf of the client. CSWs can raise client awareness of specific resources, empower and encourage clients to connect with those resources, walk clients through the process of advocating with third-party payors or with others, and engage clients in motivational approaches designed to help clients better meet their own needs going forward.

Termination and referrals K95-101

Ethical considerations with interrupting or terminating. There are times when interrupting or terminating therapy is appropriate or necessary, even when the goals of therapy have not been reached. You may become seriously ill or need to step away from your practice to care for loved ones. The client may suddenly be called to a military deployment or a new job out of state. The clinic where you are seeing the client may lose its funding. While we all hope these situations will not occur, the reality is that they sometimes do, and a social worker is ethically required to be ready for such abrupt shifts. A social worker also must take appropriate steps when this kind of situation does happen.

CSWs are ethically required to take reasonable steps to ensure continuity of services in the event that they become suddenly incapacitated or otherwise unavailable. These procedures may include emergency contact numbers where clients may reach the therapist or others able to take over client care. CSWs in private practice commonly have what is called a *professional will*, which lays out issues like who will take over client care in the event of the therapist's serious injury or death. The person assigned to take over client care must be given access to records so that they can contact clients to let them know of the change; for this reason, many CSWs include an authorization in their informed consent agreement letting clients know that a professional will exists and having clients agree that their records may be forwarded when necessary.

Having these plans in place minimizes the harm that may come to clients when a therapist is suddenly unavailable. However, treatment interruptions or sudden terminations are not always due to something happening to the therapist.

Whenever treatment must be interrupted or terminated, regardless of whether it is because of something happening to the client, the therapist, the clinic, or the larger social context, CSWs have ethical responsibilities to *non-abandonment* and appropriate *continuity of care*. Non-abandonment simply means that clients in need of continued services typically should not be left to fend for themselves; if treatment with the current CSW must be interrupted or ended, the CSW still has a responsibility to ensure that crisis needs are addressed and that any potential for harm due to the change in treatment is minimized. Continuity of care means that the client can receive continued care with another provider appropriate to their needs; most commonly, this means providing referrals that are local to the client, within their financial means, and able to treat the client's specific problem type and severity.

Social workers in fee-for-service settings may terminate care with a client when the client is unable to pay an outstanding balance. However, several specific elements must all be in place before such a termination is considered ethical: (1) The financial contract must have been made clear to the client (this often is addressed in the initial informed consent process); (2) the client must not pose an imminent danger to themselves or others; and (3) the consequences (clinical and otherwise) of the current outstanding balance must have been discussed with the client. So, a social worker who has been clear with a client about the client's financial commitment, has assessed a client for danger and found none, and who has discussed the consequences of an outstanding balance with the client is free to terminate.

As mentioned previously, social workers are ethically prohibited from terminating services in order to pursue a social, financial, or sexual relationship with a client.

Knowledge of referrals/resources to provide continuity of care. In order to make referrals when necessary, a CSW must be aware of local resources that can provide continuity of care to clients if therapy is suddenly stopped. Many CSWs maintain referral lists that include local hospitals and crisis resources, low-fee clinics, psychiatrists, other providers whose services are similar to those of the CSW, and other community resources.

Methods to facilitate transfer. There are several steps social workers can take to ensure that the transfer of a client does not result in that client being abandoned or otherwise falling through the cracks. These methods can generally be categorized as providing good referrals, ensuring client follow-through, and collaborating with their new service provider.

The social worker begins by being proactive when it comes to providing appropriate referrals: Ensuring that referrals provided are appropriate to client needs and are accepting new clients. If necessary, the social worker might even aid the client in making the initial appointment with a new provider. The social worker can create a "warm handoff" by inviting the new provider of the client's choice to join the social worker in the social worker's termination session. The social worker can ask the client to sign a release of information allowing the social worker to transfer treatment records to the new provider, and to discuss the client's case with the new provider to answer any questions the new provider may have. Similar releases might also allow the CSW to communicate with the client's partner or other close family members, to ensure that the client is able to connect with other providers.

Indicators of need to terminate or refer. The clearest indication that it is time to terminate therapy is when the client has reached their treatment goals, and no new goals have emerged. Even in the absence of having reached the goals of treatment, termination may be appropriate if the client regularly comes in appearing to no longer be in distress, and sessions are spent on ordinary social conversation. Termination may also be appropriate if the client is behaving in an aggressive, threatening, or harassing manner toward the therapist. Finally, termination (and referral) is appropriate if the client's symptoms are not appropriate for continued outpatient therapy – in other words, if they need a higher level of care. Ongoing, careful monitoring and discussion with clients about their changing needs can help determine whether and when termination or additional referrals may be necessary.

The CSW should also refer out, or terminate existing services, if:

- The CSW is impaired and unable to provide competent services
- There is a conflict of interests
- There is a dual relationship that is likely to create risk of exploitation or impair the CSW's clinical judgment

Of course, referrals are appropriate for addressing client needs that the CSW cannot immediately address. Client reports of medical symptoms suggest a need for a referral to a physician. Other needs that the CSW cannot meet, but that appear relevant to the client's functioning, may be best met through appropriate referrals.

Client is not benefiting. Even if the goals of therapy have not been reached, it is appropriate to terminate therapy if it is clear that the client is not benefiting from treatment. Further deterioration of functioning is a clear indication of treatment failure. A lack of improvement in symptoms may or may not indicate a lack of benefit from treatment; if a client entered therapy on a downward trend, simply stabilizing them and keeping them out of hospitalization can be considered a benefit. Ultimately, though, clients should experience a benefit from being in therapy. If, by their own report or by therapist or other observation of client behavior, they are not benefiting, termination should be considered – with referrals given if appropriate.

Managing termination. A good termination process starts at the beginning of therapy, with therapist and client reaching clear agreement on what the goals of therapy are and what improvements will lead to a determination that therapy can end. Discussions of progress toward termination should be a regular part of therapy. Once it is clear that termination is appropriate, a responsible CSW will provide advance notice of termination, take steps to prevent a relapse of symptoms, recognize the gains the client has made in therapy, and provide appropriate referrals for any additional needed care. The number of sessions needed for a formal termination may vary by client, but the process should not be needlessly prolonged.

Preventing abandonment or neglect. A termination process that is done too quickly or without appropriate referrals can be considered client abandonment. There may be times when a therapist needs to end therapy abruptly, either due to a medical illness, client job transfer or deployment, or for other reasons. In such circumstances, the CSW (or, in the case of the CSW's illness, someone designated by the CSW) should offer as much advance notice of termination as possible, make appropriate referrals, and follow up to ensure the clients are able to obtain continued services.

Notably, the obligation to prevent client abandonment does not mean that a client can effectively hold a CSW hostage by refusing to accept referrals. When termination is appropriate, the social worker is obligated to provide appropriate referrals and to take reasonable steps to ensure that crisis needs are addressed.

Sample Questions

See the next page for answers and rationales

1. An associate CSW has been struggling with a difficult family case. The associate's supervisor suggests that the associate record video of future sessions so that the associate and supervisor can together review what happens in session. The associate is reluctant to record sessions, fearing that the parents in the family might feel embarrassed. The associate CSW is required to:

   a. Remind the clients that, because the associate is under supervision, video recording of sessions is a common and accepted practice
   b. Obtain specific consent for recording from each adult family member prior to recording sessions
   c. Comply with the supervisor's request even if the family would prefer to not be recorded, as the associate is working under the supervisor's license
   d. Remind the clients of the limits of confidentiality prior to recording sessions

2. An LCSW is involved on a treatment team for a county social service agency. The LCSW grows frustrated that the LCSW's suggestions are rarely implemented by the team. An appropriate course of action would be for the LCSW to:

   a. Seek advice from colleagues about handling treatment team dynamics
   b. Temporarily stop providing input into team decisions until the LCSW can better understand why previous suggestions have not been implemented
   c. In the interest of transparency, directly inform clients of the LCSW's recommendations, including those that the team has rejected
   d. Demand that the team implement the LCSW's suggestions to promote the well-being of clients

Sample Questions: Answers and Rationales

1. An associate CSW has been struggling with a difficult family case. The associate's supervisor suggests that the associate record video of future sessions so that the associate and supervisor can together review what happens in session. The associate is reluctant to record sessions, fearing that the parents in the family might feel embarrassed. The associate CSW is required to:

a. **Incorrect.** Remind the clients that, because the associate is under supervision, video recording of sessions is a common and accepted practice. *While this may be a common and accepted practice, pushing the clients in this way may lead them to believe that they do not have the ability to refuse recording.*
b. **CORRECT.** Obtain specific consent for recording from each adult family member prior to recording sessions. *This is required by the NASW Code of Ethics.*
c. **Incorrect.** Comply with the supervisor's request even if the family would prefer to not be recorded, as the associate is working under the supervisor's license. *Consent for taping cannot be forced upon the clients. They should be fully informed of the risks and benefits, and choose on their own.*
d. **Incorrect.** Remind the clients of the limits of confidentiality prior to recording sessions. *While doing so may be helpful, it is not required.*

2. An LCSW is involved on a treatment team for a county social service agency. The LCSW grows frustrated that the LCSW's suggestions are rarely implemented by the team. An appropriate course of action would be for the LCSW to:

a. **CORRECT.** Seek advice from colleagues about handling treatment team dynamics. *The NASW Code of Ethics encourages LCSWs to seek advice when such consultation is in clients' best interests.*
b. **Incorrect.** Temporarily stop providing input into team decisions until the LCSW can better understand why previous suggestions have not been implemented. *Social workers are ethically obligated to be actively involved in interdisciplinary treatment teams. Stopping participation, even temporarily, would violate this standard.*
c. **Incorrect.** In the interest of transparency, directly inform clients of the LCSW's recommendations, including those that the team has rejected. *This could undermine treatment decisions made by the team, and places clients in a difficult position. It does not live up to social workers' requirement to work collaboratively with colleagues. To the degree that the LCSW seeks to have clients take the LCSW's side, this could be considered exploitation of the client.*
d. **Incorrect.** Demand that the team implement the LCSW's suggestions to promote the well-being of clients. *It is not collaborative for one member of a treatment team to make demands. Even if the team's decisions raised ethical concerns – which is not indicated by the question stem – making demands of the team is unlikely to resolve those concerns effectively.*

ETHICS

Business Practices and Policies

Scored exam questions (approximate): **7-8**

Advertising K102-104

Accurate representation. Ethically, you can only advertise those degrees or credentials you have actually earned, and which are relevant to the practice of clinical social work. If you have a master's degree in social work and a doctorate in English, you could not include your doctorate as a professional qualification. Even though you do have a doctorate, it would be a misrepresentation of the credentials you hold relative to your clinical work.

Similarly, any other professional qualifications or competencies that you advertise must be accurate. If others misrepresent your qualifications or credentials, you should take reasonable steps to correct the information. You also must accurately represent the services you provide and the results to be achieved. Any time you speak on behalf of an organization, you should accurately represent the official position of the organization.

Testimonials. The NASW Code of Ethics prohibits seeking testimonials from current clients or anyone else who might be subject to undue influence. Clients and others may feel pressured by such requests. This issue has gotten more complicated in the age of apps and web sites designed for patients to share their experiences with health care professionals. Clients sometimes provide testimonials on such sites without being prompted to by therapists. CSWs should be aware that *responding* to any online testimonial may be considered a breach of client confidentiality, even when the client is openly discussing their treatment.

Affiliations. As you would expect, CSWs cannot advertise themselves as being employees, members, partners, or associates of a group that they don't actually belong to. Any representation of employment or professional affiliations must be accurate. Social workers are also expected to be particularly cautious about recruiting clients when those clients are currently being served by other providers. Social workers should discuss the clients' needs, possible benefits and risks of receiving services through a new provider, and whether consultation with the other provider will be helpful.

Social workers are ethically prohibited from charging a private fee for services that the client is entitled to receive through the social worker's employer or agency. In other words, you cannot use an employer's marketing and recruitment efforts to then steer potential clients toward your own private practice.

Maintaining records K105-108

Generating records. Professional ethics demand that treatment records be accurate and reflect the services provided. Documentation should also be completed in a timely manner to ensure continuity of care. When a CSW is suddenly unavailable, due to illness or any other reason, accurate and up-to-date records ensure that clients can be adequately cared for until the CSW is able to return.

The NASW Code of Ethics *specifically* demands that CSWs document the following:

- Informed consent for evaluation or research
- Client requests for records and, where applicable, reasons for refusing access to part or all of those records

Many other elements of documentation can be reasonably inferred from the code, even though they are not stated outright. For example, the code requires that CSWs *obtain* informed consent for therapy. While this consent does not specifically need to be in writing (and indeed, there are times when a written informed consent document may be inadequate), it is reasonable to assume that consent should be documented in some form.

The NASW code also addresses information that does *not* belong in a client's record. Documentation should only include information that is directly relevant to the services being provided. This helps to protect the privacy of clients.

Protecting the confidentiality of records. CSWs should protect the confidentiality of client records while services are being delivered and after the services have been completed. Possible methods for protecting the confidentiality of records include but are not limited to:

- Keeping paper records in a secure, locked file cabinet
- Keeping electronic records in a secure, encrypted format
- Carefully controlling who has access to client files
- Shredding paper files to dispose of them at the proper time

Maintenance of records. Under state law, records must be maintained for at least 7 years following the last professional contact. If you are working with a minor, records must be maintained for at least 7 years after the minor turns 18. The NASW Code of Ethics reinforces this legal standard.

CSWs have an ethical responsibility to store records in ways that allow reasonable future access to them. At the same time, you should take reasonable steps to ensure they remain secure and confidential. When the time comes that you dispose of old client records, this disposal should also be done in a manner that protects security and confidentiality. A CSW should never simply throw old client files in the trash.

Client access to records. Clients generally have a legal and ethical right to access their records, though there are some limitations on this. They may request that records be released to themselves or to a third party. Unless you believe that the release of records to the client would be harmful, you must comply with their request in a timely manner, as described in the Law section.

If you believe that releasing records to a client would be harmful to them, you may refuse to do so. If you refuse, you need to document the request and your reason for refusal. Recall from the Law section that the client may then request that a third-party professional review the records to see whether that third party agrees with you that the record should not be released.

Couple, family, and group treatment present challenges when one client requests records but the others involved in treatment are either unaware of the request or do not agree to it. The NASW Code of Ethics requires CSWs to seek clarity, as early as possible, about policies for confidentiality from all participants in couple, family, or group therapy.

When clients are given access to records that identify or discuss other individuals, the CSW should act to protect the confidentiality of those other individuals. This may involve releasing a treatment summary as allowed by law. Note that a summary is typically not appropriate for removing records of one family member's participation in couple or family based treatment; all adult family members who participated in therapy should consent before such records are released.

Social workers have a specific ethical responsibility to develop and inform clients about policies related to the use of technology to give clients access to their records.

Helping clients and others understand records. Because clients are typically not trained mental health professionals, it may be easy for them to misunderstand or misinterpret the information contained in their records. CSWs can minimize this risk by using clear language in their documentation, going through the record with the client upon release, explaining diagnoses and other clinical decisions, and providing the client the opportunity to ask questions about their records if they wish.

Other professional roles K109-110

Clarifying roles. Because social workers serve clients in a variety of ways and in a variety of contexts, it is important to clarify the CSW's role at the beginning of services. This includes clarifying what services will be provided and who is considered the client. While not all dual relationships are avoidable, especially in rural settings, where the potential for a dual relationship exists the CSW should clarify their role and take steps to reduce the risk of exploitation or impaired judgment. Clarifying their role can be part of that process.

Engaging in conflicting roles. Generally, CSWs should avoid situations that amount to a conflict of interest, as discussed previously. However, in some situations it may become unavoidable for the CSW to engage in conflicting roles. For example, the CSW may be compelled by a judge to testify in a court case involving a client. When such instances occur, the CSW should clarify their role with all parties involved and take steps to minimize conflicts of interest.

Technology and social media K111-113

Potential for harm. Technology has proven indispensable during the COVID-19 pandemic, as most mental health services have been provided through telehealth platforms. Such technologies offer clients convenience and access to care that may not have been achievable without the technology. However, social workers' use of telehealth platforms, social media, and other technology also carries risks.

Let's first look at client care provided via telehealth. When a client goes into crisis or has some other form of emergency in a CSW's office, the CSW knows what to do, whom to call, and where to send the client for immediate help. Over telehealth, that may not be the case. Clients may go into crisis without the CSW being aware of the client's location or where to send them – or even that the crisis is happening. When a CSW fails to respond in a timely manner to a client in crisis, damage to the therapeutic relationship can be lasting, and of course the client may remain at risk for suicide without the risk being addressed until the CSW makes contact.

When social workers post personal information online that is later discovered by clients, or when social workers engage clients in personal relationships on social media or other digital platforms, a number of harms can result. Clients may become confused about the CSW's role or the nature of their relationship. Professional boundaries become more difficult to uphold. Ultimately, an inappropriate dual relationship may result, damaging client confidence in the CSW and in the services being provided.

As it relates to clients' information, CSWs who fail to meet their responsibilities to protect client data may expose that data to hackers or others who could use information from social work services to blackmail the client or steal their identity. They also could simply make the information public, which could itself cause the client significant harm.

Ethical standards. Technology-specific obligations operate *on top of* all the regular ethical requirements for social work, not in place of them. CSWs providing services via telemedicine are ethically obligated to:

- Be aware of cultural and economic barriers to technology-based care, and work to reduce those barriers
- Inform clients of the risks and benefits specific to telemedicine
- Discuss policies regarding the use of technology
- Verify the identity and location of clients
- Assess client appropriateness for telehealth
- Identify alternate service methods for clients who prefer not to utilize telehealth
- Comply with all applicable legal standards for practice in the location where the social worker is *and* the location where the client is
- Avoid using technology for personal or non-work related communications with clients
- Protect confidentiality of technological communication and electronic records
- Notify clients of any breaches of confidential data

Risks and limitations. While current scientific research is generally finding mental health services provided via technology to be as effective as care provided in-person, there remain some specific risks and limitations associated with the use of technology in service delivery. Some examples of these risks include:

- Technology failure or inconsistent performance
- Added difficulty in clinical assessment or observation
- Data breaches

In addition, some CSWs may experience telehealth as hindering their ability to connect with some clients. It is common for clinicians to express challenges in working with children, couples, and families online, for example.

One key limitation of technology in all of its forms is that it is not accessible to everyone. While telehealth has certainly increased access to care in rural or isolated areas, clients need access to a relatively recent computer or smart phone with a camera, as well as sufficient internet access, to participate in video-based services.

Fees K114-119

Determining fees. There are many factors you can consider when setting fees, such as a client's income, the fees generally charged for services in your area, your own qualifications, and so on. There are three things you *can't* do when determining fees:

- You can't enter into an agreement with other independent practitioners or clinics to set a common fee (or common minimum fee) in your area. This would be a violation of antitrust law.
- You can't set different fees based on race, national origin, or any other protected class in anti-discrimination rules.
- You can't set fees that are exploitive (i.e., high fees that take advantage of clients' vulnerability or wealth).

Fees must be fair, reasonable, and aligned with the services that clients are paying for. You can raise or lower fees whenever you wish, even for existing clients. You simply need to make sure that your fee changes are within the rules listed above.

Payment for referrals prohibited. As noted in the Law section, CSWs are both legally and ethically prohibited from giving or receiving payment for referrals. Referrals should be made solely on the basis of what is in the best interests of the client.

Bartering. Bartering – that is, exchanging clinical services for some other product or service, rather than money – comes with a lot of potential problems. There is risk of exploitation if the market value of the goods or services the client offers as payment exceeds the usual fee the CSW charges. There is also the risk that the therapy relationship will be impacted, if the therapist particularly likes or dislikes the goods or services received, or if they hold strong sentimental value for the client.

In spite of those problems, bartering is not completely prohibited. The NASW Code of Ethics allows CSWs to "explore and [...] participate in bartering only in very limited circumstances" (standard 1.13(b)). Under the NASW code, bartering is only acceptable if *all* of these conditions are met (reformatted here into a list):

"(a) such arrangements are an accepted practice among professionals in the local community,
(b) considered to be essential for the provision of services,
(c) negotiated without coercion, and
(d) entered into at the client's initiative and
(e) with the client's informed consent."

Generally, you should not enter into a bartering arrangement with clients. If bartering ultimately presents a problem, the burden is on the CSW to show that the bartering arrangement was not detrimental to the client. However, under the limited circumstances described above, there may be rare instances when bartering for services is preferable to interrupting or discontinuing treatment.

Collecting unpaid balances. While the collection of debts is not specifically addressed in the NASW Code of Ethics, based on existing standards it appears to be ethical to use collection agencies for the purposes of collecting unpaid balances. It would be reasonable to conclude that a CSW who uses such agencies should clarify in their informed consent documentation that they do so. And of course, any client information provided to a collection agency should only be the minimum information necessary to collect the balance, and should not include any details about the treatment itself.

Continuation of treatment. The NASW Code of Ethics goes so far as to specifically *allow* termination of therapy based on non-payment of fees, as long as the client does not pose an immediate danger, their financial responsibilities were made clear to them, and the impact of nonpayment has been discussed. When a CSW is unable or unwilling, for any reason, to provide continued care to a client, the CSW must assist the client in making appropriate arrangements for continuation of treatment.

Providing services paid for by third-party payors. When services will be paid for by a third party, such as an insurance company, CSWs are obligated to inform clients of the requirements of that payor that might limit services. (For example, insurers commonly cover individual therapy to treat a diagnosed mental health disorder, but may not cover therapy to treat conflict in a couple or family relationship.) In addition, CSWs should only provide information to the third-party payor when the client has provided specific authorization for the information sharing.

Gifts K120-121

Giving and receiving gifts. While some professional standards have gotten stricter over time, the standards around giving and receiving gifts have actually grown more flexible. This is due largely to increased recognition of the cultural significance of gifts in many populations. Refusing a small gift may be culturally insensitive. The current NASW Code of Ethics does not mention gifts at all, though the existing standards around non-exploitation would prohibit a CSW from placing their own interests above the client's in deciding whether to accept a gift. CSWs commonly consider the effect of giving or receiving the gift on the client, and the potential impact of the gift on the therapy process.

Giving a gift to a client, or accepting a gift from a client, does come with some risks. The client might perceive that the gift changes the nature of their relationship with you to a more personal one. They might hold an expectation that any gift should be reciprocated. They might expect preferential treatment in scheduling or other elements of therapy. In each of these instances (and surely many others you could come up with), the integrity of the therapeutic process can be impacted. Whether you accept or reject a client gift, it is good practice to document your decision-making on the issue. You might consider factors like the cost, nature, and meaning of the gift, how it fits within cultural norms, and its potential impact on therapy.

Research ethics K122-125

Procedures for safeguarding research participants. The most important safeguard for research participants is the process of informed consent. Just as a client should be fully informed of the processes, risks, and potential benefits of therapy, a research participant should be fully informed of the processes, risks, and benefits of their participation in a study. Most studies are overseen by some form of Institutional Review Board, which reviews the protocols and protections the researchers have in place.

Necessary disclosures to research participants. Under the NASW Code of Ethics, research participants need to be informed of potential risks and benefits from participating. They should also be clearly informed of what participation entails: What is being asked of them, and for how long? Participants should be informed of the limits to confidentiality that apply to their participation, the steps being taken to preserve their confidentiality, and how long records of the research will be retained before being destroyed. Finally, participants must be informed that they can withdraw their consent and end participation at any time, without penalty.

Some forms of research, like naturalistic observation or archival research, do not involve informed consent processes. The NASW code notes that these methods should only be employed without informed consent when “a rigorous and responsible review” has found the research worthwhile, and when alternatives that involve informed consent are not feasible.

Client rights when participating in research. In addition to the right to be informed about the research they are participating in, clients also have the right to decline or withdraw their participation in a study at any time. They have a right to confidentiality unless they sign a waiver specifically authorizing the release of information from their participation. (If the study is a study involving therapy services, the same limits of confidentiality would apply as ordinarily apply in therapy, and the clients should be informed of this as part of the informed consent process.) Under the NASW code, they have the right to be protected from unwarranted danger or distress.

Confidentiality of research data. Unless clients provide a written waiver, CSWs consider any information they learn about a research participant to be confidential, subject to the exceptions to confidentiality outlined earlier. If others may be able to gain access to a participant's research data, the CSW should explain this possibility at the beginning of the study and share their plan for protecting confidentiality.

Unethical or incompetent colleagues K126-127

CSWs not only need to be able to recognize when their own ability to provide therapy is compromised. They also must be aware of times when a *colleague's* ability to provide ethical and effective therapy is compromised.

Situations that can impair the integrity or effectiveness of therapy include multiple relationships (subject to the boundaries previously described); therapist substance abuse, mental illness, or emotional disturbance; bias or discrimination by the therapist; exploitation; and many more.

Unlike some other states, California does not have any rules allowing clinical social workers to directly report colleagues who are behaving in unethical or incompetent ways. If a client tells you about bad behavior on the part of their previous therapist, you are required to keep this information confidential, subject to the same rules as any other confidential information. Reporting it to the board yourself, or directly confronting the colleague, would be a breach of confidentiality. If a client grants permission for you to talk with the other therapist (through a written release of information), you could then address the other therapist, but it would be important to avoid taking the client's report at face value. There are often two very different sides to such stories, and social workers treat each other with respect.

Addressing unethical or incompetent colleagues. If you learn of another therapist's unethical or incompetent behavior *directly from that therapist*, you may have more options. For example, if you learn that a colleague in your clinic is struggling with an alcohol abuse problem, you could encourage your colleague to seek treatment and to discontinue seeing clients until the problem is under control. The NASW Code of Ethics encourages CSWs to offer assistance to colleagues who are impaired and need to take remedial action. Doing so would certainly be in the best interests of their clients. If the other therapist refuses, you must carefully balance competing standards. The NASW code generally requires social workers avoid unwarranted criticism of colleagues. At the same time, the code demands that social workers who become aware of a colleague's impaired, unethical, or incompetent behavior attempt to consult with and assist that colleague (subject to the normal legal limitations surrounding confidentiality). If those efforts fail, you should take action through appropriate channels, if it is feasible to do so.

What is most important in a situation like this is that you take appropriate action to promote the welfare of clients. While confidentiality laws may prevent you from reporting it yourself when a client tells you that another therapist is behaving unethically or incompetently, you can (and often should) encourage the client to report that behavior themselves. You can't *require* the client to make that report – that would be putting your wishes above the client's – but you can encourage it.

Supervision K128

Supervisors have several specific responsibilities defined in the NASW Code of Ethics. Supervisors are ethically obligated to:

- Have the necessary skills and knowledge to supervise, getting consultation when needed
- Set clear, appropriate, and culturally sensitive boundaries
- Avoid multiple relationships where there is risk of impaired judgment or exploitation
- Evaluate supervisee performance in a manner that is fair, respectful, and based on clearly established criteria
- Ensure clients are aware when services are being provided by students (this ethical standard applies to fieldwork instructors)

Sample Questions

See the next page for answers and rationales

1. An LCSW is providing couple therapy to a separated couple with two young children. Both partners have given the LCSW permission to testify at an upcoming court hearing where the judge may approve their temporary custody agreement. The LCSW has agreed to testify. As the hearing approaches, the LCSW notices that each partner seems to be trying to win the LCSW's favor, complimenting the LCSW on small changes in their office or offering small gifts. How should the LCSW manage their ethical responsibilities?

   a. Clarify the LCSW's role as a treatment provider, and differentiate this from the role of a custody evaluator
   b. Remind the couple that it is not legally appropriate to attempt to bribe a future witness
   c. Draft a Testimony Agreement that clearly defines court testimony as a separate service with a separate fee
   d. Rescind the LCSW's agreement to testify, as it should not have been given

2. An LCSW is being interviewed for a podcast. The interviewers ask about her training and clinical work, and repeatedly refer to her as "Doctor," even though her highest degree is a master's degree. The LCSW should:

   a. End the interview and ask that it not be released
   b. No action is called for, as the interview does not qualify as advertising
   c. Continue the interview, and afterward, remind the interviewer of her proper title
   d. Politely correct the interviewers, and ensure that the correction is included on any edited version of the interview used in the podcast

Sample Questions: Answers and Rationales

1. An LCSW is providing couple therapy to a separated couple with two young children. Both partners have given the LCSW permission to testify at an upcoming court hearing where the judge may approve their temporary custody agreement. The LCSW has agreed to testify. As the hearing approaches, the LCSW notices that each partner seems to be trying to win the LCSW's favor, complimenting the LCSW on small changes in their office or offering small gifts. How should the LCSW manage their ethical responsibilities?

   a. **CORRECT.** Clarify the LCSW's role as a treatment provider, and differentiate this from the role of a custody evaluator
   b. **Incorrect.** Remind the couple that it is not legally appropriate to attempt to bribe a future witness
   c. **Incorrect.** Draft a Testimony Agreement that clearly defines court testimony as a separate service with a separate fee
   d. **Incorrect.** Rescind the LCSW's agreement to testify, as it should not have been given

While it is acceptable for the LCSW to testify on the couple's behalf, clarifying roles is an ethical responsibility of the LCSW when working in multiple roles as they are here. The purpose of the LCSW's testimony is not clear from the question, but the treatment provider's role is separate from that of a custody evaluator, and it would not be appropriate for the LCSW to take on a custody evaluator role for a couple the LCSW had been treating. It is not clear what the parents hope they will achieve in court through their efforts.

2. An LCSW is being interviewed for a podcast. The interviewers ask about her training and clinical work, and repeatedly refer to her as “Doctor,” even though her highest degree is a master's degree. The LCSW should:

a. **Incorrect.** End the interview and ask that it not be released. *Ending the interview would be a drastic and probably unnecessary step.*
b. **Incorrect.** No action is called for, as the interview does not qualify as advertising. *Because the interview discussed her clinical work, the interview may be considered advertising. A correction is needed to ensure listeners are not misled as to the LCSW’s education.*
c. **Incorrect.** Continue the interview, and afterward, remind the interviewer of her proper title. *Reminding the interviewer afterward of her proper title might mean that the incorrect title is used many more times during the recording, misleading listeners.*
d. **CORRECT.** Politely correct the interviewers and ensure that the correction is included on any edited version of the interview used in the podcast. *The NASW Code of Ethics requires social workers to correct misinformation about their qualifications.*

Mini-Mock Exam

Introduction to the Mini-Mock

The exam itself will not simply ask you to recount facts from the preceding pages. Instead, it will ask you to *apply and integrate* the legal and ethical standards that govern the field. That's why the sample questions in this book, like the questions on the real exam, take the form of case vignettes instead of simple memorization. Over the next few pages, you'll get some more practice, in the form of a 25-question mini-mock exam.

What makes these questions a bit different (and, indeed, a bit tougher) from the ones you've seen already is that 1) you don't know which areas of knowledge you're being tested on for each item, and 2) items may ask you to combine multiple areas of knowledge when determining the correct answer. You may need to pull from several content areas to rule out incorrect responses and determine the correct one.

In each question, unless the question says otherwise, assume the therapist is a California LCSW acting within their professional role. Remember that, as is the case on the test itself, questions may be complex, and they may require careful reading – but they aren't designed to trick you. There's a single, best answer for each question.

Items on this mini-mock exam are proportioned correctly based on the actual exam. In other words, just like the real thing, this mini-mock exam includes 40% Law questions (10 out of 25) and 60% Ethics questions (15 out of 25).

California LCSW Law & Ethics Mini-Mock Exam

1. ____	8. ____	15. ____	22. ____
2. ____	9. ____	16. ____	23. ____
3. ____	10. ____	17. ____	24. ____
4. ____	11. ____	18. ____	25. ____
5. ____	12. ____	19. ____	
6. ____	13. ____	20. ____	
7. ____	14. ____	21. ____	

1. An LCSW is working with an individual client who is employed in the movie industry. The client is emotionally unstable following a breakup. The client informs the LCSW that the client will be travelling out of state for the next three weeks to work on a film, and asks whether the LCSW can continue to work with the client by phone during that time. The LCSW should first:

a. Assess the severity of the client's symptoms to determine whether phone therapy is appropriate, and if so, proceed with phone sessions
b. Determine whether they have the requisite qualifications to practice in the state to which the client is travelling
c. Determine the client's state of residency
d. Inquire with the BBS as to the appropriateness and legality of phone sessions for this client

2. A female LCSW finds herself becoming increasingly blunt and even harsh with a client who is overweight and experiencing depression. The LCSW realizes she is judging the client for the client's weight and her apparent lack of interest in resolving any of the personal or relational struggles that the LCSW believes are perpetuating the client's depressive symptoms. The client continues attending therapy and reporting attempts to complete homework assigned by the therapist, but without improvement. The LCSW should:

a. Seek consultation and attempt to repair the therapeutic relationship
b. Seek consultation and refer the client to a therapist who does not share the LCSW's weight bias
c. Refer the client out and seek additional training to recognize and not blame the client for common correlates to depression
d. Refer the client out as it does not appear that therapy has a reasonable likelihood of success

3. An LCSW in private practice has a new adult client, who describes a variety of troubling experiences in prior therapy with another local LCSW. As the client describes it, the prior therapist pressured the client for advance payment for sessions, raised the client's fees frequently and without warning, and at one point asked the client for a significant loan. To address their ethical responsibilities, the LCSW now seeing this client should:

a. Report the colleague to the BBS based on the client description
b. Confront the colleague on their behavior, without revealing how they learned about it
c. Inform the client that descriptions of unethical or unprofessional behavior are an exception to confidentiality
d. Inform the client of the process for reporting the prior therapist's behavior

4. A military family in treatment with an LCSW for four months comes into session appearing dazed, as the mother has learned she will be deployed to another country in a matter of weeks. The family will be moving with her and will need to discontinue treatment upon their moving date, they say, even though the treatment is incomplete. The LCSW should:

a. Discuss the transition, consider increasing the frequency of sessions in the remaining weeks, and encourage the family to continue therapy with a local provider during the deployment
b. Empower the mother to delay the deployment, discuss the possibility of transition, and consider adding individual sessions with the mother
c. Assess for substance abuse, discuss the transition, and offer to provide online therapy during the deployment
d. Consider the deployment a "pause" rather than an ending of therapy, and encourage the family to continue treatment once they return

5. A family of five comes to an LCSW to address family conflict surrounding the family's business. The parents own an auto body shop. Their children, ages 16, 19, and 22, are all working there but are interested in pursuing their own careers. The parents are concerned that the body shop cannot survive if it has to hire outside workers, and they want the shop to be a place the children can rely on. The children express love and support for their parents but openly wonder whether the business should survive if it is relying on their underpaid work. How should the LCSW proceed with the family?

a. Allow the parents to set the goals of treatment, while recognizing that the 19-year-old and 22-year-old may choose not to participate
b. Attempt to define goals for therapy that all family members can agree upon
c. Separate the units of treatment to better support their specific interests, seeing the parents as a couple and each child individually
d. Refer out as this is outside of the LCSW's scope of practice

6. An adult client tells an LCSW that the client's 89-year-old mother is in hospice care. The client goes on to say that the hospice staff have been screening the mother's mail and phone calls, as they are concerned that she would fall prey to financial scammers who target the elderly. The client tells the LCSW that the mother has severe dementia and that the client believes the screening of mail and phone calls is appropriate. The client also says the staff has never refused him access to his mother. The LCSW should:

a. Obtain a release from the client, contact the hospice directly, and gather more information about the mother's diagnosis and the need for mail and calls to be screened
b. Report suspected elder abuse
c. Maintain the client's confidentiality
d. Empower the client to gather more information on the mother's diagnosis and the need for mail and calls to be screened, and ask the client to bring that information to a future session for the client and the LCSW to review together

7. An LCSW is surprised to see that her new client did not complete the LCSW's standard informed consent paperwork in the waiting room prior to their scheduled session. The LCSW brings the client into her therapy office, where the client says that he can only read and write in Spanish. He speaks English fluently, and says he prefers that his therapy sessions be in English. The LCSW only speaks and writes in English. Ethically, the therapist should:

a. Have a verbal conversation to establish informed consent, and have the client sign the informed consent document
b. Have a verbal conversation to establish informed consent, and document that conversation in session notes
c. Provide a Spanish translation of her informed consent documents as soon as possible, for the client to read and sign
d. Have a verbal conversation about informed consent, and offer to provide a Spanish language translation of her informed consent documents as soon as possible

8. An LCSW in private practice has chosen to specialize in working with "long-term married" couples, which the LCSW defines as having been married for at least 20 years. The LCSW notes that they are willing to make exceptions for same-sex couples who have been together for at least that long, as they may not have been legally able to marry when they got together. The LCSW is approached by an unmarried couple with four children, ranging in ages from 4 to 19. The couple explains that they are seeking treatment for their relationship, and they are fully committed to each other, they simply chose never to marry. The LCSW believes that the bond of marriage creates bonds and obligations for a couple that cannot be replicated outside of marriage. How should the LCSW address the ethical issues present?

a. Offer treatment to the couple, and build competency in committed, non-marital relationships
b. Refer the couple to qualified therapists who do not share the LCSW's beliefs about marriage
c. Accept the couple for treatment on a probationary basis, to assess whether their relationship is meaningfully similar to a marriage
d. Clarify the reasoning behind the policy and its connections to the LCSW's religious belief

9. A client is aware of a local wellness center that is soon to be put up for sale. The client tells her therapist, an LCSW, about the business and how much she would like to join the LCSW in buying it. She presents a detailed proposal that would have them end their therapy relationship so that they could become investment partners. The LCSW should:

a. Carefully consider the risks and benefits associated with the potential investment
b. Remind the client of the boundaries of the therapy relationship
c. Inform the client that the LCSW will only consider terminating therapy if it is clinically appropriate, and that any potential investment partnership could only be discussed once the therapeutic relationship has ended
d. Thank the client for her consideration in bringing the opportunity to the LCSW, and to protect the client from potential exploitation, offer to serve as an unpaid advisor for the buying process without investing any money

10. In January of 2015, an LCSW successfully terminated treatment with a family consisting of a married couple and their three children, who were ages 6, 8, and 12 at the time of termination. The family member who was 12 at the time of termination contacts the LCSW today to obtain a copy of records from the family's therapy, as the former client is now applying for a military job that requires security clearance. The family member presents the LCSW with a letter, signed by all other members of the family who participated in treatment, authorizing the release of records. How should the LCSW proceed?

a. Inform the client that, because treatment ended more than seven years ago, the LCSW no longer has an obligation to provide records
b. Inform the client that, because treatment ended more than seven years ago, the LCSW no longer is in possession of the records
c. Provide the records as requested
d. Provide the portion of records relevant to the client's request for security clearance, redacting all information pertaining to other family members who participated in treatment

11. A client diagnosed with a moderate Anxiety Disorder calls her therapist, who is an LCSW, at the client's scheduled session time. The client informs the therapist that the client will be unable to attend today's scheduled session and asks the LCSW whether they could do a phone session instead. Which step is a necessary part of the LCSW addressing their legal responsibilities?

a. Inform the client that the LCSW must have certification in telehealth to engage in phone sessions
b. Go forward with the session as scheduled, and assess for potential crisis
c. Determine and document the client's specific location
d. Inform the client that while a phone session is not allowed, they can have a session through telehealth if the client can meet using a HIPAA-compliant videoconference platform

12. To battle her flu symptoms, an LCSW working via telehealth takes an over-the-counter medication. Despite the medication containing caffeine, the LCSW soon finds herself drowsy and struggling to maintain focus in session. A couple of clients notice this and express their empathy, as well as their gratitude for the LCSW working with them via telehealth so that there is no risk of the clients becoming infected. Considering the LCSW's ethical responsibilities, the LCSW should:

a. Consult their physician and cancel remaining sessions for the day, ensuring available backup care for any clients who may be in or may go into crisis
b. Ask a colleague to monitor their work for the rest of the day to ensure they are not missing anything clinically important
c. No action is called for, as the LCSW is providing services via telehealth
d. Seek out additional training on working effectively in the presence of illness

13. An LCSW is running a therapy group for adults abused as children. Given the sensitive nature of the group, the LCSW wants to begin with a discussion about privacy. Group members ask the LCSW whether they can share information they learn in the group with their significant others at home. The most appropriate course of action would be for the LCSW to:

a. Remind group members of their legal obligation to keep information confidential
b. Discuss with the group why privacy is important to the success of the group process
c. Remind group members of their ethical obligation to keep information confidential
d. Discuss with the group what they believe the appropriate rules should be around such disclosures, as well as the consequences for violations of those rules

14. A walk-in client at a local counseling center presents with moderate suicidal ideation and racing thoughts. The front desk worker at the clinic tells an available LCSW that the client should be seen immediately, and that the clinic manager has approved skipping the usual intake paperwork to get the client in to see the LCSW as quickly as possible, as the client has verbally agreed to be seen. Legally, the LCSW must:

a. Inform the client of the fee for services, and the basis on which the fee is computed, prior to beginning treatment
b. Demand that the client complete the full standard intake paperwork for the clinic prior to beginning treatment
c. Inform the client of the limits of confidentiality prior to beginning treatment
d. Demand that the clinic manager provide approval in writing for skipping the usual intake paperwork, in order to reduce the LCSW's potential liability

15. An adult struggling with substance abuse seeks treatment from an LCSW who specializes in Substance Use Disorder. During the intake session, they both realize that they had a brief sexual relationship 20 years earlier. The client laughs and says, “It looks like you’ve done well for yourself. I’ve had a harder time, as you can see.” The LCSW asks whether the client is concerned about saying more, given their prior relationship. “No, it’s fine,” the client says. The LCSW should:

a. Assess for crisis, discontinue the session and provide appropriate referrals
b. Assess for crisis, continue treatment, and seek consultation
c. Assess for crisis, and provide the client with a copy of the brochure *Therapy Never Includes Sexual Behavior*
d. Assess for crisis, continue with initial assessment, and plan to ask again about the client’s comfort level at each session

16. An LCSW is conducting and researching a group therapy process for adolescents who have been victims of child abuse. The parents of one of the members of the group ask to have their 16-year-old child removed from the group and from the study, noting that they believe the group is making the child’s trauma symptoms worse. The parents had been informed of this risk prior to agreeing to put their child in the study. The LCSW should:

a. Remind the parents of the agreement they signed outlining the risks of the research, and attempt to convince them to keep their child in the group
b. Remind the parents of the agreement they signed outlining the risks of the research, and leave the decision about participation up to the child
c. Remove the child from the group, and take steps to resolve any negative impacts the group caused for the child
d. Take steps to resolve any negative impacts the group caused for the child, and keep the child in the group based on the parents’ initial agreement

17. An LCSW working in a middle school setting is confronted by a mother who is upset that the LCSW has not filed a child abuse report over the bullying her daughter has faced. The daughter is regularly taunted by other girls at the school and has been injured in some shoving matches. Though the daughter has sought to avoid these fights and does not fight back, the LCSW defends herself by noting that in each case the girl has been fighting with other girls around the same age and size. The daughter is a regular client of the LCSW, and the mother has attended some sessions. The LCSW must:

a. Contact her local child protective service agency to report the mother for failing to protect her child
b. Contact her local child protective service agency to report physical abuse of the daughter
c. Contact the school principal to discuss the mother's concerns
d. Calmly explain to the mother why her daughter's injuries are not considered problematic

18. An LCSW is preparing to transition from working for a nonprofit organization to launching the LCSW's own private practice. The LCSW is planning to see clients under the clients' insurance, and to submit claims electronically. In preparing for the transition, the LCSW has joined the panels of three popular insurance networks. Considering the LCSW's legal obligations, the LCSW must:

a. Conduct a formal risk analysis regarding how client data will be gathered, stored, and shared
b. Obtain from each insurance company their list of denial and exclusion criteria, and provide this to each insured client prior to beginning therapy services
c. Offer a sliding fee scale to clients who have other insurances or are paying out of pocket for mental health care
d. Review the insurance contracts to ensure that the LCSW is receiving the same per-session fee from each insurance company

19. A client who has expressed great concern about anyone knowing she is in therapy passes out in the middle of a session. The LCSW the client was seeing is able to wake her long enough to learn that she has recently been struggling with illness and has pain from a neck injury, and the LCSW knows from the client's intake paperwork that she has a blood disorder. The LCSW should:

a. Stay with the client and continue attempting to wake her
b. Call 911 and transport the client outside of the office into a public area to protect her privacy
c. Call 911 and summon paramedics without providing any information about the client or her illness
d. Call 911, summon paramedics, and inform them of the client's medical issues

20. With the client's permission, an LCSW contacts another California psychotherapist who had previously been involved in the client's treatment. The client reported to the LCSW that about a year ago, the other therapist had become confrontational with the client in several sessions, challenging the client with statements like, "Why are you acting like such a baby?" and "Drinking is the coward's way of coping, and you're a coward, so I'm sure you're going to go drink as soon as we're done here." The client reported to the LCSW that these sessions left the client struggling to get out of bed each day, and contributed to the client getting fired for missing work. During their call, the other therapist becomes defensive, and tells the LCSW that the client was unresponsive to more empathetic approaches, and so these confrontations were "I guess, my way of pushing [the client] to take some accountability. That's not a crime." How should the LCSW proceed?

a. Inform the client of their ability to report the prior therapist to the BBS
b. Inform the other therapist that their conduct was harmful and is indeed a crime
c. Ask the client to provide documentation of their decline in functioning and their job loss in response to the prior therapy
d. Seek to better understand the other therapist's clinical approach

21. Following a contentious presidential election, an LCSW in private practice is interested in providing care for supporters of the losing candidate. The LCSW advertises short-term grief therapy for the losing candidate's supporters at a 50% reduced rate. A man who was a supporter of the winning candidate asks the LCSW whether he, too, can have the reduced rate, as he is struggling with grief following the retirement of the man's mentor at work. The LCSW should:

a. Agree to the reduced rate for this client, and for anyone else who asks for it
b. Agree to the reduced rate for this client, and alter their advertising to clarify that the grief treatment must be focused on the election to qualify for a reduced rate
c. Cite the language in the LCSW's advertising and inform the client that they do not qualify for the specific rate reduction, but consider their income in setting a fee
d. Agree to the reduced rate for this client, and alter their advertising to remove mention of the election

22. Three months before a local election, a social worker is meeting with a client who serves as campaign director for a prominent local politician. The politician is facing a close race, and the social worker supports the politician in light of the politician's policies related to social and economic justice. The client appears exhausted in session, largely due to the demands of their role. The social worker decides to contact the client after the session to offer encouragement. What message should the social worker send to the client?

a. I'll be tuning in to the debate next week. Good luck.
b. Let me know how I and everyone who is on your side can make your job easier.
c. Keep your head up. I know it's hard. You can do this.
d. I've just donated $100 to your campaign. It's a small gesture, but I want you to know how much I support the campaign.

23. A 57-year-old woman has been diagnosed with a psychotic disorder by an LCSW working at a community clinic. The client has an extensive history of risk-taking behavior in manic phases, followed by periods of relative stability. She calls the LCSW to let the social worker know that she has been stable long enough that she has chosen to discontinue her medication. When asked about risk-taking, the client acknowledges having gone cliff diving, climbing to the top of a crane, and almost getting into a knife fight, all within the past 36 hours. She says she's "doing much better without help than I ever did with it." How should the social worker proceed?

a. Ask the client to come into the office for a full assessment as soon as possible
b. Ask the client for permission to contact her physician and discuss her medication decision
c. Ask the client for her current location, and begin the process of involuntary hospitalization
d. Ask the client to self-assess her own current functioning to develop insight around her risk level

24. A 31-year-old male client is on probation for assault, and one condition of the probation is that the client attend therapy to address anger and substance use concerns. Six months into therapy, the client informs the LCSW providing treatment that the client wishes to discontinue. The client reports believing he has "gotten everything out of it that I can," and that he is growing frustrated with the expense. He notes that he has not had any angry outbursts in the past three months. Considering the LCSW's ethical obligations, how should the LCSW proceed?

a. Encourage the client to remain in treatment
b. Offer to write a letter to the court describing the client's successful completion of mental health treatment and encouraging the court to release the client from their remaining obligation
c. Inform the client of the potential consequences of discontinuing treatment, including the possibility that their probation may be revoked
d. Consult with the probation office about how to proceed with a treatment mandate when treatment is no longer warranted

25. An LCSW works across the street from a major software company's offices. The LCSW begins advertising specifically to employees of the company, using the company's logo on the LCSW's website and business cards to say that the LCSW is "now proudly serving employees of" that company. One client, who works for the software company and had found the LCSW through the website, asks about the relationship between the LCSW and the software company. The LCSW should:

a. Clarify for the client that there is no formal relationship, and that the LCSW simply enjoys working with employees of the company
b. Clarify for the client that there is no formal relationship, and change the website and business cards to not use the company's logo
c. Seek to develop a more formal relationship with the company, including a contract to treat their employees
d. Change the website and business cards to indicate that the company's logo is a registered trademark used with permission

- STOP HERE -
END OF TEST

Mini-Mock Exam: Answers and Rationales

Mini-Mock Exam: Quick Answer Key

1. B
2. A
3. D
4. A
5. B
6. C
7. B
8. A
9. B
10. C
11. C
12. A
13. D
14. A
15. A
16. C
17. B
18. A
19. D
20. A
21. D
22. C
23. C
24. C
25. B

Mini-Mock Exam: Subscale Scoring

The numbers below refer to **question numbers** aligned with each of the major content areas in the exam. You can use these subscale scores to assess your strengths and weaknesses and guide additional study.

Please note: Because of the small sample sizes here, your subscale scores on the mini-mock exam may not be as reliable as subscale scores on the full-length exam. Subscale scores here may reflect knowledge of the specific questions, rather than knowledge of the topic area more broadly.

Law			**Ethics**		
Confidentiality, privilege, and consent	Limits to confidentiality, including mandated reporting	Legal standards for professional practice	Professional competence and preventing harm	Therapeutic relationship	Business practices and policies
1 10 11 18	6 17 19 23	14 20	2 9 12 15	4 5 7 8 13 21 24	3 16 22 25
Total: ____ out of 4	Total: ____ out of 4	Total: ____ out of 2	Total: ____ out of 4	Total: ____ out of 7	Total: ____ out of 4
Law Total: ____ out of 10			**Ethics Total: ____ out of 15**		

Mini-Mock Exam: Rationales

1. An LCSW is working with an individual client who is employed in the movie industry. The client is emotionally unstable following a breakup. The client informs the LCSW that the client will be travelling out of state for the next three weeks to work on a film, and asks whether the LCSW can continue to work with the client by phone during that time. The LCSW should first:

a. **Incorrect.** Assess the severity of the client's symptoms to determine whether phone therapy is appropriate, and if so, proceed with phone sessions. *There is no point in doing the assessment if the LCSW is not legally authorized to provide services in the state where the client will be.*

b. **CORRECT.** Determine whether they have the requisite qualifications to practice in the state to which the client is travelling. *Phone sessions are only an option if the therapist is legally authorized to provide services in the state to which the client will be travelling. If the therapist is also licensed in that state, or if the state has a carve-out in their licensure law allowing for short-term continuation of care with an out-of-state therapist, then the phone sessions requested here are a possibility, pending further assessment.*

c. **Incorrect.** Determine the client's state of residency. *Residency does not matter. The BBS, like most state licensure boards, considers the physical location of the client at the time of service as where the therapy takes place (and, thus, where the therapist needs to be licensed or otherwise authorized to provide care).*

d. **Incorrect.** Inquire with the BBS as to the appropriateness and legality of phone sessions for this client. *The BBS cannot provide legal advice and may not know current licensing requirements for all other states. It would be a more appropriate step to check with the licensing board of the state where the client will be, to see what the rules there are.*

2. A female LCSW finds herself becoming increasingly blunt and even harsh with a client who is overweight and experiencing depression. The LCSW realizes she is judging the client for the client's weight and her apparent lack of interest in resolving any of the personal or relational struggles that the LCSW believes are perpetuating the client's depressive symptoms. The client continues attending therapy and reporting attempts to complete homework assigned by the therapist, but without improvement. The LCSW should:

a. **CORRECT.** Seek consultation and attempt to repair the therapeutic relationship. *The client's continued efforts suggest that the therapeutic relationship has not been damaged beyond repair. The LCSW and client are both best served by the LCSW seeking to understand and correct her personal biases while continuing to treat.*
b. **Incorrect.** Seek consultation and refer the client to a therapist who does not share the LCSW's weight bias. *A therapist bias does not always require a referral. In some instances it is better to continue treatment while managing the bias and repairing the relationship. In this case, the client's continued efforts suggest that the relationship can be preserved.*
c. **Incorrect.** Refer the client out and seek additional training to recognize and not blame the client for common correlates to depression. *A therapist bias does not always require a referral. In some instances it is better to continue treatment while managing the bias and repairing the relationship. In this case, the client's continued efforts suggest that the relationship can be preserved.*
d. **Incorrect.** Refer the client out as it does not appear that therapy has a reasonable likelihood of success. *Nothing in the question stem suggests that therapy is hopeless. It is possible that the LCSW's efforts to address her own biases and repair the therapeutic relationship could lead to meaningful gains.*

3. An LCSW in private practice has a new adult client, who describes a variety of troubling experiences in prior therapy with another local LCSW. As the client describes it, the prior therapist pressured the client for advance payment for sessions, raised the client's fees frequently and without warning, and at one point asked the client for a significant loan. To address their ethical responsibilities, the LCSW now seeing this client should:

a. **Incorrect.** Report the colleague to the BBS based on the client description
b. **Incorrect.** Confront the colleague on their behavior, without revealing how they learned about it
c. **Incorrect.** Inform the client that descriptions of unethical or unprofessional behavior are an exception to confidentiality
d. **CORRECT.** Inform the client of the process for reporting the prior therapist's behavior

Unprofessional conduct does not qualify as an exception to confidentiality under California law. While social workers are ethically obligated to take appropriate action to expose and prevent the unethical conduct of colleagues, here, that must be done by informing the client of the reporting process. Reporting the colleague directly, or confronting the colleague on their behavior, would be a violation of confidentiality in this instance.

4. A military family in treatment with an LCSW for four months comes into session appearing dazed, as the mother has learned she will be deployed to another country in a matter of weeks. The family will be moving with her and will need to discontinue treatment upon their moving date, they say, even though the treatment is incomplete. The LCSW should:

a. **CORRECT.** Discuss the transition, consider increasing the frequency of sessions in the remaining weeks, and encourage the family to continue therapy with a local provider during the deployment. *Given that their treatment is incomplete, it would be better for them to continue it with a local provider during the deployment than to simply wait out the deployment while family problems continue.*
b. **Incorrect.** Empower the mother to delay the deployment, discuss the possibility of transition, and consider adding individual sessions with the mother. *It is unlikely that the mother could delay the deployment; even if she could, adding individual sessions while family sessions continue would be a potential conflict of interests.*
c. **Incorrect.** Assess for substance abuse, discuss the transition, and offer to provide online therapy during the deployment. *There is nothing in the vignette to indicate heightened risk of substance abuse.*
d. **Incorrect.** Consider the deployment a "pause" rather than an ending of therapy, and encourage the family to continue treatment once they return. *Given that their treatment is incomplete, it would be better for them to continue it with a local provider during the deployment than to simply wait out the deployment while family problems continue.*

5. A family of five comes to an LCSW to address family conflict surrounding the family's business. The parents own an auto body shop. Their children, ages 16, 19, and 22, are all working there but are interested in pursuing their own careers. The parents are concerned that the body shop cannot survive if it has to hire outside workers, and they want the shop to be a place the children can rely on. The children express love and support for their parents but openly wonder whether the business should survive if it is relying on their underpaid work. How should the LCSW proceed with the family?

a. **Incorrect.** Allow the parents to set the goals of treatment, while recognizing that the 19-year-old and 22-year-old may choose not to participate
b. **CORRECT.** Attempt to define goals for therapy that all family members can agree upon
c. **Incorrect.** Separate the units of treatment to better support their specific interests, seeing the parents as a couple and each child individually
d. **Incorrect.** Refer out as this is outside of the LCSW's scope of practice

This is an example of a situation in which family treatment could present a conflict of interests, as what the parents perceive as best for the family doesn't appear to align with what the kids perceive as best for the family. Rather than simply abandoning the idea of family treatment, the LCSW should first take steps to minimize the conflict, by determining whether there are shared goals that the family could align around.

6. An adult client tells an LCSW that the client's 89-year-old mother is in hospice care. The client goes on to say that the hospice staff have been screening the mother's mail and phone calls, as they are concerned that she would fall prey to financial scammers who target the elderly. The client tells the LCSW that the mother has severe dementia and that the client believes the screening of mail and phone calls is appropriate. The client also says the staff has never refused him access to his mother. The LCSW should:

a. **Incorrect.** Obtain a release from the client, contact the hospice directly, and gather more information about the mother's diagnosis and the need for mail and calls to be screened. *Even if there were evidence of abuse, the LCSW should not take on an investigator role.*
b. **Incorrect.** Report suspected elder abuse to the LCSW's local adult protective service agency. *There is no evidence of abuse here.*
c. **CORRECT.** Maintain the client's confidentiality. *It appears to the client, and as presented to the LCSW, that the hospice's actions in screening mail and phone calls are appropriate. Further, they are not refusing the client access to his mother.*
d. **Incorrect.** Empower the client to gather more information on the mother's diagnosis and the need for mail and calls to be screened, and ask the client to bring that information to a future session for the client and the LCSW to review together. *There does not appear to be reason for the LCSW to suggest concerns to the client, nor is there reason for the LCSW and client to investigate together.*

7. An LCSW is surprised to see that her new client did not complete the LCSW's standard informed consent paperwork in the waiting room prior to their scheduled session. The LCSW brings the client into her therapy office, where the client says that he can only read and write in Spanish. He speaks English fluently, and says he prefers that his therapy sessions be in English. The LCSW only speaks and writes in English. Ethically, the therapist should:

a. **Incorrect.** Have a verbal conversation to establish informed consent, and have the client sign the informed consent document. *There is no requirement or ethical preference that informed consent be provided via signature; it is enough to document informed consent in session notes.*
b. **CORRECT.** Have a verbal conversation to establish informed consent, and document that conversation in session notes. *Informed consent can be provided verbally and documented appropriately.*
c. **Incorrect.** Provide a Spanish translation of her informed consent documents as soon as possible, for the client to read and sign. *While a Spanish language version of the informed consent may be useful to have, since the LCSW does not read in Spanish, there may be issues with translation that the LCSW would not be aware of. The client may then have a different understanding of what they have consented to than the therapist would.*
d. **Incorrect.** Have a verbal conversation about informed consent, and offer to provide a Spanish language translation of her informed consent documents as soon as possible. *Since the client understands English well, the conversation is likely to be sufficient. Since the LCSW does not read in Spanish, there may be issues with translation that the LCSW would not be aware of. The client may then have a different understanding of what they have consented to than the therapist would.*

8. An LCSW in private practice has chosen to specialize in working with "long-term married" couples, which the LCSW defines as having been married for at least 20 years. The LCSW notes that they are willing to make exceptions for same-sex couples who have been together for at least that long, as they may not have been legally able to marry when they got together. The LCSW is approached by an unmarried couple with four children, ranging in ages from 4 to 19. The couple explains that they are seeking treatment for their relationship, and they are fully committed to each other, they simply chose never to marry. The LCSW believes that the bond of marriage creates bonds and obligations for a couple that cannot be replicated outside of marriage. How should the LCSW address the ethical issues present?

a. **CORRECT.** Offer treatment to the couple, and build competency in committed, non-marital relationships
b. **Incorrect.** Refer the couple to qualified therapists who do not share the LCSW's beliefs about marriage
c. **Incorrect.** Accept the couple for treatment on a probationary basis, to assess whether their relationship is meaningfully similar to a marriage
d. **Incorrect.** Clarify the reasoning behind the policy and its connections to the LCSW's religious belief

Refusing to treat the couple, or accepting them on a probationary basis when a married couple would simply be accepted into treatment, would be discriminating on the basis of marital status. That is expressly prohibited by NASW ethical standards, and any connections to the LCSW's religious belief would not change that. The only ethically acceptable option here is to accept the couple and ensure competence in treating them.

9. A client is aware of a local wellness center that is soon to be put up for sale. The client tells her therapist, an LCSW, about the business and how much she would like to join the LCSW in buying it. She presents a detailed proposal that would have them end their therapy relationship so that they could become investment partners. The LCSW should:

a. **Incorrect.** Carefully consider the risks and benefits associated with the potential investment. *While what is proposed in the question would be, technically, a business venture with a* former *patient, termination should be based on sound clinical judgment and not on a financial opportunity arising. The LCSW should not accept this offer regardless of the balance of risks and benefits associated with the investment.*
b. **CORRECT.** Remind the client of the boundaries of the therapy relationship. *Engaging in a business venture with a client is a problematic dual relationship, and ending therapy to engage in a business relationship is prohibited.*
c. **Incorrect.** Inform the client that the LCSW will only consider terminating therapy if it is clinically appropriate, and that any potential investment partnership could only be discussed once the therapeutic relationship has ended. *Ending therapy to engage in a business relationship is prohibited. Better for the LCSW to remain in a clinical role here.*
d. **Incorrect.** Thank the client for her consideration in bringing the opportunity to the LCSW, and to protect the client from potential exploitation, offer to serve as an unpaid advisor for the buying process without investing any money. *While it may be well-intentioned, advising on this purchase would be out of the LCSW's scope of practice and suggests a potentially problematic multiple relationship.*

10. In January of 2015, an LCSW successfully terminated treatment with a family consisting of a married couple and their three children, who were ages 6, 8, and 12 at the time of termination. The family member who was 12 at the time of termination contacts the LCSW today to obtain a copy of records from the family's therapy, as the former client is now applying for a military job that requires security clearance. The family member presents the LCSW with a letter, signed by all other members of the family who participated in treatment, authorizing the release of records. How should the LCSW proceed?

a. **Incorrect.** Inform the client that, because treatment ended more than seven years ago, the LCSW no longer has an obligation to provide records
b. **Incorrect.** Inform the client that, because treatment ended more than seven years ago, the LCSW no longer is in possession of the records
c. **CORRECT.** Provide the records as requested
d. **Incorrect.** Provide the portion of records relevant to the client's request for security clearance, redacting all information pertaining to other family members who participated in treatment

While LCSWs are required to maintain records for seven years after the last professional contact, when minors are involved in treatment that seven-year clock doesn't start until the minor turns 18. The LCSW is obligated to continue maintaining records of the family's treatment at least until the youngest child who participated in treatment turns 25. That will be roughly 19 years after termination in this case. The LCSW may work with the client to see whether a treatment summary would suffice for the client's purposes, but there is no accepted process for the LCSW to provide partially-redacted records, and to do so would go against the release that all family members have signed.

11. A client diagnosed with a moderate Anxiety Disorder calls her therapist, who is an LCSW, at the client's scheduled session time. The client informs the therapist that the client will be unable to attend today's scheduled session and asks the LCSW whether they could do a phone session instead. Which step is a necessary part of the LCSW addressing their legal responsibilities?

a. **Incorrect.** Inform the client that the LCSW must have certification in telehealth to engage in phone sessions.
b. **Incorrect.** Go forward with the session as scheduled, and assess for potential crisis.
c. **CORRECT.** Determine and document the client's specific location.
d. **Incorrect.** Inform the client that while a phone session is not allowed, they can have a session through telehealth if the client can meet using a HIPAA-compliant videoconference platform.

Phone sessions are legal (ruling out option D), and are considered telehealth. Telehealth has its own set of legal requirements established in state regulation. Among those requirements is that the LCSW must document the client's specific location (C) at every instance of telehealth. This serves in part to ensure that the therapist is not accidentally practicing across state lines. The LCSW is not obligated to carry on with the session (B), and would be violating the law to go forward with the session without fulfilling their other telehealth responsibilities first. The LCSW does not need specific telehealth certification (A) to engage in telehealth.

12. To battle her flu symptoms, an LCSW working via telehealth takes an over-the-counter medication. Despite the medication containing caffeine, the LCSW soon finds herself drowsy and struggling to maintain focus in session. A couple of clients notice this and express their empathy, as well as their gratitude for the LCSW working with them via telehealth so that there is no risk of the clients becoming infected. Considering the LCSW's ethical responsibilities, the LCSW should:

a. **CORRECT.** Consult their physician and cancel remaining sessions for the day, ensuring available backup care for any clients who may be in or may go into crisis
b. **Incorrect.** Ask a colleague to monitor their work for the rest of the day to ensure they are not missing anything clinically important
c. **Incorrect.** No action is called for, as the LCSW is providing services via telehealth
d. **Incorrect.** Seek out additional training on working effectively in the presence of illness

While it may not fit into the same mental framework as a clinician abusing substances or struggling with a mental illness, this question is asking about a form of impairment. Clients are noticing the LCSW's difficulty, indicating that it is obvious in – and likely interfering with – sessions. This doesn't reasonably require additional training for the clinician or an outside monitor (which would raise confidentiality concerns); the LCSW should get the treatment they need to resolve the impairment, which likely means resting and focusing on getting healthy.

13. An LCSW is running a therapy group for adults abused as children. Given the sensitive nature of the group, the LCSW wants to begin with a discussion about privacy. Group members ask the LCSW whether they can share information they learn in the group with their significant others at home. The most appropriate course of action would be for the LCSW to:

a. **Incorrect.** Remind group members of their legal obligation to keep information confidential.
b. **Incorrect.** Discuss with the group why privacy is important to the success of the group process.
c. **Incorrect.** Remind group members of their ethical obligation to keep information confidential.
d. **CORRECT.** Discuss with the group what they believe the appropriate rules should be around such disclosures, as well as the consequences for violations of those rules.

Group members do not have legal or ethical obligations particular to being a client (A and C). Clear guidelines are needed, but the group can come up with their preferred guidelines with the therapist's guidance. Simply discussing why privacy is important (B) would not answer the group members' question about whether sharing information in a limited context with a trusted partner would be allowed.

14. A walk-in client at a local counseling center presents with moderate suicidal ideation and racing thoughts. The front desk worker at the clinic tells an available LCSW that the client should be seen immediately, and that the clinic manager has approved skipping the usual intake paperwork to get the client in to see the LCSW as quickly as possible, as the client has verbally agreed to be seen. Legally, the LCSW must:

a. **CORRECT.** Inform the client of the fee for services, and the basis on which the fee is computed, prior to beginning treatment. *Informing the client of the fee and the basis on which it was computed are legal obligations. While the client is experiencing moderate suicidal ideation, there is no further evidence in the vignette to suggest that the LCSW could not take the minimal amount of time needed to fulfill these obligations, or that doing so would somehow be dangerous.*
b. **Incorrect.** Demand that the client complete the full standard intake paperwork for the clinic prior to beginning treatment. *This may not be necessary, as the standard paperwork may include a great deal of information gathering that is not legally or ethically required and that may be reasonably deprioritized to assess for safety.*
c. **Incorrect.** Inform the client of the limits of confidentiality prior to beginning treatment. *This is an ethical, rather than a legal, obligation.*
d. **Incorrect.** Demand that the clinic manager provide approval in writing for skipping the usual intake paperwork, in order to reduce the LCSW's potential liability. *While the LCSW should document their permission from the clinic manager, and to have it in writing might be particularly helpful, this is not a legal requirement, and placing such a demand ahead of caring for the client is to place the LCSW's interests ahead of those of the client.*

15. An adult struggling with substance abuse seeks treatment from an LCSW who specializes in Substance Use Disorder. During the intake session, they both realize that they had a brief sexual relationship 20 years earlier. The client laughs and says, “It looks like you’ve done well for yourself. I’ve had a harder time, as you can see.” The LCSW asks whether the client is concerned about saying more, given their prior relationship. “No, it’s fine,” the client says. The LCSW should:

a. **CORRECT.** Assess for crisis, discontinue the session, and provide appropriate referrals
b. **Incorrect.** Assess for crisis, continue treatment, and seek consultation
c. **Incorrect.** Assess for crisis, and provide the client with a copy of the brochure *Therapy Never Includes Sexual Behavior*
d. **Incorrect.** Assess for crisis, continue with initial assessment, and plan to ask again about the client’s comfort level at each session

Regardless of how long ago the relationship occurred or how brief it was, the social worker cannot engage in therapy with a prior sexual partner. The social worker should discontinue the session and provide appropriate referrals.

16. An LCSW is conducting and researching a group therapy process for adolescents who have been victims of child abuse. The parents of one of the members of the group ask to have their 16-year-old child removed from the group and from the study, noting that they believe the group is making the child's trauma symptoms worse. The parents had been informed of this risk prior to agreeing to put their child in the study. The LCSW should:

a. **Incorrect.** Remind the parents of the agreement they signed outlining the risks of the research, and attempt to convince them to keep their child in the group.
b. **Incorrect.** Remind the parents of the agreement they signed outlining the risks of the research, and leave the decision about participation up to the child.
c. **CORRECT.** Remove the child from the group, and take steps to resolve any negative impacts the group caused for the child.
d. **Incorrect.** Take steps to resolve any negative impacts the group caused for the child, and keep the child in the group based on the parents' initial agreement.

One of the rights of research participants is the right to withdraw participation at any time; with minors, this includes the right of parents to withdraw their child's participation. The fact that the parents signed an agreement at the beginning of the study, indicating that they understood the risks of the study, does not change their right to withdraw their child.

17. An LCSW working in a middle school setting is confronted by a mother who is upset that the LCSW has not filed a child abuse report over the bullying her daughter has faced. The daughter is regularly taunted by other girls at the school and has been injured in some shoving matches. Though the daughter has sought to avoid these fights and does not fight back, the LCSW defends herself by noting that in each case the girl has been fighting with other girls around the same age and size. The daughter is a regular client of the LCSW, and the mother has attended some sessions. The LCSW must:

a. **Incorrect.** Contact her local child protective service agency to report the mother for failing to protect her child. *It is not the mother's job to protect the child while the child is at school.*
b. **CORRECT.** Contact her local child protective service agency to report physical abuse of the daughter. *While there is an exception to the physical abuse reporting standards when children engage in willful mutual combat ("a mutual affray between minors," according to section 11165.6 of the Penal Code), the fact that the girl here is seeking to avoid these fights is critical. It means that they cannot accurately be described as mutual. Even when the combatants are of similar age and size, if one is being pushed into combat against their will, it can qualify as physical abuse under the law.*
c. **Incorrect.** Contact the school principal to discuss the mother's concerns. *This would raise confidentiality concerns and would not resolve the LCSW's reporting responsibility.*
d. **Incorrect.** Calmly explain to the mother why her daughter's injuries are not considered problematic. *This would not resolve the LCSW's reporting responsibility (see the rationale above for response B).*

18. An LCSW is preparing to transition from working for a nonprofit organization to launching the LCSW's own private practice. The LCSW is planning to see clients under the clients' insurance, and to submit claims electronically. In preparing for the transition, the LCSW has joined the panels of three popular insurance networks. Considering the LCSW's legal obligations, the LCSW must:

a. **CORRECT.** Conduct a formal risk analysis regarding how client data will be gathered, stored, and shared
b. **Incorrect.** Obtain from each insurance company their list of denial and exclusion criteria, and provide this to each insured client prior to beginning therapy services
c. **Incorrect.** Offer a sliding fee scale to clients who have other insurances or are paying out of pocket for mental health care
d. **Incorrect.** Review the insurance contracts to ensure that the LCSW is receiving the same per-session fee from each insurance company

The fact that the LCSW is planning to submit insurance claims for payment electronically establishes that they will be a "covered entity" under HIPAA, and the risk analysis is a required component of HIPAA compliance. None of the other options here reflect a legal obligation. The LCSW is free to accept different rates from different insurers if they so choose, as long they are not violating the terms of any individual contract by doing so. Sliding fee scales for cash-pay clients also may be offered if they do not violate the terms of any specific insurance contract, but sliding scales for cash-pay clients are not legally required. The LCSW does not need to provide information about a client's insurance coverage to the client prior to beginning services.

19. A client who has expressed great concern about anyone knowing she is in therapy passes out in the middle of a session. The LCSW the client was seeing is able to wake her long enough to learn that she has recently been struggling with illness and has pain from a neck injury, and the LCSW knows from the client's intake paperwork that she has a blood disorder. The LCSW should:

a. **Incorrect.** Stay with the client and continue attempting to wake her. *Passing out mid-session may be indicative of a medical emergency. Absent other information, it should be treated as an emergency.*
b. **Incorrect.** Call 911 and transport the client outside of the office into a public area to protect her privacy. *Calling 911 is appropriate, but attempting to transport the client is not, particularly given her known neck injury. Further, it is difficult to argue that moving the client to a public area from a private one would protect her privacy.*
c. **Incorrect.** Call 911 and summon paramedics without providing any information about the client or her illness. *Paramedics may need information on the woman's recent illness, neck injury, and blood disorder in order to treat her appropriately. It is acceptable to share this information with other health care providers in an emergency, and the LCSW can do so without revealing anything about the woman's therapy.*
d. **CORRECT.** Call 911, summon paramedics, and inform them of the client's medical issues. LCSW*s are allowed to share medical information in an emergency situation, and the LCSW in this instance can do so without revealing any information about the client's therapy.*

20. With the client's permission, an LCSW contacts another California psychotherapist who had previously been involved in the client's treatment. The client reported to the LCSW that about a year ago, the other therapist had become confrontational with the client in several sessions, challenging the client with statements like, "Why are you acting like such a baby?" and "Drinking is the coward's way of coping, and you're a coward, so I'm sure you're going to go drink as soon as we're done here." The client reported to the LCSW that these sessions left the client struggling to get out of bed each day, and contributed to the client getting fired for missing work. During their call, the other therapist becomes defensive, and tells the LCSW that the client was unresponsive to more empathetic approaches, and so these confrontations were "I guess, my way of pushing [the client] to take some accountability. That's not a crime." How should the LCSW proceed?

a. **CORRECT.** Inform the client of their ability to report the prior therapist to the BBS
b. **Incorrect.** Inform the other therapist that their conduct was harmful and is indeed a crime
c. **Incorrect.** Ask the client to provide documentation of their decline in functioning and their job loss in response to the prior therapy
d. **Incorrect.** Seek to better understand the other therapist's clinical approach

No accepted form of psychotherapy involves the clinician directly insulting their client in this manner. It is reckless and caused harm, which is a violation of unprofessional conduct standards. The LCSW does not need to further investigate, either by attempting to learn more about the other clinician's approach or demanding supporting documentation from the client. The LCSW should empower the client to make a report of unprofessional conduct to the BBS if the client chooses to do so. While there may be utility in informing the other therapist of the harm their actions caused to the client, the LCSW cannot determine on their own that the other therapist's actions violated the law (and even if they did, the other therapist's actions technically would have violated administrative, not criminal, law).

21. Following a contentious presidential election, an LCSW in private practice is interested in providing care for supporters of the losing candidate. The LCSW advertises short-term grief therapy for the losing candidate's supporters at a 50% reduced rate. A man who was a supporter of the winning candidate asks the LCSW whether he, too, can have the reduced rate, as he is struggling with grief following the retirement of the man's mentor at work. The LCSW should:

a. **Incorrect.** Agree to the reduced rate for this client, and for anyone else who asks for it
b. **Incorrect.** Agree to the reduced rate for this client, and alter their advertising to clarify that the grief treatment must be focused on the election to qualify for a reduced rate
c. **Incorrect.** Cite the language in the LCSW's advertising and inform the client that they do not qualify for the specific rate reduction, but consider their income in setting a fee
d. **CORRECT.** Agree to the reduced rate for this client, and alter their advertising to remove mention of the election

The NASW Code of Ethics non-discrimination standard prohibits discrimination on the basis of political belief, and providing a reduced rate to those who have one set of political beliefs while denying it to others would be discriminatory. Providing the reduced rate upon request (A or B) does little good if the LCSW's advertising continues to suggest discriminatory rate-setting; prospective clients who do not share the LCSW's political preferences would not know to ask. Refusing to provide this client the reduced rate but offering a different kind of rate reduction (C) also does nothing to resolve the apparent discrimination in the LCSW's advertising.

22. Three months before a local election, a social worker is meeting with a client who serves as campaign director for a prominent local politician. The politician is facing a close race, and the social worker supports the politician in light of the politician's policies related to social and economic justice. The client appears exhausted in session, largely due to the demands of their role. The social worker decides to contact the client after the session to offer encouragement. What message should the social worker send to the client?

a. **Incorrect.** I'll be tuning in to the debate next week. Good luck.
b. **Incorrect.** Let me know how I and everyone who is on your side can make your job easier.
c. **CORRECT.** Keep your head up. I know it's hard. You can do this.
d. **Incorrect.** I've just donated $100 to your campaign. It's a small gesture, but I want you to know how much I support the campaign.

Since this is a clinical relationship, contacts that are political rather than clinical in nature would be considered non-work-related. All of the options here suggest support for the candidate or the campaign, rather than the client, except for option C. This option is most clearly and specifically clinical support for the client, making it the best choice.

23. A 57-year-old woman has been diagnosed with a psychotic disorder by an LCSW working at a community clinic. The client has an extensive history of risk-taking behavior in manic phases, followed by periods of relative stability. She calls the LCSW to let the social worker know that she has been stable long enough that she has chosen to discontinue her medication. When asked about risk-taking, the client acknowledges having gone cliff diving, climbing to the top of a crane, and almost getting into a knife fight, all within the past 36 hours. She says she's "doing much better without help than I ever did with it." How should the social worker proceed?

a. **Incorrect.** Ask the client to come into the office for a full assessment as soon as possible
b. **Incorrect.** Ask the client for permission to contact her physician and discuss her medication decision
c. **CORRECT.** Ask the client for her current location, and begin the process of involuntary hospitalization
d. **Incorrect.** Ask the client to self-assess her own current functioning to develop insight around her risk level

The client's current risk-taking is dangerous, and even potentially fatal, to her. This risk-taking is a direct result of her mental health condition. She does not appear interested in receiving help on a voluntary basis. Of the options presented, beginning the process of involuntary hospitalization is the most appropriate.

24. A 31-year-old male client is on probation for assault, and one condition of the probation is that the client attend therapy to address anger and substance use concerns. Six months into therapy, the client informs the LCSW providing treatment that the client wishes to discontinue. The client reports believing he has "gotten everything out of it that I can," and that he is growing frustrated with the expense. He notes that he has not had any angry outbursts in the past three months. Considering the LCSW's ethical obligations, how should the LCSW proceed?

a. **Incorrect.** Encourage the client to remain in treatment
b. **Incorrect.** Offer to write a letter to the court describing the client's successful completion of mental health treatment and encouraging the court to release the client from their remaining obligation
c. **CORRECT.** Inform the client of the potential consequences of discontinuing treatment, including the possibility that their probation may be revoked
d. **Incorrect.** Consult with the probation office about how to proceed with a treatment mandate when treatment is no longer warranted

The client may believe they have gotten as much as they could from treatment, but the question does not specify whether the goals of treatment (in particular, those around substance use) have been met. As such, it would be premature for the social worker to declare that treatment is complete or no longer necessary. The social worker can best support the client's autonomy by informing them of the potential consequences of discontinuing at this stage.

25. An LCSW works across the street from a major software company's offices. The LCSW begins advertising specifically to employees of the company, using the company's logo on the LCSW's website and business cards to say that the LCSW is "now proudly serving employees of" that company. One client, who works for the software company and had found the LCSW through the website, asks about the relationship between the LCSW and the software company. The LCSW should:

a. **Incorrect.** Clarify for the client that there is no formal relationship, and that the LCSW simply enjoys working with employees of the company. *Clarifying this for one client who has been misled, while helpful, does not prevent others from being similarly misled by the LCSW's advertising.*
b. **CORRECT.** Clarify for the client that there is no formal relationship, and change the website and business cards to not use the company's logo. *Use of the company's logo suggests an affiliation with the company that does not exist.*
c. **Incorrect.** Seek to develop a more formal relationship with the company, including a contract to treat their employees. *The possible development of a more formal relationship with the company in the future does not make the LCSW's advertising any less misleading in the present.*
d. **Incorrect.** Change the website and business cards to indicate that the company's logo is a registered trademark used with permission. *Providing an indication that the company logo is trademarked does not solve the problem of the marketing material being misleading. Also note that this response did not include the LCSW actually obtaining that permission.*

How did you do? If you struggled a bit with these, don't worry. They're designed to help you understand the mechanics of this kind of multiple-choice test. If you've reviewed the rationales carefully, and understand *why* you missed any questions you answered incorrectly, then the mini-mock has done its job. If you are interested in taking a full-length practice test, well, that's up up next.

You've got this.

Good luck!

Practice Test: Information

Instructions

There are two answer sheets on the next two pages, which you can tear out of the book and fill in as you are taking the practice test. There are *two* sheets there to give you two attempts at the test. Hopefully if you take the practice test a second time, your score increases. However, you should interpret such increases carefully: It's better if your score improved because you deepened your understanding of the material than if your score improved simply because you memorized some of the correct answers.

Use the practice test here as you see fit! There are a number of different ways you could use it to help you prepare:

1. **Focus on understanding.** In this study method, you would take a practice test untimed, focusing on carefully examining the question and thinking through the available responses. You would then spend a fair amount of time with the *rationale* for each correct answer, making sure that you are deeply understanding the underlying concepts. While of course you hope to get a good score, your scores on the practice exams are not terribly important when understanding is your goal. Any question you answer incorrectly is simply a chance to expand your knowledge and better prepare you for the real test. After all, while the actual test will cover the same content areas as these practice exams, it is unlikely they will ask the same questions in the same ways. You need to be able to understand and apply the key legal and ethical concepts across different clinical situations.

2. **Focus on timing.** In this study method, you would time yourself on each test, making sure you finish within the 90-minute time limit. This also gives you an opportunity to practice any anxiety management techniques you may need, and to practice time management skills like skipping questions you may want to come back to later. Many examinees have reported that they spent more time on the actual test than they did on practice tests, so it's good if you have at least some amount of time left over when you complete the test here.

3. **Focus on performance.** In this study method, a good score is the only goal. As is the case in method 1 above, you still want to make sure you understand why you answered incorrectly on any items you got wrong, but this method is more about confidence-building leading up to your test day. One thing to note if you're focused on your score: Because the real exam varies in difficulty with each exam cycle, it is not safe to presume that a score on any given practice test equates with the same score on the real thing. If you're getting a significant majority of the items on a practice test right, your scores have been steadily improving, and you can understand why any incorrect answers you gave were incorrect, that is probably a better measure of preparedness than any specific score.

There are other, more creative ways you can use the material here as well, such as dividing the questions into three "mini-exams" of 25 questions each, or going through questions and rationales one at a time, flash-card style. I'm a big believer in being pragmatic where studying for an exam is concerned. Do what you know works best for you.

A few cautionary notes

While these questions and responses are written to help prepare you for the California LCSW Law and Ethics Exam, it is important to bear in mind that the practice test here (like all practice tests) is an *approximation* of the style and format of the exam itself. The actual exam changes with each 90-day test cycle; some exam cycles have a more difficult exam, while others have an easier exam. This is why the passing score cutoff changes with each cycle, to ensure that examinees aren't disadvantaged by happening into a tougher cycle of the test.

It's also worth noting that, while every effort has been made here to tie these questions with specific and identifiable legal and ethical principles, ethical decision-making isn't always clear-cut. Even on questions where there is a clear correct answer, reasonable arguments can sometimes be made for some of the other response choices. If you find yourself arguing with the rationale on a question, focus your efforts on understanding why the correct response was identified as such.

If you are using multiple practice tests from different sources (for example, if you are using this book alongside practice tests provided by a test prep company), you may find that in some instances, the different sources suggest different answers for similar questions. That can be confusing and anxiety-provoking, but usually has a good explanation. You may be able to find that even minor, technical differences between the questions account for the differences in the best answers. You may also find that one source or another has something wrong – either because the law or ethical standard has changed, or because it has been misinterpreted. All of us (myself included) make mistakes on occasion. Rest assured that for the actual exam, every item must be keyed to an objective standard, so there will always be a current, justifiable best answer. If you find yourself disagreeing with a practice item from any source, and you have a clear legal or ethical rationale supporting your response choice, you're probably in good shape for the actual test. And of course, if you'd like to discuss anything in this book that you think I may have incorrect, please email my team at support@bencaldwelllabs.com and let us know.

Finally, as a reminder of the disclaimer from the beginning of this book, you may find that some questions here resemble situations that you have actually encountered in your practice. However, real clinical situations are by nature more complex than what is typically captured in a multiple-choice exam question. For that reason, nothing here should be construed as legal advice or as a substitute for consulting with a qualified attorney.

Practice Test: Answer Sheets

California LCSW Law & Ethics Practice Exam

1. ____	21. ____	41. ____	61. ____
2. ____	22. ____	42. ____	62. ____
3. ____	23. ____	43. ____	63. ____
4. ____	24. ____	44. ____	64. ____
5. ____	25. ____	45. ____	65. ____
6. ____	26. ____	46. ____	66. ____
7. ____	27. ____	47. ____	67. ____
8. ____	28. ____	48. ____	68. ____
9. ____	29. ____	49. ____	69. ____
10. ____	30. ____	50. ____	70. ____
11. ____	31. ____	51. ____	71. ____
12. ____	32. ____	52. ____	72. ____
13. ____	33. ____	53. ____	73. ____
14. ____	34. ____	54. ____	74. ____
15. ____	35. ____	55. ____	75. ____
16. ____	36. ____	56. ____	
17. ____	37. ____	57. ____	
18. ____	38. ____	58. ____	
19. ____	39. ____	59. ____	
20. ____	40. ____	60. ____	

California LCSW Law & Ethics Practice Exam

1. ____
2. ____
3. ____
4. ____
5. ____
6. ____
7. ____
8. ____
9. ____
10. ____
11. ____
12. ____
13. ____
14. ____
15. ____
16. ____
17. ____
18. ____
19. ____
20. ____
21. ____
22. ____
23. ____
24. ____
25. ____
26. ____
27. ____
28. ____
29. ____
30. ____
31. ____
32. ____
33. ____
34. ____
35. ____
36. ____
37. ____
38. ____
39. ____
40. ____
41. ____
42. ____
43. ____
44. ____
45. ____
46. ____
47. ____
48. ____
49. ____
50. ____
51. ____
52. ____
53. ____
54. ____
55. ____
56. ____
57. ____
58. ____
59. ____
60. ____
61. ____
62. ____
63. ____
64. ____
65. ____
66. ____
67. ____
68. ____
69. ____
70. ____
71. ____
72. ____
73. ____
74. ____
75. ____

Practice Test

1. The adult client of an LCSW calls the therapist from a police station. The client is filing a police report after their roommate physically attacked the client in an argument over housework. The client asks to reschedule the next planned session and reports that they do not feel safe going home, as the roommate is still there and the client believes the roommate is still very angry. How should the LCSW proceed?

a. Ask the client for permission to speak to the police officer taking the report
b. Ensure that the client has a safe place they can go
c. Develop a plan for what to do if the roommate becomes violent or threatening again
d. Assess the client for suicidality

2. In the client's second session, the individual client of an LCSW requests a letter that would allow the client to have an emotional support dog in their apartment. The client reports that their apartment building does not typically allow dogs, but their pet dog who is currently in the care of a family member helps the client to manage their panic attacks. Considering the LCSW's legal obligations, the LCSW is required to:

a. Seek records from the client's prior treatment to support the need for an emotional support animal, prior to issuing such a letter
b. Establish at least a 30-day clinical relationship with the client, including a full clinical assessment
c. Observe the animal and the client together to directly assess the animal's impact on the client
d. Observe the animal directly in order to be able to attest to the animal's safety

3. An LCSW working in a rural area begins taking on clients who have friendships or professional relationships with other clients. The LCSW does not always know of these connections between clients when treatment begins with a new client. While the LCSW is confident in their own ability to maintain strong boundaries, they wonder what will happen if one client starts speaking about someone else in session, not knowing that the person they are speaking of is also a client. How should the LCSW address this issue?

a. Seek consultation from other therapists who are working in rural areas
b. Considering the nature of the community, ask new clients not to speak about others during therapy
c. Move part or all of their practice to telehealth to broaden their geographic service area
d. If existing clients give permission, provide new clients with a list of current clients, defining those current clients as off-limits topics for the new client's therapy

4. A supervisee expresses frustration to their LCSW supervisor that the supervisee is still having many of the same clinical challenges they were having a year ago when they started working under the supervisor. The supervisee explains to the supervisor that the supervisee has reviewed clinical records and session tapes, and still does not understand what they are doing wrong in therapy. While some of the supervisee's clients appear to be improving, many are not. Considering the supervisor's ethical obligations, how should the supervisor proceed?

a. Consider terminating the supervision relationship in light of the supervisee's lack of improvement
b. Reassure the supervisee that therapeutic growth is sometimes slow and inconsistent
c. Utilize a substitute supervisor to provide the supervisee an alternate perspective on their work
d. Provide a summary of the supervisee's strengths and weaknesses as the supervisor perceives them

5. An LCSW is conducting a home visit with a 16-year-old client who lives with their 43-year-old mother and 70-year-old grandmother. The family is poor and lives in a small apartment. The LCSW had previously met the mother when the mother provided consent for the daughter's treatment, but had not previously met the grandmother. When the client introduces the LCSW to the grandmother, the LCSW notices that the grandmother is in bed in the middle of the afternoon, appears to have an untreated infection on her arm, and the bed smells strongly of urine. The client apologizes for the mess in the apartment and says that she is working an after-school job to help her mother, who works two full-time jobs, so that they can save up for a caregiver for the grandmother, who has dementia. How should the LCSW proceed?

a. Refer the family to programs that provide in-home health care at reduced costs
b. Consider the family's socioeconomic context and their good faith efforts
c. Report suspected elder and child neglect
d. Report suspected elder neglect

6. An LCSW is providing services to an individual client through the client's insurance plan, which the LCSW serves as an in-network provider. The LCSW provides the client with treatment for major depressive disorder and for substance use disorder, but comes to find that the insurer is only paying for claims related to the depressive disorder treatment and not the substance use treatment. How should the LCSW address the legal elements of this case?

a. Inform the client that they will be fully responsible for fees related to substance abuse treatment
b. Resubmit the billing and advocate for the insurer to pay for all services the LCSW provided
c. Ask the client to provide a copy of their policy's specific exclusions and limitations
d. Continue billing under the depressive disorder diagnosis regardless of which actual problem is being worked on, to facilitate payment

7. A prospective client contacts an LCSW who offers therapy services via telehealth through a secure video platform. The client identifies themselves only as "Jose" and informs the LCSW that they are 27 years old and interested in receiving treatment for childhood trauma. The client is willing to attest that they live in California and will complete any intake paperwork the therapist sends, as long as they can sign as just "Jose." They say they are ashamed of what they experienced as a child, and this will make it easier for them to discuss it. Considering the LCSW's legal responsibilities, what must the LCSW do?

a. Require the client to provide prepayment for all services
b. Refuse to conduct sessions via telehealth unless the client is willing to provide their full name
c. Locate the hospital and crisis house closest to the client's geographic location
d. Document the client's request and the LCSW's reasons for agreeing to it

8. An LCSW is working with an individual client who is contemplating moving out of the state. The client has twin 5-year-old children with her spouse, and the client says she is prepared to let her spouse have primary custody. The client explains that her marriage is failing and she cannot find work in California, but that her family in another state is prepared to give her a place to live and help connect her with possible jobs. She says she wants to be a good parent and maintain good relationships with her spouse and children. How should the LCSW proceed?

a. Help the client develop and consider possible outcomes of the move, and possible alternatives
b. Consider the family to be the client and support maintaining the family structure until instructed otherwise by the client
c. Offer to connect the client with a therapist in what will be their new state, including sending records if the client will allow
d. Inform the client that the therapist will listen and reflect as the client weighs their options, but that the LCSW will not guide the discussion in any way

9. An online business aims to make therapy more affordable for telehealth clients by using what they call a “reverse auction” process. When a prospective client signs up with the business, the business creates a de-identified summary of client information (such as location, demographics, and presenting problem), and then allows participating therapists to “bid” on the client by posting what they would agree to charge that client per 50-minute therapy session. The therapist who has offered the lowest “bid” when the auction closes pays the business a nominal fee, and then receives the client’s full information, including their name, phone number, and email address. The client is told which therapist won the auction, what fee the therapist committed to, and the therapist’s contact information. How should LCSWs interact with this service?

a. LCSWs should not participate in this service
b. LCSWs should ensure that no actual therapy information is shared with the service
c. LCSWs should only participate in this service if the fees they charge auction clients are in line with fees they would charge to the general public
d. LCSWs should demand that the business do additional screening on potential clients, to address potential crisis issues

[Question 10 is on the next page.]

10. An LCSW is closing their private practice and planning to start a full-time job with a county mental health agency. They have been using an electronic health record (EHR) system to maintain records of their private practice cases. They plan to stop paying the monthly fee for this system in two weeks, when they begin their new job. Once they stop paying the fee, they would lose access to the EHR system. Considering their legal responsibilities, what should the LCSW do with their private practice records?

a. Continue paying the monthly fee for at least 5 years so that records can be accessed as needed
b. Once the LCSW stops paying the fee, inform all current and past private practice clients that the EHR company becomes the custodian of their records
c. Download all client records from the EHR and transfer them to the system used by the county to ensure ongoing access as needed
d. Download all client records and store them securely in a manner and location separate from the county's system

11. The parents of a developmentally delayed 16-year-old bring the teenager to therapy and provide consent for the teenager's individual therapy. The LCSW providing therapy finds the teenager to be witty and charming. The LCSW also finds the teenager to be emotionally immature and believes her intelligence to be around a second-grade level. After a few sessions where the client appears to be making limited progress, the parents express their dissatisfaction with the LCSW and inform the LCSW that they are pulling their child out of therapy. Considering the LCSW's ethical responsibilities, the LCSW should:

a. Offer to assist with continuity of care to another provider or referrals for additional services
b. Inform the parents that because the child is older than 12, the child can make their own decisions about consent for treatment
c. Advocate on behalf of the client for continuing as the client's therapist
d. Ask the client directly, in the presence of the parents, about the client's desire to remain in treatment

12. An LCSW's former client threatens a licensing board complaint after the former client requested their records be shared with their new therapist. The records were forwarded as requested, and the new therapist then informed their client that the client had been diagnosed by the LCSW with Post-Traumatic Stress Disorder. The client was surprised by the news, as they had not been previously informed of the diagnosis; treatment with the LCSW had focused on the client's social and relational functioning. The former client demands the LCSW apologize and explain why the LCSW believes the client is, as the client describes it, "broken and unfixable." The LCSW should:

a. Retract the release of the client's record, as its release has caused the client harm
b. Contact the new therapist to explain the diagnosis
c. Explain to the former client what the diagnosis means and how the LCSW determined it
d. Inform the former client of the process for filing a board complaint, and remind them of their ability to provide an addendum that would be added to the treatment record

13. An LCSW is nearing termination with a family the social worker has helped through multiple crises, including the unexpected death of a family member. The family has frequently expressed their gratitude to the social worker, saying things like "you saved us. We're still a family because of you." The LCSW is interested in using one specific, touching statement of gratitude the family shared in session on the LCSW's web site. Ethically, the LCSW should:

a. Ask the clients for their permission, and if granted, post the statement without attaching the clients' names to it
b. Wait until therapy has ended, and then post the statement without attaching the clients' names to it
c. Not post the statement, regardless of timing or client permission
d. Wait until two years after therapy has ended, and then seek the clients' permission to post the statement

14. An LCSW learns that his individual client, who is being seen for symptoms of Bipolar Disorder, is also interested in attending couple therapy with her spouse. The client asks the LCSW whether the couple could see the LCSW together for couple therapy separately from her individual sessions, and says she is willing to sign a release form such that information from her individual sessions could be discussed in couple therapy and vice versa. Ethically, the LCSW should:

a. Continue individual treatment and refer out for couple therapy
b. Continue individual treatment with the client and begin concurrent couple therapy, utilizing a separate file and separate treatment plan
c. Inform the client that it would be better to complete individual treatment before engaging in couple therapy, regardless of whether the couple therapy is with the LCSW or another provider
d. Discontinue the individual treatment in order to begin couple treatment, with the client's release in place to allow for material from the individual sessions to be discussed in couple work

15. An LCSW is working with a family where the parents are in the process of getting a divorce and are arguing over custody of their two children. Therapy has focused on maintaining effective co-parenting, as neither parent wants an extended court battle. Because the LCSW knows the family well and has seen both parents interacting with the children, the parents ask the LCSW to submit a letter to the court with the LCSW's clinical evaluation of each of their parenting skills. The best course of action for the LCSW would be to:

a. Obtain a release from all family members, and send the letter to the court, emphasizing that the evaluative statements should not be used to draw conclusions about custody
b. Obtain a release from all family members, and send the letter to the court, offering specific recommendations for custody based on the LCSW's work with the family and based on the LCSW's knowledge of the wishes of the children
c. Obtain a release from all family members, and engage in a process of testing and evaluation to draw objective conclusions before completing the letter
d. Refuse to send the letter

16. The director of an afterschool program contacts an LCSW by phone to refer a 14-year-old girl to the social worker for psychotherapy. The director says that the girl is a participant in the program and has been struggling with extreme shyness. The director further says that the program will be happy to pay for the therapy. The girl, who is with the director in an office, gets on the phone to provide the LCSW with more information. She says she does not want her parents to know she is seeking help. How should the LCSW proceed?

a. Allow the program director to consent for treatment on the minor's behalf and accept financial responsibility
b. Inform the minor that one parent must consent to her receiving treatment regardless of how it is being paid for
c. Assess the maturity of the minor
d. Allow the minor to consent for treatment on her own, and have her complete a Release of Information so that the program can be billed

17. A young adult client with a history of severe childhood trauma begins weeping in session as she connects her traumatic experiences with her current struggles in building trusting relationships. An LCSW has been providing the client with individual sessions for more than two years, and the client has only even begun to trust the therapist in the past few months. The LCSW notices that the client is having difficulty calming herself, and is shaking in her seat. The client turns to the social worker and softly asks, "Will you please just hold me for a moment, so I can catch my breath?" The client has never made such a request before. Considering her ethical responsibilities, how should the social worker proceed?

a. Briefly hold the client, and immediately afterward, discuss it in order to reinforce a strong clinical boundary
b. Briefly hold the client, to support their autonomy. Since the client has not made such a request in more than two years of treatment, it is unlikely that a clarifying conversation is needed
c. Decline the client's request, while offering a blanket or other means the client can use for calming
d. Decline the client's request, and when appropriate, re-evaluate the clinical relationship in light of the client's efforts toward dependence

18. A 23-year-old client whose family immigrated to California from Indonesia calls her LCSW to inform the therapist that the client cannot attend therapy for the next three weeks, as the client's sister just had a baby and the client is going to be helping the sister and the sister's partner. The LCSW has been treating the client for post-traumatic stress disorder and wonders whether the treatment has simply been overwhelming for the client. What steps should the LCSW take to fulfill their ethical duties?

a. Ensure crisis needs are met and a safety plan is in place if needed; schedule a next session for three weeks from now
b. Offer to reduce the intensity of sessions in exchange for the client remaining consistent in treatment
c. Seek to understand the client's behavior from a cultural perspective; treat the interruption of therapy as a crisis and intervene accordingly
d. Wish the client well for the upcoming three weeks; hold the client's usual spot on the LCSW's calendar; ask to see photos of the baby upon the client's return

19. An LCSW has been treating a 38-year-old woman who has been abusing substances. The woman has experienced a series of health problems, and lost the debit card that she uses to buy food through a state program. She leaves the social worker a voicemail one morning, saying that she is "tired of people messing with me" and that "the next person who tries to put me down or take something from me is getting dead." The social worker knows that the client carries a gun and a knife with her in most places. What should the LCSW do next?

a. Invoke *Tarasoff* and begin the process of notifying law enforcement and the client's neighbors of the potential risk
b. Notify law enforcement and attempt to contact and locate the client to initiate the process of hospitalization
c. Invoke *Tarasoff* and attempt to contact and locate the client to initiate the process of hospitalization
d. Notify law enforcement as a precautionary measure, and assume the client's statements reflect substance intoxication rather than actual physical danger

20. A private university contracts with a group practice to provide long-term therapy to university students in need of such services. The university agrees to pay the group practice for up to 20 sessions per student per year at a discounted rate. The practice owner, an LCSW, receives the first request from the university for records that will allow the university to issue payment to the practice. The university requests a list of client names, session dates, and procedure codes for all sessions held with the university's students in the past month. Legally, how should the LCSW respond?

a. Request that each client who attends the university provide a Release of Information allowing the practice to share complete records with the university for billing purposes
b. Provide the university with all data requested except for client names, which can be replaced with ID numbers
c. Provide the university with all of the requested data
d. Ask that all clients who are students of the university pay for sessions at the time of the session, and then submit receipts to the university for reimbursement

21. A client with a history of eating disorder schedules an intake session with an LCSW to discuss the client's current emotional struggles. In the intake, the client reports that prior treatment has been helpful in reducing disordered eating, but that the client still struggles with body image concerns. Referring to prior treatment, the client says, "I learned a lot about monitoring and responding to my body, but not so much about how to prepare food or specifically what to eat." Ethically, the LCSW should:

a. Diagnose the client as having an active eating disorder
b. Collaborate with the client to determine whether a referral to a dietitian is appropriate
c. Request that the client sign a Release of Information for all prior eating disorder treatment providers, allowing the LCSW to request treatment records
d. Educate the client about the typical course of eating disorder over the life span

22. An LCSW receives a phone call from a prospective new client couple. The couple reports that they moved to the US three years ago from a country the LCSW does not know well. The couple says they would like to come to therapy to work on communication difficulty in their marriage. The LCSW strives to maintain strong awareness of cultural issues, but has never worked with anyone from the clients' country of origin before. The best course of action for the LCSW would be to:

a. Refer the couple to a therapist from the clients' country
b. Encourage the clients to educate the LCSW about their country's culture and customs
c. Seek resources and consultation to become familiar with the client couple's culture and customs, and to understand how clients from that country typically present in therapy
d. Wait until the clients come in for an initial assessment to determine whether meaningful cultural differences exist

23. A couple seeks counseling from an LCSW to address conflict in their relationship. One partner in the couple identifies as asexual, while the other partner angrily suggests that "asexual" is a "cop-out" the first partner is using to avoid taking action on the first partner's lack of sexual desire, which has been a source of conflict for the couple since the birth of their child four years ago. The first partner has been medically evaluated, and was determined to be in good physical health. Considering the LCSW's ethical responsibilities, how should the LCSW proceed?

a. Gather information to determine whether the first partner qualifies as asexual
b. Treat this conflict as being no different from other forms of couple conflict, and seek to determine and address the root cause
c. Assess whether changes in the couple's diet, exercise, or sleep hygiene may lead to changes in sexual desire
d. Gather the couple's history, including information about the first partner's history of how they identify

24. Partway through an emotionally difficult session, a client tells their social worker, “My psychic said this was going to get worse before it got better. I guess this what they meant.” The LCSW is initially startled, and asks the client more about the psychic. The client notes that they have been going to the same psychic weekly for more than five years, and find the process valuable and reassuring, especially when discussing issues of grief. The LCSW should:

a. Ask the client’s permission to contact the psychic to develop a professional relationship
b. Discuss the LCSW’s concern that the psychic is exploiting the client’s fragile emotional state
c. Express to the client that while the services of the psychic may be helpful, they are not grounded in science
d. Explore the client’s relationship with the psychic to determine whether the psychic has attempted to diagnose or treat mental illness

25. An LCSW is supervising an associate clinical social worker from a different cultural background. Early in their supervision relationship, they discover that they both are part of a small social media group for health care professionals in their city who suffered abuse as children. How should the supervisor proceed?

a. Ask the supervisee to set a boundary on their social media interactions that is comfortable for the supervisee, based on the supervisee’s cultural background and expectations
b. Meet with the supervisee to establish that the supervisor will not discuss their professional relationship in the social media group or interact with the supervisee’s posts in that group; discuss what other limitations may be necessary
c. Acknowledge their professional relationship in the group, in the interest of transparency; discuss what other limitations may be necessary
d. Inform the supervisee that if they are going to work together, neither the supervisor nor the supervisee can participate in the social media group

26. A white family has been attending family therapy to address conflict among the three siblings: A 16-year-old girl, a 13-year-old girl, and a 10-year-old who identifies as nonbinary. In session, the 16-year-old admits that she and the 10-year-old sometimes wake up before the 13-year-old, and then wake the 13-year-old by climbing on top of her, slapping, and punching her. The 13-year-old has shown her parents the bruises on her face and arms that have resulted, but the parents say they did not take photos of the bruises, and the LCSW providing family therapy has not observed any bruising. The 13-year-old says she has tried to "get back" at her siblings by stealing and giving away their belongings. The parents say they feel helpless to stop the siblings' behavior toward one another. How should the LCSW proceed?

a. File a report of suspected child abuse, naming all three siblings as both victims and perpetrators
b. File a report of suspected child abuse, naming the 16-year-old and 10-year-old as perpetrators
c. File a report of suspected child neglect, naming the parents as perpetrators for failing to protect the 13-year-old
d. File a report of suspected child abuse, naming only the 16-year-old as a perpetrator

[Question 27 is on the next page.]

27. A 56-year-old male client is seeing a social worker to address the client's substance use. The client also regularly sees a psychiatrist. The client provided the social worker with the psychiatrist's name, contact information, and date of most recent visit during the intake process. When discussing the psychiatrist in session, the client asks the social worker not to contact the psychiatrist. The client says the psychiatrist "isn't real big on therapy. I don't know if they would like that I'm here." Considering the social worker's ethical responsibilities, how should the social worker proceed?

a. Contact the psychiatrist to coordinate care, as the psychiatrist is an active member of the client's treatment team
b. Inform the client that coordinated care is necessary for effective treatment, and reassure the client that only a minimal amount of information will be shared
c. Inform the client that coordinated care is necessary for effective treatment, and direct the client to sign a Release of Information form allowing the social worker to coordinate with the psychiatrist
d. Do not contact the psychiatrist, and discuss the implications of the client coming to therapy against the psychiatrist's guidance

28. A polyamorous couple experiencing difficulty in their sexual relationship presents for therapy with an LCSW who believes sexual activity outside of a monogamous relationship is inappropriate and harmful. The couple does not believe that their sexual relationships outside of their own relationship are causing their sexual problems with each other. Ethically, the LCSW should:

a. Seek to address underlying emotional issues that may be impacting the couple's sexual relationship, so as to improve the relationship without directly discussing the couple's other partners
b. Refer the couple to a therapist who does not share the LCSW's belief
c. Inform the clients in advance of her belief, allowing the clients to determine whether they would like to continue therapy with her
d. Begin therapy by explaining her belief and the underlying research, and explaining that the couple's theory that their polyamory is not related to their own sexual difficulty is unlikely to be true

29. A mother arrives late for her therapy session and is enraged. She reports that she just spent an hour dealing with police, who came to the grocery store where her car was parked and were about to break a window when she returned to the car and stopped them. The police, she said, rudely lectured her about the infant son she had left in the car while she was grocery shopping. While the car was in sunlight, it was only about 80 degrees out at the time and she had been away from the car for less than 20 minutes, she said. The LCSW should:

a. Explore the mother's feelings of anger and shame
b. Assess whether the son had suffered any harm
c. Ask for a Release of Information and offer to contact police directly to follow up
d. Report suspected child neglect

30. An LCSW is close to successful termination with a father who has been in treatment for 15 sessions. The father expresses his gratitude to the LCSW, and says he would like to find a way to help families with similar needs. The LCSW is aware of an online discussion group where the father could share his experience in therapy, steering potential clients toward the LCSW and offering hope to families experiencing similar problems to the ones his own family had experienced at the beginning of therapy. Ethically, the LCSW should:

a. Encourage the father to share his experience in the discussion group, including both positive and negative components, and including the LCSW's name so that other participants know where they can receive confidential help
b. Thank the father for his work in therapy, and discuss potential benefits and risks of several potential means by which the father could help similar families
c. Thank the father for his work in therapy, and discourage him from publicly sharing his experience in the interest of confidentiality
d. Encourage the father to share his experience in the discussion group but to do so anonymously, only naming the LCSW if he chooses to do so

31. A social worker who is part of a multidisciplinary treatment team becomes concerned when the team decides to contact the mother of an adult client and ask her to become more involved in treatment. The team made this decision based on the client's worsening symptoms, out of concern that the client may soon need to be hospitalized. The social worker notes that there is not a release in place allowing them to share information with the mother. The social worker should:

a. Respect the treatment team's decision, and not be personally involved in the efforts to contact the mother
b. Respect the treatment team's decision, and be prepared to address the client's possible feelings of betrayal
c. Contact the treatment team and ask to meet with them as soon as possible in an effort to change their decision
d. Contact the treatment team and inform them that if the team's decision goes forward, the social worker will encourage the client to report a confidentiality violation

32. The individual client of an LCSW tells the LCSW that he recently took his 94-year-old grandfather, who has been suffering from dementia, on a fishing trip to a nearby lake in a California State Park. He had grown frustrated with the quality of care the grandfather had been receiving at his nursing home, which he said was not adequate to the grandfather's medical needs. He also wanted to give his grandfather "one last hurrah," as he was concerned the grandfather's death was just weeks away. He was angry that the nursing home staff had berated him upon their return for not notifying them he was taking the grandfather for the weekend. Considering the LCSW's legal obligations, the LCSW should:

a. Report the nursing home for inadequate care, and the client for abduction
b. Report the nursing home for inadequate care
c. Report the client for abduction
d. Ask the client to clarify how the nursing home's care is inadequate

33. An LCSW in private practice grows frustrated with a client who seems to be frequently in crisis, and determines that the client needs a higher level of care than what the LCSW can provide. The LCSW informs the client in person and in writing that in 30 days the LCSW will no longer provide treatment, and offers referrals to inpatient and partial-hospitalization programs as well as other local crisis resources. As the 30 days approach their end, the client has a scheduled termination session with the LCSW. The client reports that they have not even attempted to contact any of the provided referrals, they don't feel capable of doing so, and they are feeling moderately suicidal but without a specific plan or intent. Ethically, the LCSW should:

a. Offer to assist the client during session in contacting other service providers to create a warm handoff
b. Extend the termination deadline by 30 days and encourage the client to contact the referrals previously offered
c. Terminate as scheduled, and ask the client to sign a release granting the LCSW permission to follow up with a close friend or family member to ensure the client is receiving ongoing care
d. Terminate as scheduled, and ask the client to sign a release once they are connected with a new treatment provider, so that the new provider and the LCSW can communicate

34. An LCSW with a full-time caseload finds herself on the edge of burnout. She notices she is becoming less empathetic and more combative with clients, and frequently arrives at the office in the morning still tired from the day before. A colleague she greatly respects refers her a complex case. The LCSW should:

a. Discontinue or temporarily pause treatment with some of her better-functioning clients in order to take the referral
b. Take the referral without changing any aspects of treatment for her other clients, and take other steps to manage her burnout
c. Decline the referral, and consider reducing her overall caseload
d. Accept the referral on a short-term basis, agreeing only to two sessions with the client in order to better assess their needs

35. A social worker has been working with a family for several sessions and plans a session where the entire family will participate in a ceremony relieving the oldest daughter of the responsibility she has taken on as a co-parent. Shortly before the session, the mother informs the LCSW that she will be away on a business trip and asks whether she can participate in the session by phone or videoconferencing. The mother's frequent absences are part of the reason why the daughter felt obligated to take on parenting tasks. The social worker should:

a. Contact the BBS to see whether the LCSW can include the mother in session while she is on her trip
b. Include the mother in the session and in the ceremony via phone or videoconference, and clarify that her involvement is consultation rather than therapy
c. Refuse the mother's request and reschedule the ceremony for a time she can attend in person
d. Contact the other family members to see whether they believe including the mother would be legally and ethically appropriate

36. An LCSW has been treating a 16-year-old under consent from the child's father. The child's parents are divorced, and under the terms of their joint custody agreement, either parent has the authority to consent to health care on behalf of any of the couple's three children. The mother contacts the LCSW to say that she objects to the therapy and is concerned that the LCSW has not prevented the 16-year-old from using marijuana. Consistent with the LCSW's legal responsibilities, the LCSW should:

a. Explain to the mother that the LCSW's role is not to prevent the 16-year-old from engaging in marijuana use, but rather to openly discuss such choices and support the 16-year-old's autonomy
b. Inform the client and the father of the mother's objection, and let them and the mother know that going forward, both parents' consent will be necessary to continue therapy
c. Inform the mother that unless the custody agreement allows her specifically to revoke the father's consent, the LCSW will continue treating the minor as they have been
d. Say nothing to the mother, and review the custody agreement

37. In a hospital setting, an LCSW works with patients who are involuntarily hospitalized for being a danger to themselves or others. One such patient is preparing for discharge after one night in the hospital. The treating psychiatrist interrupts the process, and insists that the patient be held for at least another 24 hours. The LCSW brings together the psychiatrist, a member of the nursing team, and a hospital administrator to discuss the case. The psychiatrist is insistent, based on their view of the patient's symptoms. While the others say they are not sure the extended hospitalization is needed, they express willingness to defer to the psychiatrist. The LCSW strongly believes that the additional night is not needed, and explains why, but the psychiatrist is unmoved. The team plans to keep the patient in the hospital for one more night. How should the LCSW proceed?

a. Accept the decision of the team, and seek to better understand the others' perspectives
b. Insist that the perspective of the LCSW be given equal weight to that of the psychiatrist
c. Re-convene the treatment team in an effort to change their minds
d. Refuse to participate in the ongoing care of this specific patient, without allowing it to impact the quality of care provided to others

[Question 38 is on the next page.]

38. An LCSW is serving as a consultant for a software company that is developing a platform where prospective clients can connect with licensed mental health treatment providers, and where providers can make referrals to one another by securely sharing client data when clients have given permission to do so. The company proposes several different pricing models for therapists who wish to participate on the platform. Which of these models could social workers participate in under state law?

a. Therapist listings are free; when the prospective client matches with a therapist on specified criteria, the therapist pays a fee to view the prospective client's full information and reach out to them
b. Therapists buy credits that are not assigned to any specific client; when a prospective client matches with a therapist on specified criteria, the therapist can spend one credit to view the prospective client's full information and reach out to them
c. Referrals, whether from clients referring themselves or from colleagues, are on a dynamic pricing model; depending on demand in the therapist's area, the therapist may need to pay a fee for a prospective referral, or may get paid a small amount to accept the referral
d. Therapists subscribe to the service to be included in its directory; for an added subscription fee, they can be notified each time a prospective client who matches with them on specified criteria joins the platform and allows clinicians to reach out to them

[Question 39 is on the next page.]

39. Following an arrest for assault, a 20-year-old man has been seeing an LCSW for private anger management and substance use counseling on orders from the court. Three months into the therapy process, and one month prior to the client's next court date, he reveals to the social worker that he recently had a relapse with methamphetamine. He asks the LCSW to keep this information private. As the court date approaches, the LCSW receives a subpoena from the court demanding all records from the client's treatment. The LCSW is obligated to:

a. Provide full and complete records to the court
b. Provide the court a treatment summary, outlining in general terms the client's participation but without specific information on recent substance use
c. Claim privilege on behalf of the client
d. Provide the court with the client's clinical file, and withhold psychotherapy notes, where the client's recent substance use are noted

40. A family from Cambodia is seeing an LCSW for family therapy. During a family session, the father tells the therapist that he sometimes disciplines his 15-year-old son the same way the father had been disciplined in Cambodia when he was young: With lashes across his back, using a stick. The mother voices her objection to this form of discipline, and notes that on multiple occasions the son was left bleeding and crying. The most appropriate action for the LCSW would be to:

a. Consider the cultural elements involved and inform the clients that such discipline may not be accepted in the US
b. Report suspected physical abuse to the local child protective service agency
c. Remind the family of the limits of confidentiality and ask whether there are any photos of the son's injuries
d. Consider the cultural elements involved and research common Cambodian disciplinary practices to determine whether the behavior is consistent with cultural norms

41. A 15-year-old girl is seeing an LCSW individually for issues related to body image and self-esteem. Her parents provided consent for the therapy and pay for her sessions, but do not participate. The girl tells the LCSW that she has been exploring her sexuality. While her parents were out of town, she had sexual intercourse with a friend's 19-year-old brother. A few days later, she had intercourse with another boy, an 18-year-old senior at her high school. The LCSW should manage their legal responsibilities by:

a. Reporting child abuse to the local child protective service agency
b. Investigating to ensure that the sexual activity was not coerced or while under the influence of drugs or alcohol
c. Notifying the parents of their daughter's high-risk sexual behavior
d. Maintaining confidentiality

42. A 20-year-old client who identifies her family background as Chinese starts therapy with an LCSW. The client describes herself as a social media influencer with about 1 million followers, and says that she posts about 20 minutes of video online each day. She tells the LCSW she is coming to therapy after family members expressed concern that she may be depressed. She tells the LCSW in session "I feel like such a faker with every video I post." Considering their ethical responsibilities, the LCSW should:

a. Anonymously review the client's public social media posts, without commenting on them
b. After session, contact the family members to learn more about their concerns
c. After session, digitally request to be added as a "friend" or "follower" on the client's social media accounts, so that the client can make an informed choice as to whether to do so
d. In session, ask the client's permission to review their public social media postings

43. During an unusually tense family session, a mother confronts an LCSW on the LCSW's recent filing of a written report of suspected child abuse. The mother feels violated and reports that she can no longer trust the LCSW. Other family members attempt to calm the mother, but share her concerns. The LCSW should:

a. Discontinue treatment, as the therapeutic relationship has been irreparably compromised
b. Remind the family of the limits of confidentiality, and seek to regain the family's trust
c. In the interest of full disclosure, inform the mother that follow-up reports to the local child protective service agency may be necessary
d. Ask to speak to the other family members without the mother present, to determine whether there is an appropriate path forward for therapy

44. A 14-year-old client consented to her own treatment at a nonprofit agency, which agreed to treat her for $5/session. The client tells the therapist (an LCSW) that the client has been abusing a friend's prescription painkillers. Legally, the LCSW should:

a. Notify the local child protective service agency
b. Notify the client's parent or guardian, as the behavior is considered high-risk
c. Work with the client to develop a plan to gradually reduce dosage and ultimately stop the client's drug use
d. Document the discussion and refer the client to a physician

45. After a family session where a family's 15-year-old daughter believed the LCSW sided with the mother instead of the daughter, the daughter comes to the next session wearing earbuds she refuses to take out, and demanding an apology from the LCSW. The LCSW should:

a. Consider whether the daughter is correct, and if appropriate, offer an apology
b. Side with the mother again, reinforcing the appropriate power hierarchy in the family
c. Refuse to go on with therapy until the 15-year-old removes her earbuds
d. Demand an apology from the 15-year-old

46. A recently-licensed LCSW is interested in helping others successfully navigate the licensure process. She posts to a closed group of licensed and prelicensed therapists on a popular social media platform about her experience taking her clinical exam. In her post, she encourages those about to take their tests to focus their diagnostic review on mood disorders and schizophrenia, as these came up multiple times on her test. Considering the LCSW's legal responsibilities, this post could result in:

a. No action against the LCSW, as she was not specific about the questions she was asked
b. No action against the LCSW, as the post was to a closed group and not the general public
c. Action against the LCSW's license
d. A jail sentence for the LCSW

47. An LCSW is working with a client on issues of anxiety and body image. The client gives the LCSW permission to consult with the client's physician, but asks the LCSW not to discuss the client's recent weight gain with the physician. The client explains that they felt shamed by the physician and pressured to lose weight despite the client being in overall good health. The LCSW contacts the physician and explains that the client appears to be learning to manage their anxiety effectively without medication. The physician asks whether the client is losing weight as instructed. How should the LCSW respond?

a. Say yes to satisfy the physician, and redirect the conversation
b. Inform the physician of the client's weight gain, considering the potential medical concerns
c. Without directly answering the question, inform the physician that the client has experienced pressure to lose weight and that such pressure may worsen the client's anxiety
d. Explain that the client's weight is not part of their therapy

48. An adult client with an extensive history of gambling seeks couple therapy with his wife of 14 years. Despite the best efforts of an LCSW, the treatment fails, and the couple chooses to divorce. The man's gambling worsens, eventually leaving him bankrupt. He sues the LCSW, claiming that the LCSW's misconduct negatively impacted his mental health, causing him to lose his job and ultimately run out of money. The LCSW believes that records of the case will ultimately lead a court to rule in the LCSW's favor, but the client refuses to release the records. Instead, the client goes on television, where he discloses his gambling and therapy history and again accuses the therapist of misconduct. Legally, how should the LCSW proceed?

a. Disclose the client file to the public, as the client has waived confidentiality with his own disclosures to the media
b. Disclose the client file to the court
c. Through an attorney, move to submit the client file into evidence
d. Through an attorney, contact the client in a good-faith effort to have the records released

49. With the client's consent, an LCSW working with an adolescent client encourages one of the client's teachers to attend sessions that will focus on the adolescent's behavior in school. While the teacher's presence is at first helpful, the teacher asks to continue coming to the sessions, and it is clear to the LCSW that the client is finding the teacher's presence gradually more intrusive and uncomfortable. The LCSW should:

a. Clarify the teacher's role in treatment, and ask the client whether they would like to continue having the teacher in session
b. Ask the client whether they would like to continue having the teacher in session, and remind the teacher of the limits to confidentiality
c. Ask the client to contact the school and request that the teacher be removed from the therapy sessions
d. Remind the client of the goals of therapy and the reasons for the teacher's presence in session

50. An LCSW is serving as the family therapist for a family where the father is also engaged in individual therapy with another provider. The family has only attended one session so far, and while the father informed the LCSW of his individual therapy, he did not provide information about the other therapist or sign a release of information. The LCSW receives a voicemail message from a local therapist, identifying themselves as the individual therapist for the father, and asking the LCSW to provide any information the LCSW may have regarding the father's history of psychosis, as the individual therapist is attempting to determine a proper diagnosis. Considering the LCSW's ethical responsibilities, the LCSW should:

a. Provide the colleague with the minimum information necessary to aid them in diagnosis
b. Provide the colleague with the client's full medical and mental health history
c. Contact the father to assess his wishes and ask him to sign a release of information
d. Contact the father to inform him that his information will be disclosed; remind him of the limits of confidentiality

51. In a mid-size college town, an LCSW is the only local mental health provider who speaks fluent Farsi. She routinely receives referrals from other providers when the other provider discovers that their client identifies as Persian or speaks Farsi, even if the client is also fluent in English. Given her ties to the local Persian community, the LCSW often finds that she is at least somewhat familiar with the new clients being referred to her. Considering her ethical responsibilities, the LCSW should:

a. Refer out clients who could effectively receive services from other providers, retaining those who speak only Farsi, unless her familiarity makes her incapable of providing unbiased care
b. Refer out clients she has any form of prior knowledge about
c. Refer out clients she has personally interacted with in the last two years, retaining the rest
d. Reach out to referring providers and let them know she cannot accept additional Farsi-speaking clients

52. A client sees an LCSW at a local community clinic for court-mandated anger management groups. The client comes to dislike the LCSW and becomes disruptive, frequently comparing the group to jail, and saying "I'm not free when I'm here." In considering her ethical responsibilities, the LCSW should:

a. Empathize and validate the client's feeling of disempowerment
b. Terminate therapy with the client and refer them back to court
c. Remind the client that he is free to attend any anger management group he wishes, or none at all
d. Tell the client the LCSW will inform the court of his statements if he continues, and encourage him to become more open to the group process

53. An LCSW is working as the Director for a non-profit agency serving the LGBTQIA+ community. As part of her role, the LCSW occasionally sits in on treatment sessions to observe the work of clinicians at the agency. In a session the LCSW is observing, the client informs the treating therapist that the client is in the process of coming out as bisexual, and is unsure of what to reveal to her parents, or when. The client notices that the Director is older than the treating therapist, and asks the Director, "what would you do in my shoes?" The Director should:

a. Avoid speaking, so as to reinforce that the treating clinician is running the session
b. Clarify the Director's role and defer to the treating clinician
c. Answer the question, and then leave the session in order to support the treating clinician in their role
d. Inform the client that it is inappropriate to ask such a question of the Director, and redirect the question to the treating clinician

54. A client on probation comes to a scheduled session with an LCSW appearing angry. The client confronts the LCSW on a report the LCSW recently filed with the probation officer, updating the probation officer on the client's attendance in therapy. (There is a release in place allowing for the report to be sent directly.) The client had been making good progress in therapy, and is disappointed that the probation officer "didn't seem to know or care." To manage their ethical responsibilities, the LCSW should:

a. Review with the client what information is sent to the probation officer, and how that information can be used
b. Review with the client their progress to date in therapy
c. Remind the client that legally, the LCSW can only inform the probation officer about their attendance in therapy, not about specific therapy content
d. Remind the client that the role of the probation officer is not to provide support or encouragement, but to ensure compliance

55. A 14-year-old girl presents for therapy at a local mental health clinic, where an LCSW is assigned to her case. During a screening interview, the girl tells the LCSW that she is struggling with anxiety around her schoolwork and social relationships. She goes on to say that she plans to pay for therapy on her own and would prefer that her parents not know she is in therapy. The LCSW should:

a. Assess the girl's ability to participate intelligently in therapy and determine whether notifying the parents would be damaging
b. Determine whether notifying the parents would be damaging and determine what adult can consent for the girl's therapy
c. Assess the girl's ability to participate intelligently in treatment and inform her that even when seen under her own consent, her parents may have the right to access her records if they become aware she is in therapy
d. Determine whether notifying the parents would be damaging and determine whether notifying the girl's school would be damaging

56. An LCSW provided therapy to a 16-year-old boy for several months with his parents' consent. A few months later, the LCSW receives a subpoena from the attorney for a classmate of the boy. The classmate accused the client of physical assault, and the classmate's family is suing to recover medical expenses. The subpoena requests complete records of the boy's treatment. The LCSW attempts to contact the client and his parents but is unsuccessful. The LCSW should:

a. Wait to respond to the subpoena until the LCSW is able to determine how the client would like the LCSW to respond
b. Wait to respond to the subpoena until the LCSW is able to determine how the parents would like the LCSW to respond
c. Respond to the subpoena by asserting privilege, and continue attempts to contact the client and his parents
d. Acknowledge the exception to privilege, turn over the client's records, and inform the client and his family as soon as possible

57. An LCSW is working with a Latina mother and her 7-year-old son in therapy, when the LCSW observes unusual bruises on the boy's face and arms. The bruises seem to be in several different stages of healing. When the LCSW asks how he got the bruises, the boy does not answer. His mother says, "He's a normal boy, he likes to play rough" and refuses to discuss the matter further. The LCSW should:

a. Report suspected child abuse
b. Consider whether physical discipline is common in Latin cultures
c. Remind the mother of the limits of confidentiality
d. Ask the child to remove his shirt to inspect his torso for additional injuries

58. A single LCSW finds herself sometimes flirting with one particular group therapy client at the end of each week's session, as the other group members are making their way outside. The group member is also single, and appears to be interested in the therapist, but is careful to not cross boundaries during session or in other situations where other group members could see. One evening, the client sends the social worker an email to express gratitude for all she has done in the group, and attaches a couple of racy photos. The LCSW should:

a. Ignore the photos, respond to the gratitude, and encourage continued growth in group
b. Do not respond via email, engage the client in a phone discussion, warn the client that the email cannot remain confidential, and consider termination from the group
c. Acknowledge the email, inform the client that they are violating the LCSW's boundaries, and inform the client that sexually explicit communications must be reported
d. Acknowledge the email, inform the client that including the photos was inappropriate, apologize for any misunderstanding about the nature of their relationship, and monitor both the LCSW's and the client's future behavior

59. An LCSW is working for an agency that contracts with a local private school to provide mental health services. The social worker is called to the school to assess a 9-year-old girl who has been falling asleep in class. The girl's teacher tells the social worker that the teacher is concerned in part because the girl recently wrote a story as part of a class assignment, and in the story a young girl wasn't allowed to sleep when she got into trouble at home. During the assessment, the girl repeatedly asks whether she can take a nap, and refuses to answer any questions about the story she wrote. Asked how things are at home, the girl will only say, "I got in trouble. I'm always getting in trouble." The girl is being raised by a single mother, and the school nurse says that the girl is otherwise in relatively good health, but that her grades have been dropping and her behavior in class has been increasingly disorganized. How should the social worker proceed?

a. Contact the mother to inform her of the child's behavior and the school's concerns
b. Contact the child's physician to request a medical assessment
c. Report suspected child abuse
d. Ask the child directly whether she is being physically abused or neglected

[Question 60 is on the next page.]

60. An older woman who has been seeing an LCSW for seven months storms out of session after her therapist started the session some 30 minutes late. The LCSW attempted to explain that another client had been in crisis, but the woman cut off the LCSW, saying that the delay was disrespectful of her time. A few days later the client calls the LCSW saying she will not come back for future sessions and requesting a copy of the treatment record be sent to her. The LCSW should:

a. Insist that the client come in for an additional session to discuss her hurt feelings, and provide a copy of the treatment record
b. Apologize for the delay, offer to discuss it further, provide options for other treatment providers, and provide a copy of the treatment record
c. Provide a copy of the treatment record, and consider whether the client's display was simply a way of resolving cognitive dissonance about the need to end treatment
d. Provide options for other treatment providers, and inform the client that the LCSW will forward the treatment record to the new provider of the client's choosing, in order to ensure that the client does remain in therapy

[Question 61 is on the next page.]

61. An LCSW with strong religious beliefs is talking with a trans male client about the client's family history. The client reveals that his parents had strong religious beliefs, but the client describes himself as atheist and says, "I just never understood why people buy into those fairy tales." The client says he has never found comfort or strength in religious or spiritual activity, and has judgment toward those who do. The LCSW should:

a. Mention the LCSW's beliefs briefly, without challenging the client's experience
b. Inform the client that religion is a source of comfort for many people, and encourage the client to keep an open mind toward it for the future
c. Connect the client's beliefs about religion with their history of family trauma
d. Show understanding of the client's beliefs and inquire further about their family history

62. An LCSW is consulting with the physician who sent a young couple to the LCSW for couple therapy. Both partners in the couple are struggling with symptoms of anxiety. The physician provides the LCSW with useful information on the couple's medications and their possible side effects. The LCSW offers the physician useful information on the progression of the couple's symptoms. Toward the end of the conversation, the physician asks whether the older partner in the couple is "still wearing that same brown sweater twice a week." The LCSW should:

a. Answer the question
b. Politely decline to answer the question, as it is not relevant to the consultation
c. Request a release from both partners to provide this type of information
d. Gently note that the physician is asking a question outside of their scope of practice

63. A middle-aged woman struggling with panic disorder asks an LCSW whether her brother can come with her to therapy, and the LCSW approves. In the intake session, the woman describes her panic symptoms, as well as the strain that her panic has caused in her relationship with her brother. She relies on him to feel safe in public situations, and becomes angry with him when he cannot be with her due to his job or other obligations. The brother agrees, saying that while he wants to help his sister as much as he can and is glad that she is seeking treatment, he is growing resentful of being her main source of support. The LCSW should:

a. Clarify whether the woman and her brother are seeking conjoint treatment to address their relationship, or whether treatment is to focus on the woman's panic
b. Ask the brother to leave the session so that the LCSW can assess the woman for possible dependent adult abuse
c. Ask the client to sign a release of information allowing for discussion of her symptoms in therapy sessions where her brother is also present
d. Provide the client with referrals to co-occurring disorder treatment

64. An LCSW has a client who lives on a boat three months of the year, as a commercial fisherman. During that time, he comes back to shore one day a week, and sees the LCSW on that day. The client is relatively poor, and asks the LCSW whether he can pay for services in fresh salmon. The client says he may need to discontinue treatment otherwise. The LCSW frequently eats salmon, and so is familiar with the fair market value of the fish. Which of the following statements of the LCSW's responsibilities is correct?

a. The LCSW should provide services pro bono, rather than accepting payment in fish
b. If the LCSW chooses to go ahead with the barter agreement, the value of the fish should approximate the fee generally charged for therapy, and there should be a clear contract
c. The LCSW should refer the client to a low-fee or no-fee clinic rather than accepting salmon as payment
d. The LCSW should consider whether other clients would also want to pay for therapy through the products they make or services they provide

65. An LCSW suffers a serious illness, and a colleague steps in to take over the LCSW's ongoing clients until the LCSW can return to practice. The LCSW agrees to continue handling billing and to review the colleague's session notes to keep up with what is happening while she is recovering. Some of the LCSW's ongoing clients pay for sessions through their health insurance. However, the colleague (who is also a licensed LCSW in private practice) is not on any insurance panels. The ill LCSW should:

a. Continue to submit insurance billing listing herself as the treatment provider
b. Continue to submit insurance billing listing the colleague as the treatment provider and herself as the supervisor
c. Either directly or through the colleague, inform clients of the difference in panel status and arrange alternate payment or referrals as needed
d. Defer to the colleague to negotiate fees independently, and otherwise presume that the LCSW's typical business practices will be followed

66. An adult client who has been seeing an LCSW in therapy for six months asks the LCSW for a copy of her treatment record. Because the LCSW has documented that she suspects the client is being dishonest in her denials of recent drug use, the LCSW worries that sharing the file would harm the therapeutic relationship. The most appropriate course of action for the LCSW would be to:

a. Turn over the records as required by law, and use it as an opportunity to address the client's possible substance use
b. Provide the client with a partial copy of the file, leaving out the suspicion of recent drug use
c. Refuse to turn over the records, offer a treatment summary instead, and inform the client that if she wishes, she can select a neutral therapist to review the file
d. Submit the client's request, and the LCSW's reason for refusing, to a district judge for review

67. An individual client acknowledges to her therapist (an LCSW) that she lied on the LCSW's intake form and actually does have several past suicide attempts in her history. She says she is not feeling suicidal now, though she has recently experienced the ending of a romantic relationship and the death of a distant relative. Legally, the LCSW should:

a. Complete a No Harm Contract with the client
b. Discontinue therapy and refer the client to a higher level of care, as she is high risk
c. Initiate the process of involuntary hospitalization
d. Assess further and break confidentiality if required to resolve any threat of suicide

68. An LCSW in an outpatient group practice setting has fallen behind on their documentation. The owner of the practice expresses concern that the delays will impact insurance billing and, ultimately, the practice's financial health. To ethically resolve this issue, the LCSW should:

a. Create at least cursory progress notes for all sessions more than 7 days in the past, even if such notes are a single sentence each, to allow billing to move forward
b. Transfer their clients to other clinicians in the group, allowing the other clinicians to create documentation of past sessions establishing themselves as the service providers and to properly submit insurance claims
c. Work diligently to catch up
d. Consider reducing their client load or, if necessary, leaving the practice

69. As a client leaves an LCSW's office, the LCSW believes the client poses a serious danger to the client's spouse. (The client had been making threats in session about what he would do to her.) The LCSW, knowing the couple lives roughly 30 minutes from the LCSW's office, calls the client immediately, and is able to resolve the danger. The client disavows any continued plan to harm his spouse, and apologizes to the LCSW for "getting so out of hand." What does the LCSW need to do to resolve the LCSW's legal responsibility?

a. Notify the spouse and law enforcement immediately
b. Notify the spouse immediately
c. Notify law enforcement within 24 hours
d. Notify the local child protective services agency

70. An LCSW has a new client who explains during the intake session that she had a hard time coming into therapy. The client says that her previous therapist asked her to go on a date with him immediately after their termination session ended. She refused, and has not spoken with the former therapist again, but the experience left her skeptical of therapists generally. Legally, the LCSW must:

a. Report the other therapist's actions to the BBS
b. Confront the other therapist on their behavior
c. Provide the client a copy of the brochure "Therapy Never Includes Sexual Behavior"
d. Maintain the client's confidentiality

71. An LCSW is interested in conducting research on her clients, in an effort to determine whether a new form of treatment developed by the LCSW is superior to existing treatments. Because the LCSW already has access to the client files and would be reporting statistics on her recent treatment results, without specifics of any individual cases, she prepares to conduct an analysis of cases she has closed over the prior year. She hopes to publish the results of her research in a prominent journal. Ethically, the LCSW should:

a. Contact those former clients, inform them of the risks and benefits of involvement in the research, and determine their willingness to have their file included as one of those analyzed
b. Take steps to protect the confidentiality of individual cases, but include all cases from the prior year in her analysis to eliminate possible selection bias
c. Contact those former clients to let them know that their files have been included in her research
d. Because she is working with archival data that will be reported in aggregate, no action is required

[Question 72 is on the next page.]

72. A 27-year-old trans female client has been receiving services from an LCSW at a reduced-fee clinic. The client has been unable to pay even her reduced fee, and over 8 weeks has built up an unpaid balance of more than $100. The client is apologetic and has reassured the LCSW that she will pay the overdue fees once her aging mother dies and she can collect her inheritance. The LCSW has informed the client while she empathizes with the client's struggles, a balance that goes unpaid for more than 30 days will result in the termination of services. This policy also appears in the informed consent document the client signed at the beginning of services. The client does not have stable food, work, or shelter, but is typically able to engage public services and shelter space when needed. How should the social worker proceed?

a. Assess whether the client poses imminent danger to self or others
b. Terminate the client for nonpayment and provide at least three community referrals
c. Pay the client's balance on the client's behalf
d. Set a specific deadline by which the full balance must be paid off to retain services

[Question 73 is on the next page.]

73. A social worker at a private nonprofit outpatient clinic is surprised to learn that the clinic has a policy of neutrality on political matters. The social worker had hoped to get the clinic to support a proposed local law that would raise sales taxes to improve local services and accessibility for those with disabilities. The clinic asks the social worker to stay out of political discussion about the proposed law, which the social worker believes would advance social justice. The director of the clinic says that she also believes the proposal is good, but is committed to the clinic policy. How should the social worker proceed?

a. Respect the wishes of the employer, and support the proposal by voting for it and potentially donating money to groups that are advocating for its passage
b. Engage in public discussion of the proposal, and describe the clinic as being in favor of it
c. Engage in public discussion of the proposal, and criticize the clinic's unwillingness to take a public stance as likely an effort to preserve their grants and contracts
d. Engage in public discussion of the proposal, but as an individual and not as a representative of the clinic

[Question 74 is on the next page.]

74. A group practice specializing in working with depression is considering implementing a new policy to build awareness of their work: As part of the consent process, clients would be required to agree to post at least once on social media about their experience in therapy, making specific mention of the group practice when they do. The policy specifies that the post does not need to be an endorsement or testimonial; even negative discussion is allowed, so long as it is truthful. Clients who have no social media presence would be exempt. Considering the LCSW's ethical responsibilities, what should the LCSW do around this policy?

a. Clarify to clients that since it is part of the consent process, they are free to go to a different provider who does not have such a policy if they wish
b. Clarify to all clients that such posts are strongly encouraged, but are not required, regardless of what the official policy may say
c. Clarify with the practice owners what the consequence would be for clients who agree to the policy but ultimately do not post about their experience
d. Refuse to implement the policy, and ask the group practice to withdraw it

[Question 75 is on the next page.]

75. In a large public mental health clinic, a social worker (Social Worker A) becomes aware of a colleague in the clinic (Social Worker B) who describes all trans, queer, nonbinary, or otherwise gender-nonconforming clients as mentally ill, and refuses to work with such clients. Supervisors are aware of the issue and make sure that the colleague is only assigned cisgender clients. A different colleague (Social Worker C), who complained about Social Worker B's behavior, was then told that Social Worker B had accused them of religious discrimination, a charge that Social Worker A believes to be false. What ethical responsibility does Social Worker A have in this circumstance?

a. Assist in Social Worker C's defense; bring Social Worker B's behavior to the attention of administrators; file a formal ethical complaint against Social Worker B if needed
b. Assist in Social Worker C's defense; demand supervisors explain why they did not take additional action
c. Because all potentially problematic behavior has been reported, allow the administrative processes of resolving all complaints to reach their conclusions; evaluate options at that point
d. File an ethics complaint against Social Worker B and their supervisor with the NASW Ethics Committee

- STOP HERE -
END OF TEST

Practice Test: Quick Answer Key

Quick Answer Key

1. B
2. B
3. A
4. D
5. D
6. B
7. B
8. A
9. A
10. D
11. A
12. C
13. C
14. A
15. D
16. C
17. C
18. A
19. B
20. C
21. B
22. C
23. D
24. A
25. B
26. B
27. D
28. B
29. D
30. B
31. C
32. D
33. A
34. C
35. C
36. D
37. A
38. D
39. A
40. B
41. D
42. D
43. B
44. D
45. A
46. C
47. D
48. C
49. A
50. C
51. A
52. C
53. B
54. A
55. A
56. C
57. A
58. D
59. C
60. B
61. D
62. B
63. A
64. B
65. C
66. C
67. D
68. C
69. C
70. D
71. A
72. A
73. D
74. D
75. A

Subscale scoring

The numbers below refer to **question numbers** aligned with each of the major content areas in the exam. You can use these subscale scores to assess your strengths and weaknesses and guide additional study.

Law			**Ethics**		
Confidentiality, privilege, and consent	Limits to confidentiality, including mandated reporting	Legal standards for professional practice	Professional competence and preventing harm	Therapeutic relationship	Business practices and policies
2	5	6	3	1	4
7	19	9	8	11	12
10	26	38	15	14	13
16	29	46	17	18	25
20	39	64	21	23	35
30	40	65	22	24	42
36	41	70	28	27	53
44	48		33	31	68
55	57		34	32	71
56	59		47	37	72
66	67		51	43	75
	69		58	45	
			61	49	
			74	50	
				52	
				54	
				60	
				62	
				63	
				73	
Total: ____ out of 11	Total: ____ out of 12	Total: ____ out of 7	Total: ____ out of 14	Total: ____ out of 20	Total: ____ out of 11
Law Total: ____ out of 30			**Ethics Total: ____ out of 45**		

Practice Test:
Answers and Rationales

1. The adult client of an LCSW calls the therapist from a police station. The client is filing a police report after their roommate physically attacked the client in an argument over housework. The client asks to reschedule the next planned session and reports that they do not feel safe going home, as the roommate is still there and the client believes the roommate is still very angry. How should the LCSW proceed?

a. **Incorrect.** Ask the client for permission to speak to the police officer taking the report
b. **CORRECT.** Ensure that the client has a safe place they can go
c. **Incorrect.** Develop a plan for what to do if the roommate becomes violent or threatening again
d. **Incorrect.** Assess the client for suicidality

There is an immediate and potentially ongoing risk to the client if they return home. When managing risks to safety, immediate physical safety is the highest priority. The LCSW should start by ensuring that the client has a safe place to go.

2. In the client's second session, the individual client of an LCSW requests a letter that would allow the client to have an emotional support dog in their apartment. The client reports that their apartment building does not typically allow dogs, but their pet dog who is currently in the care of a family member helps the client to manage their panic attacks. Considering the LCSW's legal obligations, the LCSW is required to:

a. **Incorrect.** Seek records from the client's prior treatment to support the need for an emotional support animal, prior to issuing such a letter
b. **CORRECT.** Establish at least a 30-day clinical relationship with the client, including a full clinical assessment
c. **Incorrect.** Observe the animal and the client together to directly assess the animal's impact on the client
d. **Incorrect.** Observe the animal directly in order to be able to attest to the animal's safety

Under state law, LCSWs and other therapists issuing letters for emotional support dogs must first establish a 30-day therapeutic relationship, and conduct a formal assessment, among other requirements. The therapist is not required to seek prior records, to evaluate the animal directly, or to attest to the animal's safety.

3. An LCSW working in a rural area begins taking on clients who have friendships or professional relationships with other clients. The LCSW does not always know of these connections between clients when treatment begins with a new client. While the LCSW is confident in their own ability to maintain strong boundaries, they wonder what will happen if one client starts speaking about someone else in session, not knowing that the person they are speaking of is also a client. How should the LCSW address this issue?

a. **CORRECT.** Seek consultation from other therapists who are working in rural areas
b. **Incorrect.** Considering the nature of the community, ask new clients not to speak about others during therapy
c. **Incorrect.** Move part or all of their practice to telehealth to broaden their geographic service area
d. **Incorrect.** If existing clients give permission, provide new clients with a list of current clients, defining those current clients as off-limits topics for the new client's therapy

LCSWs are expected to engage in consultation when doing so is in clients' best interests, and this is the only option that reflects an ethical obligation in this circumstance. In this instance, the LCSW is not obligated to move to telehealth, and asking clients not to speak of specific other people in their lives would make it difficult to assess or intervene in client relationships. But the LCSW may need to take steps to manage the dual relationships that can arise in rural areas, and consultation will help the LCSW determine how to best do so.

4. A supervisee expresses frustration to their LCSW supervisor that the supervisee is still having many of the same clinical challenges they were having a year ago when they started working under the supervisor. The supervisee explains to the supervisor that the supervisee has reviewed clinical records and session tapes, and still does not understand what they are doing wrong in therapy. While some of the supervisee's clients appear to be improving, many are not. Considering the supervisor's ethical obligations, how should the supervisor proceed?

a. **Incorrect.** Consider terminating the supervision relationship in light of the supervisee's lack of improvement
b. **Incorrect.** Reassure the supervisee that therapeutic growth is sometimes slow and inconsistent
c. **Incorrect.** Utilize a substitute supervisor to provide the supervisee an alternate perspective on their work
d. **CORRECT.** Provide a summary of the supervisee's strengths and weaknesses as the supervisor perceives them

While any of the options here could theoretically be useful and appropriate, only the evaluation of supervisees represents an ethical obligation.

5. An LCSW is conducting a home visit with a 16-year-old client who lives with their 43-year-old mother and 70-year-old grandmother. The family is poor and lives in a small apartment. The LCSW had previously met the mother when the mother provided consent for the daughter's treatment, but had not previously met the grandmother. When the client introduces the LCSW to the grandmother, the LCSW notices that the grandmother is in bed in the middle of the afternoon, appears to have an untreated infection on her arm, and the bed smells strongly of urine. The client apologizes for the mess in the apartment and says that she is working an after-school job to help her mother, who works two full-time jobs, so that they can save up for a caregiver for the grandmother, who has dementia. How should the LCSW proceed?

a. **Incorrect.** Refer the family to programs that provide in-home health care at reduced costs
b. **Incorrect.** Consider the family's socioeconomic context and their good faith efforts
c. **Incorrect.** Report suspected elder and child neglect
d. **CORRECT.** Report suspected elder neglect

There is no evidence in the question to suggest that the child is being neglected, but the grandmother's untreated infection and urine smell suggest that she is. While the LCSW should be sensitive to the family's circumstances, reporting in this case is an obligation. Doing so can help ensure that the grandmother receives the care she needs. Rather than attempting to punish the child or mother, the most likely outcome would be that the local adult protective service agency would connect the family with appropriate services.

6. An LCSW is providing services to an individual client through the client's insurance plan, which the LCSW serves as an in-network provider. The LCSW provides the client with treatment for major depressive disorder and for substance use disorder, but comes to find that the insurer is only paying for claims related to the depressive disorder treatment and not the substance use treatment. How should the LCSW address the legal elements of this case?

a. **Incorrect.** Inform the client that they will be fully responsible for fees related to substance abuse treatment
b. **CORRECT.** Resubmit the billing and advocate for the insurer to pay for all services the LCSW provided
c. **Incorrect.** Ask the client to provide a copy of their policy's specific exclusions and limitations
d. **Incorrect.** Continue billing under the depressive disorder diagnosis regardless of which actual problem is being worked on, to facilitate payment

Parity law demands that insurers who provide mental health care coverage do so on a level parallel to their coverage for physical health treatment, and that the mental health care coverage include substance use treatment. The insurer is obligated to pay these claims. The LCSW can best demonstrate their knowledge of parity law by resubmitting the claims and advocating for payment. Simply billing under the depression code when that is not the actual issue being treated could be considered misleading.

7. A prospective client contacts an LCSW who offers therapy services via telehealth through a secure video platform. The client identifies themselves only as "Jose" and informs the LCSW that they are 27 years old and interested in receiving treatment for childhood trauma. The client is willing to attest that they live in California and will complete any intake paperwork the therapist sends, as long as they can sign as just "Jose." They say they are ashamed of what they experienced as a child, and this will make it easier for them to discuss it. Considering the LCSW's legal responsibilities, what must the LCSW do?

a. **Incorrect.** Require the client to provide prepayment for all services
b. **CORRECT.** Refuse to conduct sessions via telehealth unless the client is willing to provide their full name
c. **Incorrect.** Locate the hospital and crisis house closest to the client's geographic location
d. **Incorrect.** Document the client's request and the LCSW's reasons for agreeing to it

A legal requirement for LCSWs at each telehealth session is that they verbally obtain and document the client's full name and current location. If the client is not willing to provide their full name, the LCSW would be violating the law by conducting the session. Prepayment is not legally required under any circumstances, and LCSWs offering telehealth must document the reasonable efforts made to locate crisis resources local to the client; that does not necessarily require them to locate the closest hospital and crisis house, especially if the client does not present concerns about risk.

8. An LCSW is working with an individual client who is contemplating moving out of the state. The client has twin 5-year-old children with her spouse, and the client says she is prepared to let her spouse have primary custody. The client explains that her marriage is failing and she cannot find work in California, but that her family in another state is prepared to give her a place to live and help connect her with possible jobs. She says she wants to be a good parent and maintain good relationships with her spouse and children. How should the LCSW proceed?

a. **CORRECT.** Help the client develop and consider possible outcomes of the move, and possible alternatives
b. **Incorrect.** Consider the family to be the client and support maintaining the family structure until instructed otherwise by the client
c. **Incorrect.** Offer to connect the client with a therapist in what will be their new state, including sending records if the client will allow
d. **Incorrect.** Inform the client that the therapist will listen and reflect as the client weighs their options, but that the LCSW will not guide the discussion in any way

The question says the client is contemplating the move, not that the decision has been made. The LCSW should not assume that the move will happen, or that it shouldn't. But the LCSW also does not need to be passive. They can best fulfill their role by helping the client see the full range of their options, and the potential outcomes of each.

9. An online business aims to make therapy more affordable for telehealth clients by using what they call a "reverse auction" process. When a prospective client signs up with the business, the business creates a de-identified summary of client information (such as location, demographics, and presenting problem), and then allows participating therapists to "bid" on the client by posting what they would agree to charge that client per 50-minute therapy session. The therapist who has offered the lowest "bid" when the auction closes pays the business a nominal fee, and then receives the client's full information, including their name, phone number, and email address. The client is told which therapist won the auction, what fee the therapist committed to, and the therapist's contact information. How should LCSWs interact with this service?

a. **CORRECT.** LCSWs should not participate in this service
b. **Incorrect.** LCSWs should ensure that no actual therapy information is shared with the service
c. **Incorrect.** LCSWs should only participate in this service if the fees they charge auction clients are in line with fees they would charge to the general public
d. **Incorrect.** LCSWs should demand that the business do additional screening on potential clients, to address potential crisis issues

The key phrase in the question is "pays the business a nominal fee." At that point the rest of the question becomes irrelevant. LCSWs cannot charge a fee or pay a fee for referrals, and this business structure would require LCSWs to pay for each specific referral the business would generate for them. It is thus against the law for LCSWs to participate in.

10. An LCSW is closing their private practice and planning to start a full-time job with a county mental health agency. They have been using an electronic health record (EHR) system to maintain records of their private practice cases. They plan to stop paying the monthly fee for this system in two weeks, when they begin their new job. Once they stop paying the fee, they would lose access to the EHR system. Considering their legal responsibilities, what should the LCSW do with their private practice records?

a. **Incorrect.** Continue paying the monthly fee for at least 5 years so that records can be accessed as needed
b. **Incorrect.** Once the LCSW stops paying the fee, inform all current and past private practice clients that the EHR company becomes the custodian of their records
c. **Incorrect.** Download all client records from the EHR and transfer them to the system used by the county to ensure ongoing access as needed
d. **CORRECT.** Download all client records and store them securely in a manner and location separate from the county's system

It is the responsibility of the clinician to ensure that records are securely maintained for at least seven years after the last professional contact. This is not the responsibility of the EHR if the therapist stops paying for it, and is not the responsibility of the county. At the same time, the therapist is not obligated to keep paying the EHR fee; they can download records for secure storage, so long as they maintain both security and appropriate access. Transferring records onto the county's system could make them available to county staffers who should not have access to them, and would thus not be appropriate.

11. The parents of a developmentally delayed 16-year-old bring the teenager to therapy and provide consent for the teenager's individual therapy. The LCSW providing therapy finds the teenager to be witty and charming. The LCSW also finds the teenager to be emotionally immature and believes her intelligence to be around a second-grade level. After a few sessions where the client appears to be making limited progress, the parents express their dissatisfaction with the LCSW and inform the LCSW that they are pulling their child out of therapy. Considering the LCSW's ethical responsibilities, the LCSW should:

a. **CORRECT.** Offer to assist with continuity of care to another provider or referrals for additional services
b. **Incorrect.** Inform the parents that because the child is older than 12, the child can make their own decisions about consent for treatment
c. **Incorrect.** Advocate on behalf of the client for continuing as the client's therapist
d. **Incorrect.** Ask the client directly, in the presence of the parents, about the client's desire to remain in treatment

It's arguably problematic that the LCSW even took on someone with a second-grade level of intelligence as an individual client, as children at this maturity level are often better served with family-based care. However, that is not what the question asks about, and it is entirely possible that the LCSW has been regularly involving the parents in treatment up to this point. The question assesses whether you understand parents' rights and responsibilities when their child does not have the ability to make effective choices on their own. While social workers "should seek to ensure that the third party [here, the parents] acts in a manner consistent with clients' wishes and interests" (Standard 1.03(c)), asking the child their wishes in the presence of the parents puts the child in a difficult and stressful position. Social workers honor the rights of clients' guardians and representatives to make treatment decisions on behalf of those in their care who are unable to make decisions for themselves.

12. An LCSW's former client threatens a licensing board complaint after the former client requested their records be shared with their new therapist. The records were forwarded as requested, and the new therapist then informed their client that the client had been diagnosed by the LCSW with Post-Traumatic Stress Disorder. The client was surprised by the news, as they had not been previously informed of the diagnosis; treatment with the LCSW had focused on the client's social and relational functioning. The former client demands the LCSW apologize and explain why the LCSW believes the client is, as the client describes it, "broken and unfixable." The LCSW should:

a. **Incorrect.** Retract the release of the client's record, as its release has caused the client harm
b. **Incorrect.** Contact the new therapist to explain the diagnosis
c. **CORRECT.** Explain to the former client what the diagnosis means and how the LCSW determined it
d. **Incorrect.** Inform the former client of the process for filing a board complaint, and remind them of their ability to provide an addendum that would be added to the treatment record

Social workers are ethically obligated to assist clients in understanding information in their records. In this instance, the client's description of themselves as "broken and unfixable" does not align with current professional thinking about PTSD, which is understood as being both understandable and treatable. The client's description suggests they may not understand what the PTSD diagnosis means.

13. An LCSW is nearing termination with a family the social worker has helped through multiple crises, including the unexpected death of a family member. The family has frequently expressed their gratitude to the social worker, saying things like “you saved us. We’re still a family because of you.” The LCSW is interested in using one specific, touching statement of gratitude the family shared in session on the LCSW’s web site. Ethically, the LCSW should:

a. **Incorrect.** Ask the clients for their permission, and if granted, post the statement without attaching the clients’ names to it
b. **Incorrect.** Wait until therapy has ended, and then post the statement without attaching the clients’ names to it
c. **CORRECT.** Not post the statement, regardless of timing or client permission
d. **Incorrect.** Wait until two years after therapy has ended, and then seek the clients’ permission to post the statement

The NASW Code of Ethics prohibits the solicitation of testimonials from current clients, and also specifically prohibits solicitation of consent to use a client’s prior statement as a testimonial endorsement. Any client statements made in the context of therapy should remain in the context of therapy.

14. An LCSW learns that his individual client, who is being seen for symptoms of Bipolar Disorder, is also interested in attending couple therapy with her spouse. The client asks the LCSW whether the couple could see the LCSW together for couple therapy separately from her individual sessions, and says she is willing to sign a release form such that information from her individual sessions could be discussed in couple therapy and vice versa. Ethically, the LCSW should:

a. **CORRECT.** Continue individual treatment and refer out for couple therapy. *This preserves continuity of care for individual treatment and keeps the LCSW out of a potential conflict of interests that would result from serving the client in multiple roles.*
b. **Incorrect.** Continue individual treatment with the client and begin concurrent couple therapy, utilizing a separate file and separate treatment plan. *Even with a release in place and a clearly different treatment plan, the therapist is likely to be more aligned with the partner being seen individually as well. Better to refer out for couple therapy to a therapist who will be more neutral.*
c. **Incorrect.** Inform the client that it would be better to complete individual treatment before engaging in couple therapy, regardless of whether the couple therapy is with the LCSW or another provider. *Concurrent treatment carries some risks, but also some potential benefits. It should not simply be dismissed as an option.*
d. **Incorrect.** Discontinue the individual treatment in order to begin couple treatment, with the client's release in place to allow for material from the individual sessions to be discussed in couple work. *Discontinuing individual treatment prematurely does not appear likely to be in the best interests of the client.*

15. An LCSW is working with a family where the parents are in the process of getting a divorce and are arguing over custody of their two children. Therapy has focused on maintaining effective co-parenting, as neither parent wants an extended court battle. Because the LCSW knows the family well and has seen both parents interacting with the children, the parents ask the LCSW to submit a letter to the court with the LCSW's clinical evaluation of each of their parenting skills. The best course of action for the LCSW would be to:

a. **Incorrect.** Obtain a release from all family members, and send the letter to the court, emphasizing that the evaluative statements should not be used to draw conclusions about custody.
b. **Incorrect.** Obtain a release from all family members, and send the letter to the court, offering specific recommendations for custody based on the LCSW's work with the family and based on the LCSW's knowledge of the wishes of the children.
c. **Incorrect.** Obtain a release from all family members, and engage in a process of testing and evaluation to draw objective conclusions before completing the letter.
d. **CORRECT.** Refuse to send the letter.

The NASW Code of Ethics requires social workers to clarify their role and avoid conflicts of interest. The parents in this case are asking the LCSW, who has been in the treatment provider role, to also take on an evaluative stance. If the LCSW were to do so, the parents would likely be less forthcoming in the future about any struggles they experienced in parenting. Options (A), (B), and (C) all place the LCSW in an evaluator position that should be avoided if the LCSW has provided clinical treatment.

16. The director of an afterschool program contacts an LCSW by phone to refer a 14-year-old girl to the social worker for psychotherapy. The director says that the girl is a participant in thc program and has been struggling with extreme shyness. The director further says that the program will be happy to pay for the therapy. The girl, who is with the director in an office, gets on the phone to provide the LCSW with more information. She says she does not want her parents to know she is seeking help. How should the LCSW proceed?

a. **Incorrect.** Allow the program director to consent for treatment on the minor's behalf and accept financial responsibility
b. **Incorrect.** Inform the minor that one parent must consent to her receiving treatment regardless of how it is being paid for
c. **CORRECT.** Assess the maturity of the minor
d. **Incorrect.** Allow the minor to consent for treatment on her own, and have her complete a Release of Information so that the program can be billed

While minors as young as 12 can consent for their own treatment, this is conditioned upon the clinician determining that the minor is mature enough to participate intelligently in treatment. The LCSW should assess the minor's maturity level to determine whether the minor can consent on her own, or whether she will need the consent of a parent or guardian.

17. A young adult client with a history of severe childhood trauma begins weeping in session as she connects her traumatic experiences with her current struggles in building trusting relationships. An LCSW has been providing the client with individual sessions for more than two years, and the client has only even begun to trust the therapist in the past few months. The LCSW notices that the client is having difficulty calming herself, and is shaking in her seat. The client turns to the social worker and softly asks, "Will you please just hold me for a moment, so I can catch my breath?" The client has never made such a request before. Considering her ethical responsibilities, how should the social worker proceed?

a. **Incorrect.** Briefly hold the client, and immediately afterward, discuss it in order to reinforce a strong clinical boundary
b. **Incorrect.** Briefly hold the client, to support their autonomy. Since the client has not made such a request in more than two years of treatment, it is unlikely that a clarifying conversation is needed
c. **CORRECT.** Decline the client's request, while offering a blanket or other means the client can use for calming
d. **Incorrect.** Decline the client's request, and when appropriate, re-evaluate the clinical relationship in light of the client's efforts toward dependence

The NASW Code of Ethics requires social workers to avoid physical contact when that contact includes the possibility of causing psychological harm to the client. Here, that possibility exists; the client might become dependent on the social worker, or might experience their relationship in a different way. The social worker can be soothing to the client without physically holding them, and that is the most appropriate course of action.

18. A 23-year-old client whose family immigrated to California from Indonesia calls her LCSW to inform the therapist that the client cannot attend therapy for the next three weeks, as the client's sister just had a baby and the client is going to be helping the sister and the sister's partner. The LCSW has been treating the client for post-traumatic stress disorder and wonders whether the treatment has simply been overwhelming for the client. What steps should the LCSW take to fulfill their ethical duties?

a. **CORRECT.** Ensure crisis needs are met and a safety plan is in place if needed; schedule a next session for three weeks from now
b. **Incorrect.** Offer to reduce the intensity of sessions in exchange for the client remaining consistent in treatment
c. **Incorrect.** Seek to understand the client's behavior from a cultural perspective; treat the interruption of therapy as a crisis and intervene accordingly
d. **Incorrect.** Wish the client well for the upcoming three weeks; hold the client's usual spot on the LCSW's calendar; ask to see photos of the baby upon the client's return

When treatment needs to be interrupted, regardless of the reason why, it is the responsibility of the social worker to ensure that any crisis needs are met. Option B is not correct as the question does not establish any reason why a three-week break in treatment may be detrimental to the point where continuity would become more important than the client's other wishes and obligations. Option C treats the break itself as a crisis, which is not established in the question. Option D is a supportive response but does not provide appropriate protection in the event that a crisis emerges.

19. An LCSW has been treating a 38-year-old woman who has been abusing substances. The woman has experienced a series of health problems, and lost the debit card that she uses to buy food through a state program. She leaves the social worker a voicemail one morning, saying that she is “tired of people messing with me” and that “the next person who tries to put me down or take something from me is getting dead.” The social worker knows that the client carries a gun and a knife with her in most places. What should the LCSW do next?

a. **Incorrect.** Invoke *Tarasoff* and begin the process of notifying law enforcement and the client’s neighbors of the potential risk
b. **CORRECT.** Notify law enforcement and attempt to contact and locate the client to initiate the process of hospitalization
c. **Incorrect.** Invoke *Tarasoff* and attempt to contact and locate the client to initiate the process of hospitalization
d. **Incorrect.** Notify law enforcement as a precautionary measure, and assume the client’s statements reflect substance intoxication rather than actual physical danger

While the client is potentially dangerous, this is not a *Tarasoff* situation as the client poses a general danger to others, and not a specific danger to reasonably identifiable others. As a result, we can immediately rule out response choices that involve *Tarasoff*. Notifying law enforcement is appropriate, as is attempting to contact and locate the client. Depending on the client’s history, their statements may or may not be a result of intoxication; with only the information in the question, the LCSW would err on the side of caution and take steps to protect public safety.

20. A private university contracts with a group practice to provide long-term therapy to university students in need of such services. The university agrees to pay the group practice for up to 20 sessions per student per year at a discounted rate. The practice owner, an LCSW, receives the first request from the university for records that will allow the university to issue payment to the practice. The university requests a list of client names, session dates, and procedure codes for all sessions held with the university's students in the past month. Legally, how should the LCSW respond?

a. **Incorrect.** Request that each client who attends the university provide a Release of Information allowing the practice to share complete records with the university for billing purposes
b. **Incorrect.** Provide the university with all data requested except for client names, which can be replaced with ID numbers
c. **CORRECT.** Provide the university with all of the requested data
d. **Incorrect.** Ask that all clients who are students of the university pay for sessions at the time of the session, and then submit receipts to the university for reimbursement

The law creates a clear and specific exception to confidentiality for information that is necessary for billing purposes. In this case, it is reasonable for the university to request client names, so that the university can verify that each client is indeed a student. The university is not asking for diagnoses or other treatment details beyond the scope of what is necessary to facilitate billing. The LCSW is free to provide the information requested, understanding that they should only provide the minimum information necessary to achieve the purposes of the disclosure.

21. A client with a history of eating disorder schedules an intake session with an LCSW to discuss the client's current emotional struggles. In the intake, the client reports that prior treatment has been helpful in reducing disordered eating, but that the client still struggles with body image concerns. Referring to prior treatment, the client says, "I learned a lot about monitoring and responding to my body, but not so much about how to prepare food or specifically what to eat." Ethically, the LCSW should:

a. **Incorrect.** Diagnose the client as having an active eating disorder
b. **CORRECT.** Collaborate with the client to determine whether a referral to a dietitian is appropriate
c. **Incorrect.** Request that the client sign a Release of Information for all prior eating disorder treatment providers, allowing the LCSW to request treatment records
d. **Incorrect.** Educate the client about the typical course of eating disorder over the life span

Providing a diagnosis or specific education may prove to be wise, but this would be a clinical decision, not an ethical one. The question asks for your ethical judgment. Social workers are expected to refer clients to other professionals when specialized knowledge is necessary to more fully meet the client's needs.

22. An LCSW receives a phone call from a prospective new client couple. The couple reports that they moved to the US three years ago from a country the LCSW does not know well. The couple says they would like to come to therapy to work on communication difficulty in their marriage. The LCSW strives to maintain strong awareness of cultural issues, but has never worked with anyone from the clients' country of origin before. The best course of action for the LCSW would be to:

a. **Incorrect.** Refer the couple to a therapist from the clients' country. *Referring the couple out would be discrimination based on national origin.*
b. **Incorrect.** Encourage the clients to educate the LCSW about their country's culture and customs. *Relying solely on the clients to educate the therapist on cultural issues is not sufficient; the LCSW is expected to do additional work on their own to develop competence where it is lacking.*
c. **CORRECT.** Seek resources and consultation to become familiar with the client couple's culture and customs, and to understand how clients from that country typically present in therapy. *This best summarizes the LCSW's responsibilities. Understanding typical client presentation based on the client culture does not mean the LCSW should or would assume that the particular case will match cultural norms, but at least provides a useful reference point for assessment.*
d. **Incorrect.** Wait until the clients come in for an initial assessment to determine whether meaningful cultural differences exist. *Waiting until the clients come in leaves the LCSW vulnerable to their own blind spots related to cultural difference, and may lead to incorrect assessment of the couple.*

23. A couple seeks counseling from an LCSW to address conflict in their relationship. One partner in the couple identifies as asexual, while the other partner angrily suggests that "asexual" is a "cop-out" the first partner is using to avoid taking action on the first partner's lack of sexual desire, which has been a source of conflict for the couple since the birth of their child four years ago. The first partner has been medically evaluated, and was determined to be in good physical health. Considering the LCSW's ethical responsibilities, how should the LCSW proceed?

a. **Incorrect.** Gather information to determine whether the first partner qualifies as asexual
b. **Incorrect.** Treat this conflict as being no different from other forms of couple conflict, and seek to determine and address the root cause
c. **Incorrect.** Assess whether changes in the couple's diet, exercise, or sleep hygiene may lead to changes in sexual desire
d. **CORRECT.** Gather the couple's history, including information about the first partner's change in how they identify

"Asexual" is generally understood to be a sexual orientation, and sexual orientation is an element of identity determined by the individual, not by the clinician. Conflict over sexual orientation should not be treated the same way as conflict over housework; to do so would likely bring forth a range of oppressive and discriminatory clinical acts. Assessing diet, exercise, and sleep suggest that the first partner's asexuality is a problem to be solved, rather than a sexual orientation to be accepted and affirmed. The clinician should gather the couple's history as part of the assessment process. Gathering information about the first partner's history of how they identify is consistent with that process, and can be done in an affirming manner.

24. Partway through an emotionally difficult session, a client tells their social worker, "My psychic said this was going to get worse before it got better. I guess this what they meant." The LCSW is initially startled, and asks the client more about the psychic. The client notes that they have been going to the same psychic weekly for more than five years, and find the process valuable and reassuring, especially when discussing issues of grief. The LCSW should:

a. **CORRECT.** Ask the client's permission to contact the psychic to develop a professional relationship
b. **Incorrect.** Discuss the LCSW's concern that the psychic is exploiting the client's fragile emotional state
c. **Incorrect.** Express to the client that while the services of the psychic may be helpful, they are not grounded in science
d. **Incorrect.** Explore the client's relationship with the psychic to determine whether the psychic has attempted to diagnose or treat mental illness

Social workers are ethically obligated to develop positive working relationships with other professionals when doing so serves the client. Whatever the LCSW's personal beliefs about the psychic may be, the client clearly finds the interactions with the psychic comforting. The simple fact that the client has been seeing the psychic regularly for five years does not suggest inappropriate behavior on the part of the psychic, either in terms of exploitation or stepping beyond their appropriate scope.

25. An LCSW is supervising an associate clinical social worker from a different cultural background. Early in their supervision relationship, they discover that they both are part of a small social media group for health care professionals in their city who suffered abuse as children. How should the supervisor proceed?

a. **Incorrect.** Ask the supervisee to set a boundary on their social media interactions that is comfortable for the supervisee, based on the supervisee's cultural background and expectations
b. **CORRECT.** Meet with the supervisee to establish that the supervisor will not discuss their professional relationship in the social media group or interact with the supervisee's posts in that group; discuss what other limitations may be necessary
c. **Incorrect.** Acknowledge their professional relationship in the group, in the interest of transparency; discuss what other limitations may be necessary
d. **Incorrect.** Inform the supervisee that if they are going to work together, neither the supervisor nor the supervisee can participate in the social media group

Particular caution around potential multiple relationships is necessary when interacting online. Supervisors, not supervisees (A), are responsible for setting appropriate boundaries around such relationships. In this group, there is risk of potential harm to the supervisee, if the supervisor were to learn more about the supervisee's abuse through the process of supervision. That the supervisor, we hope, would not share this additional information in the social media group does not remove the risk that they could; that risk is reason enough for caution. Simply being transparent about the professional relationship (C) does not do enough to resolve that risk, while declaring that neither the supervisor nor the supervisee can continue to participate in the group (D) is likely an over-reaction. At most, it would seem that one of them, not both, may wish to step away from the online group.

26. A white family has been attending family therapy to address conflict among the three siblings: A 16-year-old girl, a 13-year-old girl, and a 10-year old who identifies as nonbinary. In session, the 16 year old admits that she and the 10-year-old sometimes wake up before the 13-year-old, and then wake the 13-year-old by climbing on top of her, slapping, and punching her. The 13-year-old has shown her parents the bruises on her face and arms that have resulted, but the parents say they did not take photos of the bruises, and the LCSW providing family therapy has not observed any bruising. The 13-year-old says she has tried to "get back" at her siblings by stealing and giving away their belongings. The parents say they feel helpless to stop the siblings' behavior toward one another. How should the LCSW proceed?

a. **Incorrect.** File a report of suspected child abuse, naming all three siblings as both victims and perpetrators
b. **CORRECT.** File a report of suspected child abuse, naming the 16-year-old and 10-year-old as perpetrators
c. **Incorrect.** File a report of suspected child neglect, naming the parents as perpetrators for failing to protect the 13-year-old
d. **Incorrect.** File a report of suspected child abuse, naming only the 16-year-old as a perpetrator

While the child abuse reporting law in California does make an exception to the physical abuse reporting requirement for a "mutual affray" among minors, the violence here is not mutual. It is leaving the 13-year-old with physical injuries. That abuse must be reported, even when the perpetrator is another minor. The 13-year-old's efforts to get back at her siblings are clinically troubling, but do not legally qualify as abuse. A report of suspected physical abuse should be filed, naming the 16-year-old and 10-year-old as perpetrators and the 13-year-old as a victim.

27. A 56-year-old male client is seeing a social worker to address the client's substance use. The client also regularly sees a psychiatrist. The client provided the social worker with the psychiatrist's name, contact information, and date of most recent visit during the intake process. When discussing the psychiatrist in session, the client asks the social worker not to contact the psychiatrist. The client says the psychiatrist "isn't real big on therapy. I don't know if they would like that I'm here." Considering the social worker's ethical responsibilities, how should the social worker proceed?

a. **Incorrect.** Contact the psychiatrist to coordinate care, as the psychiatrist is an active member of the client's treatment team
b. **Incorrect.** Inform the client that coordinated care is necessary for effective treatment, and reassure the client that only a minimal amount of information will be shared
c. **Incorrect.** Inform the client that coordinated care is necessary for effective treatment, and direct the client to sign a Release of Information form allowing the social worker to coordinate with the psychiatrist
d. **CORRECT.** Do not contact the psychiatrist, and discuss the implications of the client coming to therapy against the psychiatrist's guidance

In this instance, the law allows for the sharing of information between active treatment providers for the purposes of treatment planning, but does not require such sharing. The client may thus make determinations about whether they would like their information to be shared, and the social worker is (with some exceptions) expected to honor those wishes. Here, the social worker can follow both the law and their ethics code by respecting the client's wish not to have information about the therapy shared with the psychiatrist.

28. A polyamorous couple experiencing difficulty in their sexual relationship presents for therapy with an LCSW who believes sexual activity outside of a monogamous relationship is inappropriate and harmful. The couple does not believe that their sexual relationships outside of their own relationship are causing their sexual problems with each other. Ethically, the LCSW should:

a. **Incorrect.** Seek to address underlying emotional issues that may be impacting the couple's sexual relationship, so as to improve the relationship without directly discussing the couple's other partners *While the couple certainly may be correct in their reporting that polyamory is not a problem for them, avoiding discussion of it in therapy is likely to quickly become awkward given that they are there to address couple relationship issues.*
b. **CORRECT.** Refer the couple to a therapist who does not share the LCSW's belief. *The therapist's belief is closely related to the issue for which the couple is seeking treatment, and is likely to interfere with that treatment.*
c. **Incorrect.** Inform the clients in advance of her belief, allowing the clients to determine whether they would like to continue therapy with her. *It is the therapist's responsibility, not the client's, to determine when the therapist's values are likely to interfere with effective care.*
d. **Incorrect.** Begin therapy by explaining her belief and the underlying research, and explaining that the couple's theory that their polyamory is not related to their own sexual difficulty is unlikely to be true. *This explanation serves only to defend the therapist's belief and presupposes the cause of the couple's problems.*

29. A mother arrives late for her therapy session and is enraged. She reports that she just spent an hour dealing with police, who came to the grocery store where her car was parked and were about to break a window when she returned to the car and stopped them. The police, she said, rudely lectured her about the infant son she had left in the car while she was grocery shopping. While the car was in sunlight, it was only about 80 degrees out at the time and she had been away from the car for less than 20 minutes, she said. The LCSW should:

a. **Incorrect.** Explore the mother's feelings of anger and shame. *Exploring her feelings may be clinically useful, but is not required; a report of suspected child neglect is required.*
b. **Incorrect.** Assess whether the son had suffered any harm. *Unlike with other forms of child abuse, children do not need to have suffered any actual injuries to qualify as having been neglected.*
c. **Incorrect.** Ask for a Release of Information and offer to contact police directly to follow up. *Contacting police to follow up on the incident is offered here without a rationale, so it is unclear whether this would serve any meaningful clinical purpose. To the degree that it may help with the decision of reporting, it places the LCSW in an investigator role.*
d. **CORRECT.** Report suspected child neglect. *Leaving an infant alone in a car in direct sunlight, on a warm day with the windows up, presents significant danger to the child. Even if the child did not suffer actual harm, a report is justified.*

30. An LCSW is close to successful termination with a father who has been in treatment for 15 sessions. The father expresses his gratitude to the LCSW, and says he would like to find a way to help families with similar needs. The LCSW is aware of an online discussion group where the father could share his experience in therapy, steering potential clients toward the LCSW and offering hope to families experiencing similar problems to the ones his own family had experienced at the beginning of therapy. Ethically, the LCSW should:

a. **Incorrect.** Encourage the father to share his experience in the discussion group, including both positive and negative components, and including the LCSW's name so that other participants know where they can receive confidential help. *Asking for the LCSW's name to be included would amount to solicitation of a testimonial from a current client, which is ethically prohibited.*
b. **CORRECT.** Thank the father for his work in therapy, and discuss potential benefits and risks of several potential means by which the father could help similar families. *Confidentiality is the client's right, and they are free to share information from the therapy as they see fit.*
c. **Incorrect.** Thank the father for his work in therapy, and discourage him from publicly sharing his experience in the interest of confidentiality. *Since the father would like to use the family's experience to help others, it does not make sense to discourage him from doing so. This would arguably interfere with his autonomy.*
d. **Incorrect.** Encourage the father to share his experience in the discussion group but to do so anonymously, only naming the LCSW if he chooses to do so. *Unless the therapist can foresee a specific harm to the client from doing so, it does not make sense to discourage the client from using his own name if he wishes.*

31. A social worker who is part of a multidisciplinary treatment team becomes concerned when the team decides to contact the mother of an adult client and ask her to become more involved in treatment. The team made this decision based on the client's worsening symptoms, out of concern that the client may soon need to be hospitalized. The social worker notes that there is not a release in place allowing them to share information with the mother. The social worker should:

a. **Incorrect.** Respect the treatment team's decision, and not be personally involved in the efforts to contact the mother
b. **Incorrect.** Respect the treatment team's decision, and be prepared to address the client's possible feelings of betrayal
c. **CORRECT.** Contact the treatment team and ask to meet with them as soon as possible in an effort to change their decision
d. **Incorrect.** Contact the treatment team and inform them that if the team's decision goes forward, the social worker will encourage the client to report a confidentiality violation

When a treatment team makes a decision that a social worker believes raises ethical concerns, as is the case here, the social worker should seek to resolve the disagreement through appropriate channels – not just defer to the team. However, such challenges should be addressed in ways *consistent with the client's well-being.* Threatening the team, or encouraging the client to report a violation, makes the client a pawn in the dispute and is likely to be counter to their best interests.

32. The individual client of an LCSW tells the LCSW that he recently took his 94-year-old grandfather, who has been suffering from dementia, on a fishing trip to a nearby lake in a California State Park. He had grown frustrated with the quality of care the grandfather had been receiving at his nursing home, which he said was not adequate to the grandfather's medical needs. He also wanted to give his grandfather "one last hurrah," as he was concerned the grandfather's death was just weeks away. He was angry that the nursing home staff had berated him upon their return for not notifying them he was taking the grandfather for the weekend. Considering the LCSW's legal obligations, the LCSW should:

a. **Incorrect.** Report the nursing home for inadequate care, and the client for abduction. *While the nursing home care may be inadequate, the simple fact that a family member describes it as such does not mean it is so, and it certainly does not mean the problems in care rise to the level of being abusive or neglectful. (Note that a direct report of suspected abuse* <u>from the victim</u> *generally triggers reporting responsibility for elder or dependent adult abuse.) Also see the rationale for response C below.*
b. **Incorrect.** Report the nursing home for inadequate care. *While the nursing home care may be inadequate, the simple fact that a family member describes it as such does not mean it is so, and it certainly does not mean the problems in care rise to the level of being abusive or neglectful.*
c. **Incorrect.** Report the client for abduction. *The simple fact that the client took his grandfather on a fishing trip does not mean the grandfather was abducted. The definition of abduction in elder abuse reporting law specifically requires that the victim have been taken outside of California.*
d. **CORRECT.** Ask the client to clarify how the nursing home's care is inadequate. *There is nothing reportable in this vignette. While the nursing home care may be inadequate, the simple fact that a family member describes it as such does not mean it is so, and it certainly does not mean the problems in care rise to the level of being abusive or neglectful. While the LCSW does not want to take on the role of investigator, inquiring about the client's frustrations with his grandfather's care is clinically appropriate, and this is the only response option that is consistent with the LCSW's legal obligations.*

33. An LCSW in private practice grows frustrated with a client who seems to be frequently in crisis, and determines that the client needs a higher level of care than what the LCSW can provide. The LCSW informs the client in person and in writing that in 30 days the LCSW will no longer provide treatment, and offers referrals to inpatient and partial-hospitalization programs as well as other local crisis resources. As the 30 days approach their end, the client has a scheduled termination session with the LCSW. The client reports that they have not even attempted to contact any of the provided referrals, they don't feel capable of doing so, and they are feeling moderately suicidal but without a specific plan or intent. Ethically, the LCSW should:

a. **CORRECT.** Offer to assist the client during session in contacting other service providers to create a warm handoff
b. **Incorrect.** Extend the termination deadline by 30 days and encourage the client to contact the referrals previously offered
c. **Incorrect.** Terminate as scheduled, and ask the client to sign a release granting the LCSW permission to follow up with a close friend or family member to ensure the client is receiving ongoing care
d. **Incorrect.** Terminate as scheduled, and ask the client to sign a release once they are connected with a new treatment provider, so that the new provider and the LCSW can communicate

This question assesses your knowledge of the ethical requirement to prevent client abandonment. While extending the termination deadline does prevent abandonment in the immediate term, it does little more than kick the can down the road – and may have the result of encouraging future client crises if the client feels that voicing a crisis is necessary to keep the LCSW involved. (The client's voicing of a new crisis may actually support the notion that the client needs a higher level of care than the LCSW can provide.) A better answer is to take necessary steps in session to assist the client in connecting with appropriate providers, ensuring that a transition occurs without crisis needs falling through the cracks.

34. An LCSW with a full-time caseload finds herself on the edge of burnout. She notices she is becoming less empathetic and more combative with clients, and frequently arrives at the office in the morning still tired from the day before. A colleague she greatly respects refers her a complex case. The LCSW should:

a. **Incorrect.** Discontinue or temporarily pause treatment with some of her better-functioning clients in order to take the referral.
b. **Incorrect.** Take the referral without changing any aspects of treatment for her other clients, and take other steps to manage her burnout.
c. **CORRECT.** Decline the referral, and consider reducing her overall caseload.
d. **Incorrect.** Accept the referral on a short-term basis, agreeing only to two sessions with the client in order to better assess their needs.

Interrupting treatment with other clients in order to take a new referral (A) may be considered abandonment of those existing clients, and is putting the therapist's needs above those of the clients. Maintaining the same caseload while adding a complex case (B) is likely to only worsen the LCSW's burnout; she needs to recognize her impairment and not add to her workload. Accepting the referral on a short-term basis (D) is not likely to be in the best interests of a complex case, and does nothing to move toward resolving the burnout that may be impacting *all* of the LCSW's caseload.

35. A social worker has been working with a family for several sessions and plans a session where the entire family will participate in a ceremony relieving the oldest daughter of the responsibility she has taken on as a co-parent. Shortly before the session, the mother informs the LCSW that she will be away on a business trip and asks whether she can participate in the session by phone or videoconferencing. The mother's frequent absences are part of the reason why the daughter felt obligated to take on parenting tasks. The social worker should:

a. **Incorrect.** Contact the BBS to see whether the LCSW can include the mother in session while she is on her trip. *The BBS does not provide legal advice, and even asking the question may require providing information that is confidential.*
b. **Incorrect.** Include the mother in the session and in the ceremony via phone or videoconference, and clarify that her involvement is consultation rather than therapy. *Simply calling the mother's involvement consultation does not make it something different from therapy. This is especially true considering that the entire purpose of her presence in session is to be involved in a therapeutic intervention that the LCSW designed.*
c. **CORRECT.** Refuse the mother's request and reschedule the ceremony for a time she can attend in person. LCSW*s are required to carefully assess whether telemedicine services are appropriate in a given case. Here, the mother's absence would likely have a major impact on the planned ceremony; having her participate by phone or videoconference rather than in person appears likely to impact the effectiveness of the intervention.*
d. **Incorrect.** Contact the other family members to see whether they believe including the mother would be legally and ethically appropriate. *While the family may be able to offer useful clinical feedback on this question, it is not the role of the family to resolve the LCSW's legal and ethical concerns.*

36. An LCSW has been treating a 16-year-old under consent from the child's father. The child's parents are divorced, and under the terms of their joint custody agreement, either parent has the authority to consent to health care on behalf of any of the couple's three children. The mother contacts the LCSW to say that she objects to the therapy and is concerned that the LCSW has not prevented the 16-year-old from using marijuana. Consistent with the LCSW's legal responsibilities, the LCSW should:

a. **Incorrect.** Explain to the mother that the LCSW's role is not to prevent the 16-year-old from engaging in marijuana use, but rather to openly discuss such choices and support the 16-year-old's autonomy
b. **Incorrect.** Inform the client and the father of the mother's objection, and let them and the mother know that going forward, both parents' consent will be necessary to continue therapy
c. **Incorrect.** Inform the mother that unless the custody agreement allows her specifically to revoke the father's consent, the LCSW will continue treating the minor as they have been
d. **CORRECT.** Say nothing to the mother, and review the custody agreement

In the absence of a release of information, the mother has no right to any information about the minor's treatment – including even that the minor is a client of the LCSW. Any response to the mother that acknowledges the minor is a client could be seen as a breach of confidentiality. Further, the question stem specifically notes that either parent can consent for treatment, so the LCSW does not need to establish a rule that both parents must consent. (The LCSW *can* establish such a rule, but they are not required to do so.) The best option is to say nothing to the mother in order to protect confidentiality, and to review the custody agreement to determine whether the mother has the right to revoke consent provided by the father. Such a scenario is unlikely, but possible, and the agreement may also include other language that is instructive to the LCSW.

37. In a hospital setting, an LCSW works with patients who are involuntarily hospitalized for being a danger to themselves or others. One such patient is preparing for discharge after one night in the hospital. The treating psychiatrist interrupts the process, and insists that the patient be held for at least another 24 hours. The LCSW brings together the psychiatrist, a member of the nursing team, and a hospital administrator to discuss the case. The psychiatrist is insistent, based on their view of the patient's symptoms. While the others say they are not sure the extended hospitalization is needed, they express willingness to defer to the psychiatrist. The LCSW strongly believes that the additional night is not needed, and explains why, but the psychiatrist is unmoved. The team plans to keep the patient in the hospital for one more night. How should the LCSW proceed?

a. **CORRECT.** Accept the decision of the team, and seek to better understand the others' perspectives
b. **Incorrect.** Insist that the perspective of the LCSW be given equal weight to that of the psychiatrist
c. **Incorrect.** Re-convene the treatment team in an effort to change their minds
d. **Incorrect.** Refuse to participate in the ongoing care of this specific patient, without allowing it to impact the quality of care provided to others

The team made a clinical decision that appears to be based on clinical factors. The social worker fulfilled their responsibility in contributing to the team's process, and was outvoted. This happens, and is not indicative of an ethical violation or problem. The social worker should continue to work collaboratively with colleagues, appreciating the perspective of each of their professions.

38. An LCSW is serving as a consultant for a software company that is developing a platform where prospective clients can connect with licensed mental health treatment providers, and where providers can make referrals to one another by securely sharing client data when clients have given permission to do so. The company proposes several different pricing models for therapists who wish to participate on the platform. Which of these models could social workers participate in under state law?

a. **Incorrect.** Therapist listings are free; when the prospective client matches with a therapist on specified criteria, the therapist pays a fee to view the prospective client's full information and reach out to them
b. **Incorrect.** Therapists buy credits that are not assigned to any specific client; when a prospective client matches with a therapist on specified criteria, the therapist can spend one credit to view the prospective client's full information and reach out to them
c. **Incorrect.** Referrals, whether from clients referring themselves or from colleagues, are on a dynamic pricing model; depending on demand in the therapist's area, the therapist may need to pay a fee for a prospective referral, or may get paid a small amount to accept the referral
d. **CORRECT.** Therapists subscribe to the service to be included in its directory; for an added subscription fee, they can be notified each time a prospective client who matches with them on specified criteria joins the platform and allows clinicians to reach out to them

Each of the first three options amounts to paying for referrals, which is specifically prohibited by law. (In the third case, therapists might also get paid for accepting referrals; that is also legally prohibited.) The final option operates like traditional advertising, which LCSWs can legally pay for.

39. Following an arrest for assault, a 20-year-old man has been seeing an LCSW for private anger management and substance use counseling on orders from the court. Three months into the therapy process, and one month prior to the client's next court date, he reveals to the social worker that he recently had a relapse with methamphetamine. He asks the LCSW to keep this information private. As the court date approaches, the LCSW receives a subpoena from the court demanding all records from the client's treatment. The LCSW is obligated to:

a. **CORRECT.** Provide full and complete records to the court
b. **Incorrect.** Provide the court a treatment summary, outlining in general terms the client's participation but without specific information on recent substance use
c. **Incorrect.** Claim privilege on behalf of the client
d. **Incorrect.** Provide the court with the client's clinical file, and withhold psychotherapy notes, where the client's recent substance use are noted

When therapy is taking place by court order, privilege does not apply. The social worker should provide the court with complete records. California does not protect psychotherapy notes from subpoena, so if the LCSW was keeping separate psychotherapy notes for this client, those too would need to be provided.

40. A family from Cambodia is seeing an LCSW for family therapy. During a family session, the father tells the therapist that he sometimes disciplines his 15-year-old son the same way the father had been disciplined in Cambodia when he was young: With lashes across his back, using a stick. The mother voices her objection to this form of discipline, and notes that on multiple occasions the son was left bleeding and crying. The most appropriate action for the LCSW would be to:

a. **Incorrect.** Consider the cultural elements involved and inform the clients that such discipline may not be accepted in the US. *While LCSWs must consider cultural influences when designing and implementing treatment, the reporting standards for physical abuse are written to be as objective as possible: If the intentional striking of a child leaves an injury, it is reportable as physical abuse. Failing to report suspected abuse is a legal violation.*
b. **CORRECT.** Report suspected physical abuse to the local child protective service agency. *If the intentional striking of a child leaves an injury, it is reportable as physical abuse. It is up to the local child protective service agency to determine whether and how to involve cultural factors in their response to the abuse.*
c. **Incorrect.** Remind the family of the limits of confidentiality and ask whether there are any photos of the son's injuries. *Asking for photos places the LCSW in the role of investigator rather than treating clinician.*
d. **Incorrect.** Consider the cultural elements involved and research common Cambodian disciplinary practices to determine whether the behavior is consistent with cultural norms. *While LCSWs should consider cultural influences when designing and implementing treatment, the reporting standards for physical abuse are written to be as objective as possible: If the intentional striking of a child leaves an injury, it is reportable as physical abuse. Failing to report suspected abuse is a legal violation.*

41. A 15-year-old girl is seeing an LCSW individually for issues related to body image and self-esteem. Her parents provided consent for the therapy and pay for her sessions, but do not participate. The girl tells the LCSW that she has been exploring her sexuality. While her parents were out of town, she had sexual intercourse with a friend's 19-year-old brother. A few days later, she had intercourse with another boy, an 18-year-old senior at her high school. The LCSW should manage their legal responsibilities by:

a. **Incorrect.** Reporting child abuse to the local child protective service agency
b. **Incorrect.** Investigating to ensure that the sexual activity was not coerced or while under the influence of drugs or alcohol
c. **Incorrect.** Notifying the parents of their daughter's high-risk sexual behavior
d. **CORRECT.** Maintaining confidentiality

The age combination of the partners, in both instances of sexual activity, does not require reporting (A). If either boy were 21 or over, or under 14, these combinations would be reportable. While it may be clinically relevant to explore the context of the sexual activity in more detail, the LCSW is not obligated to do so, and in fact should not position themselves as an investigator (B). While the parents may be able to access their daughter's treatment records, the LCSW does not have a responsibility to proactively inform them of sexual behavior; further, there is nothing in the question that would necessarily classify this girl's behavior as "high-risk" (C). In the absence of a legal requirement or allowance for disclosure, the LCSW is legally obligated to maintain confidentiality.

42. A 20-year-old client who identifies her family background as Chinese starts therapy with an LCSW. The client describes herself as a social media influencer with about 1 million followers, and says that she posts about 20 minutes of video online each day. She tells the LCSW she is coming to therapy after family members expressed concern that she may be depressed. She tells the LCSW in session "I feel like such a faker with every video I post." Considering their ethical responsibilities, the LCSW should:

a. **Incorrect.** Anonymously review the client's public social media posts, without commenting on them
b. **Incorrect.** After session, contact the family members to learn more about their concerns
c. **Incorrect.** After session, digitally request to be added as a "friend" or "follower" on the client's social media accounts, so that the client can make an informed choice as to whether to do so
d. **CORRECT.** In session, ask the client's permission to review their public social media postings

Even when clients' web sites or social media profiles are public-facing, social workers are expected to seek permission to review this information unless there is "compelling clinical reason" to do otherwise. Here, there's no reason why the LCSW couldn't ask permission in session, and they should do so. Social workers should not become "friends" with clients on social media, and should not contact family in the absence of permission to do so or an applicable exception to confidentiality, neither of which appears to be present here.

43. During an unusually tense family session, a mother confronts an LCSW on the LCSW's recent filing of a written report of suspected child abuse. The mother feels violated and reports that she can no longer trust the LCSW. Other family members attempt to calm the mother, but share her concerns. The LCSW should:

a. **Incorrect.** Discontinue treatment, as the therapeutic relationship has been irreparably compromised. *While there may have been damage to the therapeutic relationship, attempts to repair are appropriate before deciding that therapy is a lost cause.*
b. **CORRECT.** Remind the family of the limits of confidentiality, and seek to regain the family's trust. *The ethics code reminds LCSWs that circumstances may require multiple discussions of the limits of confidentiality.*
c. **Incorrect.** In the interest of full disclosure, inform the mother that follow-up reports to the local child protective service agency may be necessary. *When written reports are filed, the therapist has discharged their responsibility by filing the report, and does not need to file follow-up reports unless new instances of abuse emerge.*
d. **Incorrect.** Ask to speak to the other family members without the mother present, to determine whether there is an appropriate path forward for therapy. *Speaking to other family members without the mother present would likely only further her distrust of the LCSW and harm the therapeutic relationship.*

44. A 14-year-old client consented to her own treatment at a nonprofit agency, which agreed to treat her for $5/session. The client tells the therapist (an LCSW) that the client has been abusing a friend's prescription painkillers. Legally, the LCSW should:

a. **Incorrect.** Notify the local child protective service agency.
b. **Incorrect.** Notify the client's parent or guardian, as the behavior is considered high-risk.
c. **Incorrect.** Work with the client to develop a plan to gradually reduce dosage and ultimately stop the client's drug use.
d. **CORRECT.** Document the discussion and refer the client to a physician.

Drug use, in and of itself, is not considered child abuse (a). No such report is needed. Since the client consented to treatment on their own, the parents do not have a right to the client's records; even a high-risk behavior would not be disclosed (b) unless doing so was to prevent imminent danger. Advising the client on reducing prescription drug dosage would be considered giving medical advice and is out of an LCSW's scope of practice. A referral to a physician (d) is appropriate.

45. After a family session where a family's 15-year-old daughter believed the LCSW sided with the mother instead of the daughter, the daughter comes to the next session wearing earbuds she refuses to take out, and demanding an apology from the LCSW. The LCSW should:

a. **CORRECT.** Consider whether the daughter is correct, and if appropriate, offer an apology.
b. **Incorrect.** Side with the mother again, reinforcing the appropriate power hierarchy in the family.
c. **Incorrect.** Refuse to go on with therapy until the 15-year-old removes her earbuds.
d. **Incorrect.** Demand an apology from the 15-year-old.

Remember that this test is asking about your *legal and ethical responsibilities,* not your clinical skills. (Those will be tested in the Clinical Exam.) This question is about preserving the therapeutic relationship with each individual client in a family system. That may mean offering an apology to a client who feels wronged. There may be clinical reasons in support of the other response choices, but only option A addresses the ethical need to manage conflicts that can arise when working with more than one family member in the room.

46. A recently-licensed LCSW is interested in helping others successfully navigate the licensure process. She posts to a closed group of licensed and prelicensed therapists on a popular social media platform about her experience taking her clinical exam. In her post, she encourages those about to take their tests to focus their diagnostic review on mood disorders and schizophrenia, as these came up multiple times on her test. Considering the LCSW's legal responsibilities, this post could result in:

a. **Incorrect.** No action against the LCSW, as she was not specific about the questions she was asked
b. **Incorrect.** No action against the LCSW, as the post was to a closed group and not the general public
c. **CORRECT.** Action against the LCSW's license
d. **Incorrect.** A jail sentence for the LCSW

While the LCSW's post doesn't reveal specific test questions, it does provide detailed enough information to give those who see it an unfair advantage on their tests. Even though it is not open to the public, the social media group still includes prelicensed therapists who may soon be taking the test themselves. The LCSW's post could be considered "subverting a license exam," which is one of the recognized categories of unprofessional conduct. Unprofessional conduct can result in actions against one's license or registration, but these administrative actions are different from criminal charges that could result in jail time.

47. An LCSW is working with a client on issues of anxiety and body image. The client gives the LCSW permission to consult with the client's physician, but asks the LCSW not to discuss the client's recent weight gain with the physician. The client explains that they felt shamed by the physician and pressured to lose weight despite the client being in overall good health. The LCSW contacts the physician and explains that the client appears to be learning to manage their anxiety effectively without medication. The physician asks whether the client is losing weight as instructed. How should the LCSW respond?

a. **Incorrect.** Say yes to satisfy the physician, and redirect the conversation
b. **Incorrect.** Inform the physician of the client's weight gain, considering the potential medical concerns
c. **Incorrect.** Without directly answering the question, inform the physician that the client has experienced pressure to lose weight and that such pressure may worsen the client's anxiety
d. **CORRECT.** Explain that the client's weight is not part of their therapy

The LCSW should respect the client's request for their weight to not be discussed with the physician. At the same time, the LCSW does not need to lie or argue with the physician to accomplish this. Best to simply explain that the client's weight is not part of their therapy and move on in the conversation. This protects the client's rights while preserving the LCSW's role.

48. An adult client with an extensive history of gambling seeks couple therapy with his wife of 14 years. Despite the best efforts of an LCSW, the treatment fails, and the couple chooses to divorce. The man's gambling worsens, eventually leaving him bankrupt. He sues the LCSW, claiming that the LCSW's misconduct negatively impacted his mental health, causing him to lose his job and ultimately run out of money. The LCSW believes that records of the case will ultimately lead a court to rule in the LCSW's favor, but the client refuses to release the records. Instead, the client goes on television, where he discloses his gambling and therapy history and again accuses the therapist of misconduct. Legally, how should the LCSW proceed?

a. **Incorrect.** Disclose the client file to the public, as the client has waived confidentiality with his own disclosures to the media
b. **Incorrect.** Disclose the client file to the court
c. **CORRECT.** Through an attorney, move to submit the client file into evidence
d. **Incorrect.** Through an attorney, contact the client in a good-faith effort to have the records released

The client's accusation of therapist breach of duty is an exception to privilege, but it is the role of the court, and not the therapist, to make that determination. The therapist should move to submit the client file into evidence, and the client can raise privilege claims in dispute of this if they wish. The file should not be disclosed unless and until a judge has determined that privilege does not apply.

49. With the client's consent, an LCSW working with an adolescent client encourages one of the client's teachers to attend sessions that will focus on the adolescent's behavior in school. While the teacher's presence is at first helpful, the teacher asks to continue coming to the sessions, and it is clear to the LCSW that the client is finding the teacher's presence gradually more intrusive and uncomfortable. The LCSW should:

a. **CORRECT.** Clarify the teacher's role in treatment, and ask the client whether they would like to continue having the teacher in session. *When third parties are brought into treatment, that does not mean that the presence of these third parties is permanent or unmanageable. Clarifying roles on an ongoing basis in helpful and expected. Permission for third parties to be involved in therapy can be revoked in many circumstances.*
b. **Incorrect.** Ask the client whether they would like to continue having the teacher in session, and remind the teacher of the limits to confidentiality. *Reminding the teacher of the limits of confidentiality may or may not alleviate the client's concern about the teacher's presence.*
c. **Incorrect.** Ask the client to contact the school and request that the teacher be removed from the therapy sessions. *Having the client contact the school about the teacher's presence in therapy places an undue burden of responsibility on both the client and the school; if the client wants the teacher removed and the therapist believes the teacher's presence is harmful, the therapist should take responsibility for ensuring that the teacher is removed.*
d. **Incorrect.** Remind the client of the goals of therapy and the reasons for the teacher's presence in session. *Reminding the adolescent of the goals of treatment may or may not alleviate the client's concern about the teacher's presence.*

50. An LCSW is serving as the family therapist for a family where the father is also engaged in individual therapy with another provider. The family has only attended one session so far, and while the father informed the LCSW of his individual therapy, he did not provide information about the other therapist or sign a release of information. The LCSW receives a voicemail message from a local therapist, identifying themselves as the individual therapist for the father, and asking the LCSW to provide any information the LCSW may have regarding the father's history of psychosis, as the individual therapist is attempting to determine a proper diagnosis. Considering the LCSW's ethical responsibilities, the LCSW should:

a. **Incorrect.** Provide the colleague with the minimum information necessary to aid them in diagnosis
b. **Incorrect.** Provide the colleague with the client's full medical and mental health history
c. **CORRECT.** Contact the father to assess his wishes and ask him to sign a release of information
d. **Incorrect.** Contact the father to inform him that his information will be disclosed; remind him of the limits of confidentiality

It's important to note in this question that you are being tested on knowledge of the LCSW's ethical responsibilities, not the laws around disclosure. While it is legally permissible for two active treatment providers to share information without a release when the disclosure is for the purposes of diagnosis or treatment planning, the fact that such releases are *allowed* does not mean they are *required*. So social workers should consider their ethical responsibilities before choosing to disclose such information. One such responsibility is to "inform clients, to the extent possible, about the disclosure of confidential information and the potential consequences, when feasible before the disclosure is made" (Standard 1.07(d)). Since this situation is not an emergency, it would be most appropriate to contact the client prior to any disclosure, to determine his wishes and ask him to formally authorize the release. You can contrast this question with question 30, which asked specifically about the *laws* around disclosure of billing information.

51. In a mid-size college town, an LCSW is the only local mental health provider who speaks fluent Farsi. She routinely receives referrals from other providers when the other provider discovers that their client identifies as Persian or speaks Farsi, even if the client is also fluent in English. Given her ties to the local Persian community, the LCSW often finds that she is at least somewhat familiar with the new clients being referred to her. Considering her ethical responsibilities, the LCSW should:

a. **CORRECT.** Refer out clients who could effectively receive services from other providers, retaining those who speak only Farsi, unless her familiarity makes her incapable of providing unbiased care
b. **Incorrect.** Refer out clients she has any form of prior knowledge about
c. **Incorrect.** Refer out clients she has personally interacted with in the last two years, retaining the rest
d. **Incorrect.** Reach out to referring providers and let them know she cannot accept additional Farsi-speaking clients

If the LCSW is the only local provider who can provide services in Farsi, this adds complexity to the consideration of how to manage potential dual relationships. The simple fact of familiarity, in and of itself, is not enough for the LCSW to be required to turn away clients (B). Her obligation is to consider whether a dual relationship would impair her clinical judgment or increase the risk of exploitation. This obligation is best balanced with her ability to provide culturally appropriate services in option A. There is no rule related to personal interactions in the past two years (C). And turning away any new Farsi-speaking clients simply because they speak Farsi (D) would leave local Farsi speakers without any local providers.

52. A client sees an LCSW at a local community clinic for court-mandated anger management groups. The client comes to dislike the LCSW and becomes disruptive, frequently comparing the group to jail, and saying "I'm not free when I'm here." In considering her ethical responsibilities, the LCSW should:

a. **Incorrect.** Empathize and validate the client's feeling of disempowerment.
b. **Incorrect.** Terminate therapy with the client and refer them back to court.
c. **CORRECT.** Remind the client that he is free to attend any anger management group he wishes, or none at all.
d. **Incorrect.** Tell the client the LCSW will inform the court of his statements if he continues, and encourage him to become more open to the group process.

Empathy and validation (A) may be clinically appropriate but do not address any legal or ethical responsibilities. Termination (B) is premature, given that client frustration with mandated treatment is relatively normal and often can be resolved. While repeated disclosures of the limits of confidentiality are encouraged, using those limits as threats (D) undermines efforts to work collaboratively with the court system. Option C supports client autonomy and maximizes client choice. While failure to attend groups may have legal consequences for the client, they do have the right to make that choice. The client can attend any group, or none; the social worker is not holding the client against their will.

53. An LCSW is working as the Director for a non-profit agency serving the LGBTQIA+ community. As part of her role, the LCSW occasionally sits in on treatment sessions to observe the work of clinicians at the agency. In a session the LCSW is observing, the client informs the treating therapist that the client is in the process of coming out as bisexual, and is unsure of what to reveal to her parents, or when. The client notices that the Director is older than the treating therapist, and asks the Director, “what would you do in my shoes?” The Director should:

a. **Incorrect.** Avoid speaking, so as to reinforce that the treating clinician is running the session
b. **CORRECT.** Clarify the Director’s role and defer to the treating clinician
c. **Incorrect.** Answer the question, and then leave the session in order to support the treating clinician in their role
d. **Incorrect.** Inform the client that it is inappropriate to ask such a question of the Director, and redirect the question to the treating clinician

Unless the client had been previously instructed not to engage with the Director, they haven’t done anything wrong by asking the question. The Director is also not required to take an extreme stance here, such as avoiding speaking entirely or leaving the room immediately after they respond. The Director’s ethical obligation, since they are an LCSW but not serving in a direct treatment role, is to clarify the Director role.

54. A client on probation comes to a scheduled session with an LCSW appearing angry. The client confronts the LCSW on a report the LCSW recently filed with the probation officer, updating the probation officer on the client's attendance in therapy. (There is a release in place allowing for the report to be sent directly.) The client had been making good progress in therapy, and is disappointed that the probation officer "didn't seem to know or care." To manage their ethical responsibilities, the LCSW should:

a. **CORRECT.** Review with the client what information is sent to the probation officer, and how that information can be used
b. **Incorrect.** Review with the client their progress to date in therapy
c. **Incorrect.** Remind the client that legally, the LCSW can only inform the probation officer about their attendance in therapy, not about specific therapy content
d. **Incorrect.** Remind the client that the role of the probation officer is not to provide support or encouragement, but to ensure compliance

While roles within a treatment team should be clarified among the professionals involved, it is generally not the LCSW's place to describe the roles of others (D). A release of information can request or allow whatever information the client wishes to be sent, and is not limited to attendance (C). Reviewing client progress (B) may be helpful, but would be a clinical determination and not an ethical one. The ethical responsibility here is to review confidentiality and its limitations as needed throughout the therapeutic process. That reasonably includes what information is sent and how it can be used (or, as in this case, not used).

55. A 14-year-old girl presents for therapy at a local mental health clinic, where an LCSW is assigned to her case. During a screening interview, the girl tells the LCSW that she is struggling with anxiety around her schoolwork and social relationships. She goes on to say that she plans to pay for therapy on her own and would prefer that her parents not know she is in therapy. The LCSW should:

a. **CORRECT.** Assess the girl's ability to participate intelligently in therapy and determine whether notifying the parents would be damaging. *Minors 12 and older can independently consent for treatment if the therapist considers them mature enough to participate intelligently. No adult needs to consent on their behalf. This law also requires therapists to contact the parents unless doing so would be damaging.*
b. **Incorrect.** Determine whether notifying the parents would be damaging and determine what adult can consent for the girl's therapy. *Minors 12 and older can independently consent for treatment if the therapist considers them mature enough to participate intelligently. No adult needs to consent on their behalf.*
c. **Incorrect.** Assess the girl's ability to participate intelligently in treatment and inform her that even when seen under her own consent, her parents may have the right to access her records if they become aware she is in therapy. *When a minor consents for their own therapy, the parents do not have a right to records of treatment.*
d. **Incorrect.** Determine whether notifying the parents would be damaging and determine whether notifying the girl's school would be damaging. *Notifying the school without the client's permission could be a breach of confidentiality.*

56. An LCSW provided therapy to a 16-year-old boy for several months with his parents' consent. A few months later, the LCSW receives a subpoena from the attorney for a classmate of the boy. The classmate accused the client of physical assault, and the classmate's family is suing to recover medical expenses. The subpoena requests complete records of the boy's treatment. The LCSW attempts to contact the client and his parents but is unsuccessful. The LCSW should:

a. **Incorrect.** Wait to respond to the subpoena until the LCSW is able to determine how the client would like the LCSW to respond. *Failing to respond to a subpoena may land the LCSW in trouble with the court.*
b. **Incorrect.** Wait to respond to the subpoena until the LCSW is able to determine how the parents would like the LCSW to respond. *Failing to respond to a subpoena may land the LCSW in trouble with the court.*
c. **CORRECT.** Respond to the subpoena by asserting privilege, and continue attempts to contact the client and his parents. *When clients cannot be reached to determine their preferred response to a subpoena, asserting privilege on their behalf is a reasonable default position to take.*
d. **Incorrect.** Acknowledge the exception to privilege, turn over the client's records, and inform the client and his family as soon as possible. *It is up to a judge, and not the therapist, to determine whether an exception to privilege applies.*

57. An LCSW is working with a Latina mother and her 7-year-old son in therapy, when the LCSW observes unusual bruises on the boy's face and arms. The bruises seem to be in several different stages of healing. When the LCSW asks how he got the bruises, the boy does not answer. His mother says, "He's a normal boy, he likes to play rough" and refuses to discuss the matter further. The LCSW should:

a. **CORRECT.** Report suspected child abuse.
b. **Incorrect.** Consider whether physical discipline is common in Latin cultures.
c. **Incorrect.** Remind the mother of the limits of confidentiality.
d. **Incorrect.** Ask the child to remove his shirt to inspect his torso for additional injuries.

While the injuries, and both clients' response to the therapist's inquiries, are not a guarantee that abuse has taken place, remember that the therapist does not need to be certain. They just need to reasonably suspect abuse. The location of the injuries, the fact that they are in multiple stages of healing, and the refusal to explain them would amount to reasonable suspicion in almost any LCSW's mind. B would not be correct because the abuse reporting standards do not change on the basis of client culture. C is not correct because it would be an insufficient response to what appears to be abuse. D is not correct because this would place the LCSW in the role of an investigator, which is not the proper role of a therapist.

58. A single LCSW finds herself sometimes flirting with one particular group therapy client at the end of each week's session, as the other group members are making their way outside. The group member is also single, and appears to be interested in the therapist, but is careful to not cross boundaries during session or in other situations where other group members could see. One evening, the client sends the social worker an email to express gratitude for all she has done in the group, and attaches a couple of racy photos. The LCSW should:

a. **Incorrect.** Ignore the photos, respond to the gratitude, and encourage continued growth in group
b. **Incorrect.** Do not respond via email, engage the client in a phone discussion, warn the client that the email cannot remain confidential, and consider termination from the group
c. **Incorrect.** Acknowledge the email, inform the client that they are violating the LCSW's boundaries, and inform the client that sexually explicit communications must be reported
d. **CORRECT.** Acknowledge the email, inform the client that including the photos was inappropriate, apologize for any misunderstanding about the nature of their relationship, and monitor both the LCSW's and the client's future behavior

There is no legal or ethical standard that requires the social worker to report sexually explicit communications from the client. At the same time, the client's boundary-testing should not be simply ignored, as this may lead the client to believe that their efforts are welcomed. The LCSW should enforce a boundary around sexual contact with clients (sexual communications in this case would be considered sexual contact), and monitor her and her client's behavior closely going forward.

59. An LCSW is working for an agency that contracts with a local private school to provide mental health services. The social worker is called to the school to assess a 9-year-old girl who has been falling asleep in class. The girl's teacher tells the social worker that the teacher is concerned in part because the girl recently wrote a story as part of a class assignment, and in the story a young girl wasn't allowed to sleep when she got into trouble at home. During the assessment, the girl repeatedly asks whether she can take a nap, and refuses to answer any questions about the story she wrote. Asked how things are at home, the girl will only say, "I got in trouble. I'm always getting in trouble." The girl is being raised by a single mother, and the school nurse says that the girl is otherwise in relatively good health, but that her grades have been dropping and her behavior in class has been increasingly disorganized. How should the social worker proceed?

a. **Incorrect.** Contact the mother to inform her of the child's behavior and the school's concerns
b. **Incorrect.** Contact the child's physician to request a medical assessment
c. **CORRECT.** Report suspected child abuse
d. **Incorrect.** Ask the child directly whether she is being physically abused or neglected

The child's statements and behavior are enough to reasonably suspect that she is being kept from sleeping at home as a punishment. While the social worker does not have certainty, such certainty is not required to develop reasonable suspicion. A report here (under the category of "Willful harm or endangerment") is appropriate.

60. An older woman who has been seeing an LCSW for seven months storms out of session after her therapist started the session some 30 minutes late. The LCSW attempted to explain that another client had been in crisis, but the woman cut off the LCSW, saying that the delay was disrespectful of her time. A few days later the client calls the LCSW saying she will not come back for future sessions and requesting a copy of the treatment record be sent to her. The LCSW should:

a. **Incorrect.** Insist that the client come in for an additional session to discuss her hurt feelings, and provide a copy of the treatment record. *The client cannot be forced to come back in, and making the discussion about the client's hurt feelings suggests that the client is to blame for feeling hurt. This is not likely to improve the fractured therapeutic relationship.*
b. **CORRECT.** Apologize for the delay, offer to discuss it further, provide options for other treatment providers, and provide a copy of the treatment record. *When treatment is terminated, even if the termination is conflictual, LCSWs are obligated to provide additional treatment options for continuity of care, and this response option includes this key step.*
c. **Incorrect.** Provide a copy of the treatment record, and consider whether the client's display was simply a way of resolving cognitive dissonance about the need to end treatment. *Even if the client's departure was a way of resolving dissonance around leaving therapy -- a big leap from the information in the vignette -- referrals still must be provided to ensure continuity of care.*
d. **Incorrect.** Provide options for other treatment providers, and inform the client that the LCSW will forward the treatment record to the new provider of the client's choosing, in order to ensure that the client does remain in therapy. *The LCSW cannot hold records hostage and demand that the client continue treatment. Doing so violates the client's autonomy. The client requested that records be sent to her, so the LCSW should either take steps to provide those records or establish why doing so would be harmful.*

61. An LCSW with strong religious beliefs is talking with a trans male client about the client's family history. The client reveals that his parents had strong religious beliefs, but the client describes himself as atheist and says, "I just never understood why people buy into those fairy tales." The client says he has never found comfort or strength in religious or spiritual activity, and has judgment toward those who do. The LCSW should:

a. **Incorrect.** Mention the LCSW's beliefs briefly, without challenging the client's experience
b. **Incorrect.** Inform the client that religion is a source of comfort for many people, and encourage the client to keep an open mind toward it for the future
c. **Incorrect.** Connect the client's beliefs about religion with their history of family trauma
d. **CORRECT.** Show understanding of the client's beliefs and inquire further about their family history

There is nothing in the question to indicate that the client's beliefs are causing him suffering. There's no obligation or evidence of likely clinical benefit for the LCSW to raise their own beliefs. For the social worker to mention their own beliefs, to try to change the client to a position of openness for future changes in belief, or to conclude that the client's beliefs must be related to trauma *in the absence of any evidence of trauma*, would be inappropriate.

62. An LCSW is consulting with the physician who sent a young couple to the LCSW for couple therapy. Both partners in the couple are struggling with symptoms of anxiety. The physician provides the LCSW with useful information on the couple's medications and their possible side effects. The LCSW offers the physician useful information on the progression of the couple's symptoms. Toward the end of the conversation, the physician asks whether the older partner in the couple is "still wearing that same brown sweater twice a week." The LCSW should:

a. **Incorrect.** Answer the question. *Even without a release, the LCSW could answer questions directly related to diagnosis or treatment planning; however, since this question does not appear to fall in either category, it falls outside of that allowance in HIPAA.*
b. **CORRECT.** Politely decline to answer the question, as it is not relevant to the consultation. *When taking part in a consultation, an LCSW only provides information relevant to the purposes of that consultation.*
c. **Incorrect.** Request a release from both partners to provide this type of information. *While the LCSW could get a release from the clients allowing the LCSW to discuss whatever the clients want the LCSW to discuss, this does not change the LCSW's ethical responsibilities around consultations, which include refusing to share information that is not relevant to the reason for the consult.*
d. **Incorrect.** Gently note that the physician is asking a question outside of their scope of practice. *It is not the LCSW's proper role to inform a physician of their own scope. The physician may have reasons for asking the question that relate to the partner's physical symptoms or mental health.*

63. A middle-aged woman struggling with panic disorder asks an LCSW whether her brother can come with her to therapy, and the LCSW approves. In the intake session, the woman describes her panic symptoms, as well as the strain that her panic has caused in her relationship with her brother. She relies on him to feel safe in public situations, and becomes angry with him when he cannot be with her due to his job or other obligations. The brother agrees, saying that while he wants to help his sister as much as he can and is glad that she is seeking treatment, he is growing resentful of being her main source of support. The LCSW should:

a. **CORRECT.** Clarify whether the woman and her brother are seeking conjoint treatment to address their relationship, or whether treatment is to focus on the woman's panic
b. **Incorrect.** Ask the brother to leave the session so that the LCSW can assess the woman for possible dependent adult abuse
c. **Incorrect.** Ask the client to sign a release of information allowing for discussion of her symptoms in therapy sessions where her brother is also present
d. **Incorrect.** Provide the client with referrals to co-occurring disorder treatment

There is no evidence here of substance use (co-occurring disorder) or dependent adult abuse (while the brother's resentment is a potential risk factor warranting assessment for violence, panic disorder alone does not make someone a dependent adult). A release of information may be warranted if treatment is to go forward as individual treatment. But the first thing the LCSW needs to do here is determine who exactly is the "client," and asking about the focus of treatment is a good way to get there.

64. An LCSW has a client who lives on a boat three months of the year, as a commercial fisherman. During that time, he comes back to shore one day a week, and sees the LCSW on that day. The client is relatively poor, and asks the LCSW whether he can pay for services in fresh salmon. The client says he may need to discontinue treatment otherwise. The LCSW frequently eats salmon, and so is familiar with the fair market value of the fish. Which of the following statements of the LCSW's responsibilities is correct?

a. **Incorrect.** The LCSW should provide services pro bono, rather than accepting payment in fish. *Reducing fees is an acceptable resolution to the dilemma, but this response uses the word "should," suggesting that this solution is better than bartering. The carve-out in the ethics code for bartering appears to be made for precisely this type of situation.*
b. **CORRECT.** If the LCSW chooses to go ahead with the barter agreement, the value of the fish should approximate the fee generally charged for therapy, and there should be a clear contract. *While LCSWs* ordinarily *do not accept goods or services as payment, in limited circumstances it can be acceptable. In this case, the client has specifically requested the barter arrangement, a fair value for the salmon can be easily determined, and there does not appear to be any distortion to the professional relationship that would occur. As the alternative is discontinuation of treatment, it would be ethically appropriate to at least consider the barter arrangement.*
c. **Incorrect.** The LCSW should refer the client to a low-fee or no-fee clinic rather than accepting salmon as payment. *Referring out is an acceptable resolution to the dilemma, but this option uses the word "should," suggesting that this solution is better than bartering. The carve-out in the ethics codes for bartering appear to be made for precisely this type of situation.*
d. **Incorrect.** The LCSW should consider whether other clients would also want to pay for therapy through the products they make or services they provide. *Whether a barter agreement would be appropriate for another client is not relevant to the consideration of appropriateness for this specific client.*

65. An LCSW suffers a serious illness, and a colleague steps in to take over the LCSW's ongoing clients until the LCSW can return to practice. The LCSW agrees to continue handling billing and to review the colleague's session notes to keep up with what is happening while she is recovering. Some of the LCSW's ongoing clients pay for sessions through their health insurance. However, the colleague (who is also a licensed LCSW in private practice) is not on any insurance panels. The ill LCSW should:

a. **Incorrect.** Continue to submit insurance billing listing herself as the treatment provider. *This would be a misrepresentation and may be considered insurance fraud.*
b. **Incorrect.** Continue to submit insurance billing listing the colleague as the treatment provider and herself as the supervisor. *Because the colleague is taking over treatment, the colleague is indeed the treatment provider. Listing herself as the supervisor, however, is problematic as the colleague is apparently neither employed nor supervised by the LCSW. This would be a misrepresentation and may be considered insurance fraud.*
c. **CORRECT.** Either directly or through the colleague, inform clients of the difference in panel status and arrange alternate payment or referrals as needed.
d. **Incorrect.** Defer to the colleague to negotiate fees independently, and otherwise presume that the LCSW's typical business practices will be followed. *Each of these issues help establish why a professional will is so important. It should clarify whether the colleague can change client fees, and what business practices the LCSW expects the colleague to follow. It is not safe to simply presume that the colleague's business practices will be the same as the LCSW's.*

66. An adult client who has been seeing an LCSW in therapy for six months asks the LCSW for a copy of her treatment record. Because the LCSW has documented that she suspects the client is being dishonest in her denials of recent drug use, the LCSW worries that sharing the file would harm the therapeutic relationship. The most appropriate course of action for the LCSW would be to:

a. **Incorrect.** Turn over the records as required by law, and use it as an opportunity to address the client's possible substance use. LCSW*s are not required to turn over requested records if the LCSW believes the release would be harmful to the client.*
b. **Incorrect.** Provide the client with a partial copy of the file, leaving out the suspicion of recent drug use. *While providing a treatment summary is legal and often appropriate, simply providing a partial copy of the file and leaving out the suspicion of drug use is not an option under the law. It may even be considered fraudulent if it is presented as if it were the complete record.*
c. **CORRECT.** Refuse to turn over the records, offer a treatment summary instead, and inform the client that if she wishes, she can select a neutral therapist to review the file. *The LCSW has good reason to believe that releasing the full treatment record could harm the therapeutic relationship and thus harm the client. Under the law, the LCSW is allowed to offer a treatment summary instead. Further, when an LCSW refuses to release records due to the risk of harm, the LCSW must also inform the client of their right to a third-party review of the record by another therapist.*
d. **Incorrect.** Submit the client's request, and the LCSW's reason for refusing, to a district judge for review. *Turning over the records to a judge in the absence of a release of information from the client would be a breach of confidentiality.*

67. An individual client acknowledges to her therapist (an LCSW) that she lied on the LCSW's intake form and actually does have several past suicide attempts in her history. She says she is not feeling suicidal now, though she has recently experienced the ending of a romantic relationship and the death of a distant relative. Legally, the LCSW should:

a. **Incorrect.** Complete a No Harm Contract with the client. *No Harm Contracts have largely fallen out of favor, replaced by safety plans; either way, such a response here would likely be considered inadequate to the client's level of risk.*
b. **Incorrect.** Discontinue therapy and refer the client to a higher level of care, as she is high risk. *Discontinuing therapy is not a legal requirement and may be clinically harmful, leaving the client with the lesson that they will be punished if they openly discuss their history of suicidality.*
c. **Incorrect.** Initiate the process of involuntary hospitalization. *While the client does pose an elevated level of risk, the fact that she denies current suicidality means that an attempt to initiate involuntary hospitalization would likely be considered a breach of confidentiality -- and that hospitals would likely turn her away to keep room available for higher-risk patients who are more actively suicidal.*
d. **CORRECT.** Assess further and break confidentiality if required to resolve any threat of suicide. LCSW*s are legally obligated to take steps necessary to prevent a threatened suicide, and may break confidentiality if necessary as part of that process.*

68. An LCSW in an outpatient group practice setting has fallen behind on their documentation. The owner of the practice expresses concern that the delays will impact insurance billing and, ultimately, the practice's financial health. To ethically resolve this issue, the LCSW should:

a. **Incorrect.** Create at least cursory progress notes for all sessions more than 7 days in the past, even if such notes are a single sentence each, to allow billing to move forward
b. **Incorrect.** Transfer their clients to other clinicians in the group, allowing the other clinicians to create documentation of past sessions establishing themselves as the service providers and to properly submit insurance claims
c. **CORRECT.** Work diligently to catch up
d. **Incorrect.** Consider reducing their client load or, if necessary, leaving the practice

The NASW Code of Ethics demands that social workers produce accurate and timely documentation that adequately reflects the services provided. One-sentence progress notes (A) likely would not be sufficient (they would not meaningfully reflect the services provided, and they would not be useful if a need for continuity of service with another clinician emerged), having other clinicians present themselves as the service providers for past sessions (B) would not be accurate, and reducing client load or leaving the practice (D) does nothing to resolve the issues related to the notes for sessions already conducted. There's also no other evidence in the question to suggest that the LCSW is impaired in such a way that would support reducing their client load or potentially leaving the practice. The most ethical thing for the social worker to do here is make a priority of catching up, in accordance with those ethical standards.

69. As a client leaves an LCSW's office, the LCSW believes the client poses a serious danger to the client's spouse. (The client had been making threats in session about what he would do to her.) The LCSW, knowing the couple lives roughly 30 minutes from the LCSW's office, calls the client immediately, and is able to resolve the danger. The client disavows any continued plan to harm his spouse, and apologizes to the LCSW for "getting so out of hand." What does the LCSW need to do to resolve the LCSW's legal responsibility?

a. **Incorrect.** Notify the spouse and law enforcement immediately
b. **Incorrect.** Notify the spouse immediately
c. **CORRECT.** Notify law enforcement within 24 hours
d. **Incorrect.** Notify the local child protective services agency

While warning an intended victim in a *Tarasoff* situation grants the LCSW certain additional legal protections, it is not always necessary or appropriate to do so. In this case, the LCSW was able to fully resolve the threat on their own, before notifying the intended victim or law enforcement. Still, under state law, the fact that the LCSW's *Tarasoff* responsibilities were triggered *at all* means that the LCSW must report the threatening person to law enforcement within 24 hours, even if notifying law enforcement was not necessary to resolve the initial threat. As noted in the study guide, the idea of this law is to prevent potentially dangerous individuals from buying guns.

70. An LCSW has a new client who explains during the intake session that she had a hard time coming into therapy. The client says that her previous therapist asked her to go on a date with him immediately after their termination session ended. She refused, and has not spoken with the former therapist again, but the experience left her skeptical of therapists generally. Legally, the LCSW must:

a. **Incorrect.** Report the other therapist's actions to the BBS. *The LCSW could report the other therapist to the BBS, if the client signed a release of information allowing them to do so – but this is not a legal obligation, and it would be better for the client to report directly.*
b. **Incorrect.** Confront the other therapist on their behavior. *The LCSW has no legal obligation to confront the other therapist, and doing so in the absence of a release of information from the client would be a breach of confidentiality.*
c. **Incorrect.** Provide the client a copy of the brochure "Therapy Never Includes Sexual Behavior." *Providing the brochure would be a legal obligation if the client reported having had a sexual relationship with the prior therapist. However, such a relationship never began. The LCSW can provide the brochure here, but is not required to do so.*
d. **CORRECT.** Maintain the client's confidentiality. *None of the other options are actual legal obligations in these circumstances. The prior therapist's behavior was romantic but not overtly sexual in nature, and occurred after the psychotherapist-client relationship had been terminated.*

71. An LCSW is interested in conducting research on her clients, in an effort to determine whether a new form of treatment developed by the LCSW is superior to existing treatments. Because the LCSW already has access to the client files and would be reporting statistics on her recent treatment results, without specifics of any individual cases, she prepares to conduct an analysis of cases she has closed over the prior year. She hopes to publish the results of her research in a prominent journal. Ethically, the LCSW should:

a. **CORRECT.** Contact those former clients, inform them of the risks and benefits of involvement in the research, and determine their willingness to have their file included as one of those analyzed. *The NASW Code of Ethics requires that research participants provide informed consent for their participation, including information about risks and benefits and the opportunity to choose not to participate. While the NASW ethics code allows exceptions for some archival research, this is only appropriate when obtaining consent is not feasible. Here, it would be possible to obtain consent.*
b. **Incorrect.** Take steps to protect the confidentiality of individual cases, but include all cases from the prior year in her analysis to eliminate possible selection bias. *While there is reasonable concern that those clients who choose not to participate might skew results, participants' rights outweigh concerns about possible selection bias.*
c. **Incorrect.** Contact those former clients to let them know that their files have been included in her research. *Simply informing them after the fact that they were included would not meet professional standards. It neglects an informed consent process for research and does not give the clients the opportunity to choose against being part of that research.*
d. **Incorrect.** Because she is working with archival data that will be reported in aggregate, no action is required. *Even though results will be reported in aggregate, the LCSW's clients had not been informed that they were also research participants. They must be given the opportunity to choose whether to be involved in the research. While the NASW ethics code allows exceptions for archival research, this is only appropriate when obtaining consent is not feasible. Here, the clinician presumably has contact information for her former clients, and could obtain consent from prospective participants.*

72. A 27-year-old trans female client has been receiving services from an LCSW at a reduced-fee clinic. The client has been unable to pay even her reduced fee, and over 8 weeks has built up an unpaid balance of more than $100. The client is apologetic and has reassured the LCSW that she will pay the overdue fees once her aging mother dies and she can collect her inheritance. The LCSW has informed the client while she empathizes with the client's struggles, a balance that goes unpaid for more than 30 days will result in the termination of services. This policy also appears in the informed consent document the client signed at the beginning of services. The client does not have stable food, work, or shelter, but is typically able to engage public services and shelter space when needed. How should the social worker proceed?

a. **CORRECT.** Assess whether the client poses imminent danger to self or others
b. **Incorrect.** Terminate the client for nonpayment and provide at least three community referrals
c. **Incorrect.** Pay the client's balance on the client's behalf
d. **Incorrect.** Set a specific deadline by which the full balance must be paid off to retain services

Under the NASW Code of Ethics, termination for nonpayment of an overdue balance is allowed, but a social worker first needs to engage in a number of specific steps. One of those steps is determining that the client is not an imminent danger to self or others. While nothing in the question suggests such danger, the ethical standard suggests that it should be actively determined prior to terminating with the client. Once such a determination is made, the social worker is free to terminate the client.

73. A social worker at a private nonprofit outpatient clinic is surprised to learn that the clinic has a policy of neutrality on political matters. The social worker had hoped to get the clinic to support a proposed local law that would raise sales taxes to improve local services and accessibility for those with disabilities. The clinic asks the social worker to stay out of political discussion about the proposed law, which the social worker believes would advance social justice. The director of the clinic says that she also believes the proposal is good, but is committed to the clinic policy. How should the social worker proceed?

a. **Incorrect.** Respect the wishes of the employer, and support the proposal by voting for it and potentially donating money to groups that are advocating for its passage
b. **Incorrect.** Engage in public discussion of the proposal, and describe the clinic as being in favor of it
c. **Incorrect.** Engage in public discussion of the proposal, and criticize the clinic's unwillingness to take a public stance as likely an effort to preserve their grants and contracts
d. **CORRECT.** Engage in public discussion of the proposal, but as an individual and not as a representative of the clinic

Under the NASW code, social workers should not allow employer policies to prevent them from the ethical practice of social work – including the pursuit of social justice. At the same time, social workers have a responsibility to treat colleagues with fairness and respect; describing the clinic as in favor of the proposal would not be accurate when the clinic has taken no formal position, and criticizing the clinic's non-stance as money-driven in the absence of any evidence of such is not fair to the clinic. The social worker should publicly support the proposal, but should do so on their own.

74. A group practice specializing in working with depression is considering implementing a new policy to build awareness of their work: As part of the consent process, clients would be required to agree to post at least once on social media about their experience in therapy, making specific mention of the group practice when they do. The policy specifies that the post does not need to be an endorsement or testimonial; even negative discussion is allowed, so long as it is truthful. Clients who have no social media presence would be exempt. Considering the LCSW's ethical responsibilities, what should the LCSW do around this policy?

a. **Incorrect.** Clarify to clients that since it is part of the consent process, they are free to go to a different provider who does not have such a policy if they wish
b. **Incorrect.** Clarify to all clients that such posts are strongly encouraged, but are not required, regardless of what the official policy may say
c. **Incorrect.** Clarify with the practice owners what the consequence would be for clients who agree to the policy but ultimately do not post about their experience
d. **CORRECT.** Refuse to implement the policy, and ask the group practice to withdraw it

Even though the policy says that the content of the social media post doesn't matter, this policy, if enacted, would likely be considered solicitation of endorsements from current clients, which is expressly prohibited in the NASW Code of Ethics. In any case, the proposed policy is inherently exploitive, meant to place the business interests of the practice ahead of the clinical needs of clients. The fact that it applies to all clients with social media accounts means that even clients who are deeply depressed or otherwise desperate to receive services would be bound by it. The LCSW should not implement such a policy, and should work with the employer to withdraw it.

75. In a large public mental health clinic, a social worker (Social Worker A) becomes aware of a colleague in the clinic (Social Worker B) who describes all trans, queer, nonbinary, or otherwise gender-nonconforming clients as mentally ill, and refuses to work with such clients. Supervisors are aware of the issue and make sure that the colleague is only assigned cisgender clients. A different colleague (Social Worker C), who complained about Social Worker B's behavior, was then told that Social Worker B had accused them of religious discrimination, a charge that Social Worker A believes to be false. What ethical responsibility does Social Worker A have in this circumstance?

a. **CORRECT.** Assist in Social Worker C's defense; bring Social Worker B's behavior to the attention of administrators; file a formal ethical complaint against Social Worker B if needed
b. **Incorrect.** Assist in Social Worker C's defense; demand supervisors explain why they did not take additional action
c. **Incorrect.** Because all potentially problematic behavior has been reported, allow the administrative processes of resolving all complaints to reach their conclusions; evaluate options at that point
d. **Incorrect.** File an ethics complaint against Social Worker B and their supervisor with the NASW Ethics Committee

Social workers are obligated to "defend and assist colleagues who are unjustly charged with unethical conduct" (NASW standard 2.10e), and should not condone or participate in discrimination. They should report unethical or incompetent behavior through proper formal channels; if the supervisors' actions have not addressed the issue, Social Worker A should attempt to address the issue through clinic administration. Social Worker A is not in a position to make demands of supervisors related to their actions surrounding a colleague, but can take additional steps if the problem does not appear to be resolved. However, a complaint to NASW against the supervisor would be premature, without knowing what steps the supervisor had taken in addition to restricting the clients served by Social Worker B.

Appendix:
Exam Plan with Index

Board of Behavioral Sciences
Licensed Clinical Social Worker
California Law and Ethics Examination Outline

The following document provides detailed information about the LCSW California Law and Ethics Examination, including a description of each content area, subarea and the associated task and knowledge statements. **Each question in the examination is linked to this content.**

Note: The exam outline, including all task and knowledge statements, comes from the BBS outline published online. Page numbers refer to where the relevant information can be found within this text.

I. Law (40%)

This area assesses the candidate's ability to identify and apply legal mandates to clinical social work practice.

IA. Confidentiality, Privilege, and Consent (14%)

Task Statement	*Knowledge Statement*	*Page*
T1. Comply with legal requirements regarding the maintenance/dissemination of confidential information to protect the client's privacy.	K1. Knowledge of laws regarding confidential communications within the therapeutic relationship.	37
	K2. Knowledge of laws regarding the disclosure of confidential information to other individuals, professionals, agencies, or authorities.	37
T2. Identify holder of privilege by evaluating client's age, legal status, and/or content of therapy to determine requirements for providing therapeutic services.	K3. Knowledge of laws regarding holder of privilege.	39
	K4. Knowledge of laws regarding privileged communication.	38
T3. Comply with legal requirements regarding the disclosure of privileged information to protect client's privacy in judicial/legal matters.	K4. Knowledge of laws regarding privileged communication.	38
	K5. Knowledge of laws regarding the release of privileged information.	39
	K6. Knowledge of legal requirements for responding to subpoenas and court orders.	39

Task Statement	*Knowledge Statement*	*Page*
T4. Comply with legal requirements regarding providing therapeutic services to minor clients.	K1. Knowledge of laws regarding confidential communications within the therapeutic relationship. K2. Knowledge of laws regarding the disclosure of confidential information to other individuals, professionals, agencies, or authorities. K3. Knowledge of laws regarding holder of privilege. K4. Knowledge of laws regarding privileged communication. K7. Knowledge of legal criteria and requirements for providing therapeutic services to minors.	37 37 39 38 40
T5. Maintain client records by adhering to legal requirements regarding documentation, storage, and disposal to protect the client's privacy and/or the therapeutic process.	K8. Knowledge of laws regarding documentation of therapeutic services. K9. Knowledge of laws pertaining to the maintenance/disposal of client records.	41 41
T6. Respond to requests for records by adhering to applicable laws and regulations to protect client's rights and/or safety.	K10. Knowledge of laws pertaining to client's access to treatment records. K11. Knowledge of laws pertaining to the release of client records to other individuals, professionals, or third parties.	41 42
T7. Provide services via information and communication technologies by complying with "telehealth" regulations.	K12. Knowledge of laws regarding the consent to and delivery of services via information and communication technologies.	43
T8. Comply with the Health Information Portability and Accountability Act (HIPAA) regulations as mandated by law.	K13. Knowledge of legal requirements of the Health Information Portability and Accountability Act (HIPAA).	44

IB. Limits to Confidentiality / Mandated Reporting (16%)

Task Statement	*Knowledge Statement*	*Page*
T9. Report known or suspected abuse, neglect, or exploitation of dependent adult client(s) to protective authorities.	K14. Knowledge of indicators of abuse, neglect, or exploitation of dependent adults.	57
	K15. Knowledge of laws pertaining to the reporting of known or suspected incidents of abuse, neglect, or exploitation of dependent adults.	55
T10. Report known or suspected abuse, neglect, or exploitation of elderly client(s) to protective authorities.	K16. Knowledge of indicators of abuse, neglect, or exploitation of elderly clients.	57
	K17. Knowledge of laws pertaining to the reporting of known or suspected incidents of abuse, neglect, or exploitation of elderly clients.	55
T11. Report known or suspected abuse or neglect of a child or adolescent to protective authorities.	K18. Knowledge of indicators of abuse/neglect of children and adolescents.	54
	K19. Knowledge of laws pertaining to the reporting of known or suspected incidents of abuse/neglect of children and adolescents.	51
T12. Comply with legal requirements regarding breaking confidentiality to protect the client in the presence of indictors of danger to self/others and/or grave disability.	K20. Knowledge of symptoms of mental impairment that may indicate the need for involuntary hospitalization.	58
	K21. Knowledge of protocols for initiating involuntary hospitalization.	59
	K22. Knowledge of laws regarding confidentiality in situations of client danger to self or others.	59

Task Statement	*Knowledge Statement*	*Page*
T13. Comply with legal requirements to report and protect when client expresses intent to cause harm to people or property.	K23. Knowledge of methods/criteria for identifying situations where client poses a danger to others.	60
	K24. Knowledge of laws pertaining to duty to protect when client indicates intent to cause harm.	61
	K25. Knowledge of situations/conditions that constitute reasonable indicators of client's intent to cause harm.	62
T14. Comply with legal requirements regarding privilege exceptions in client litigation or in response to breach of duty accusations.	K26. Knowledge of laws regarding privilege exceptions in litigation involving client's mental or emotional condition as raised by the client or client's representative.	62
	K27. Knowledge of laws regarding privilege exceptions where client alleges breach of duty.	62
T15. Comply with legal requirements regarding privilege exceptions in court-appointed and/or defendant-requested evaluation/therapy.	K28. Knowledge of laws regarding privilege exceptions in court-appointed evaluation or therapy.	62
	K29. Knowledge of laws pertaining to privilege exceptions in defendant-requested evaluation or therapy.	62
T16. Comply with legal requirements regarding reporting instances of crime perpetrated against minor clients.	K30. Knowledge of laws pertaining to the reporting of crimes perpetrated against a minor.	62
	K31. Knowledge of laws regarding privilege exceptions in crime or tort involving minors.	62

IC. Legal Standards for Professional Practice (10%)

Task Statement	*Knowledge Statement*	*Page*
T17. Comply with laws regarding sexual contact, conduct, and relations between therapist and client to prevent harm to the client and/or the therapeutic relationship.	K32. Knowledge of laws regarding sexual conduct between therapist and client.	69
	K33. Knowledge of legal requirements for providing client with the brochure *Professional Therapy Never Includes Sex*.	69
T18. Comply with legal parameters regarding scope of practice.	K34. Knowledge of laws that define the scope of clinical practice.	70
T19. Comply with legal parameters regarding professional conduct.	K35. Knowledge of laws that define professional conduct for licensed practitioners.	70
T20. Disclose fee structure prior to initiating therapeutic services.	K36. Knowledge of laws regarding disclosures required prior to initiating therapeutic services.	73
T21. Comply with legal regulations regarding providing treatment when interacting with third-party payers.	K37. Knowledge of laws and regulations regarding third-party reimbursement.	73
	K38. Knowledge of parity laws regarding the provision of mental health services.	74
T22. Comply with laws regarding advertisement of services and professional qualifications.	K39. Knowledge of laws regarding advertisement and dissemination of information of professional qualifications, education, and professional affiliations.	75
T23. Comply with laws pertaining to the payment or acceptance of money or other consideration for referrals.	K40. Knowledge of legal requirements regarding payment or acceptance of money or other considerations for referral of services.	76

II. Ethics (60%)

This area assesses the candidate's ability to identify and apply ethical standards for professional conduct.

IIA. Professional Competence and Preventing Harm (18%)

Task Statement	*Knowledge Statement*	*Page*
T24. Consult with other professionals and/or seek additional education, training, and/or supervision to address therapeutic issues that arise outside therapist's scope of competence.	K41. Knowledge of limitations of professional experience, education, and training to determine issues outside scope of competence.	81
	K42. Knowledge of situations that indicate a need for consultation with colleagues or other professionals.	81
	K43. Knowledge of ethical standards regarding the protection of client rights when engaging in consultation/collaboration with other professionals.	82
	K44. Knowledge of ethical methods of developing additional areas of practice or expanding competence.	82
	K45. Knowledge of the ethical responsibility to remain current on developments in the profession.	83
T25. Consult with other professionals to address questions regarding ethical obligations or practice responsibilities that arise during treatment.	K42. Knowledge of situations that indicate a need for consultation with colleagues or other professionals.	81
	K43. Knowledge of ethical standards regarding the protection of client rights when engaging in consultation/collaboration with other professionals.	82

Task Statement	*Knowledge Statement*	*Page*
T26. Evaluate therapist's own mental, emotional, or physical problems/impairments to determine impact on ability to provide competent therapeutic services.	K42. Knowledge of situations that indicate a need for consultation with colleagues or other professionals.	81
	K46. Knowledge of problems/impairments that interfere with the process of providing therapeutic services.	83
	K47. Knowledge of referrals and resources to assist in meeting the needs of clients.	84
	K48. Knowledge of methods to facilitate transfer when referrals to other professionals are made.	84
T27. Provide referral(s) to qualified professionals when adjunctive/alternate treatment would benefit the client.	K41. Knowledge of limitations of professional experience, education, and training to determine issues outside scope of competence.	81
	K43. Knowledge of ethical standards regarding the protection of client rights when engaging in consultation/collaboration with other professionals.	82
	K47. Knowledge of referrals and resources to assist in meeting the needs of clients.	84
	K48. Knowledge of methods to facilitate transfer when referrals to other professionals are made.	84
	K49. Knowledge of methods for collaborating with client to determine if referral(s) or other resources are clinically indicated.	82
T28. Manage therapist's personal values, attitudes, and/or beliefs to prevent interference with effective provision of therapeutic services and/or the therapeutic relationship.	K50. Knowledge of the potential impact of therapist's personal values, attitudes, and/or beliefs on the therapeutic relationship.	84
	K51. Knowledge of methods for managing the impact of therapist's personal values, attitudes, and/or beliefs on the client or the therapeutic relationship.	85

Task Statement	*Knowledge Statement*	*Page*
T29. Evaluate potential conflict of interest situations to determine the impact on the client or the therapeutic process.	K52. Knowledge of conditions/situations that could potentially exploit or cause harm to the client.	87
	K53. Knowledge of methods for managing boundaries and/or professional relationships with the client.	86
	K54. Knowledge of ethical standards regarding protecting the client's wellbeing in potential conflict of interest situations.	87
T30. Maintain professional boundaries with client to prevent situations or relationships that adversely impact the provision of therapeutic services.	K52. Knowledge of conditions/situations that could potentially exploit or cause harm to the client.	87
	K53. Knowledge of methods for managing boundaries and/or professional relationships with the client.	86
	K55. Knowledge of relationships that can be potentially detrimental to the client and/or therapeutic relationship.	88
	K56. Knowledge of methods to prevent impairment to clinical judgment and/or harm to the client in situations where multiple relationships are unavoidable.	88
T31. Adhere to ethical guidelines regarding sexual activity or contact with prospective, current, or former clients and/or those with whom the client has a personal relationship to avoid causing harm or exploitation of the client.	K57. Knowledge of the potential for client harm or exploitation associated with sexual activity or contact between therapist and client.	88
	K58. Knowledge of ethical standards regarding engaging in sexual activity or contact with client and/or others with whom the client has/had a personal relationship.	89
	K59. Knowledge of ethical standards regarding entering into a therapeutic relationship with former sexual partners.	90

IIB. Therapeutic Relationship/Services (27%)

Task Statement	*Knowledge Statement*	*Page*
T32. Obtain informed consent by providing client with information regarding the therapist and the treatment process to facilitate client's ability to make decisions.	K60. Knowledge of the ethical responsibility to provide client with information regarding the therapeutic process.	95
	K61. Knowledge of disclosures that facilitate client's ability to make informed decisions regarding treatment.	95
	K62. Knowledge of client's right to self-determination in making decisions regarding therapeutic services received.	96
	K63. Knowledge of methods for communicating information pertaining to informed consent in a manner consistent with developmental and cultural factors.	96
	K64. Knowledge of the right and responsibility of legal guardian/ representative to make decisions on behalf of clients unable to make informed decisions.	97
	K65. Knowledge of methods for protecting client's welfare when client is unable to provide voluntary consent.	97
T33. Evaluate for current relationships with other service providers to determine impact of entering into a relationship with a new service provider.	K66. Knowledge of the effects of concurrent mental health treatments on the provision of therapeutic services.	98
	K67. Knowledge of methods for establishing collaborative professional relationships to improve the welfare of the client.	98
	K68. Knowledge of ethical standards regarding the protection of client rights when engaging in consultation/collaboration with other professionals.	99

Task Statement	*Knowledge Statement*	*Page*
T34. Address confidentiality and/or therapeutic issues associated with therapist's role, treatment modality, and involvement of third parties to protect the client's rights and/or the therapeutic relationship.	K69. Knowledge of methods for identifying the "client" and the nature of relationships when providing therapeutic services to more than one person.	100
	K70. Knowledge of the impact of client unit, treatment modality, and involvement of multiple systems on confidentiality.	101
	K71. Knowledge of the factors that impact the therapeutic relationship.	101
	K72. Knowledge of methods for managing confidentiality and privacy issues when providing concurrent therapy.	101
	K73. Knowledge of methods for managing confidentiality and privacy issues when treatment involves multiple systems or third parties.	102
T35. Manage the impact of confidentiality/limits of confidentiality on the therapeutic relationship by discussing with the client issues/implications that arise during the therapeutic process.	K74. Knowledge of ethical standards regarding the management of confidentiality issues that arise in the therapeutic process.	102
	K75. Knowledge of methods for managing the impact of confidentiality issues on the therapeutic relationship.	102
T36. Manage the impact of safety and/or crisis situations by evaluating risk factors to protect the client/others.	K76. Knowledge of methods for assessing level of potential danger or harm to client or others.	103
	K77. Knowledge of ethical obligations regarding the management of safety needs.	103
	K78. Knowledge of methods and procedures for managing safety needs.	104

Task Statement	*Knowledge Statement*	*Page*
T37. Manage the impact of legal and ethical obligations that arise during the therapeutic process to protect the client/therapist relationship.	K79. Knowledge of the impact of legal and ethical obligations on the therapeutic relationship.	105
	K80. Knowledge of methods for protecting the best interest of the client in situations where legal and ethical obligations conflict.	106
	K81. Knowledge of methods for protecting the best interest of the client in situations where agency and ethical obligations conflict.	106
T38. Manage diversity factors in the therapeutic relationship by applying and/or gaining knowledge and awareness necessary to provide services sensitive to client needs.	K82. Knowledge of diversity factors that potentially impact the therapeutic process.	107
	K83. Knowledge of ethical standards regarding nondiscrimination.	106
	K84. Knowledge of ethical standards for providing therapeutic services congruent with client diversity.	108
	K85. Knowledge of methods to gain knowledge, awareness, sensitivity, and skills necessary for working with clients from diverse populations.	108
T39. Provide treatment that respects the client's inherent dignity and right to self-determination.	K86. Knowledge of the collaborative role between therapist and client in the therapeutic process.	108
	K87. Knowledge of the client's right to make decisions regarding therapeutic services.	109
	K88. Knowledge of methods to assist client to make decisions and clarify goals.	109
T40. Contribute to multidisciplinary team by collaborating with colleagues/other professionals to provide services that promote the wellbeing of the client.	K43. Knowledge of ethical standards regarding the protection of client rights when engaging in consultation/collaboration with other professionals.	82
	K89. Knowledge of methods for establishing collaborative professional relationships to improve welfare of the client.	110
	K90. Knowledge of ethical standards for participating as a member of an interdisciplinary team.	110

Task Statement	*Knowledge Statement*	*Page*
T41. Advocate with and/or on behalf of the client by addressing barriers and/or increasing access to assist client in receiving services.	K91. Knowledge of methods for evaluating client's capacity to advocate on own behalf.	111
	K92. Knowledge of ethical standards pertaining to interacting with third-party payers.	111
	K93. Knowledge of ethical standards pertaining to interacting with other service delivery systems.	111
	K94. Knowledge of methods for enhancing client's ability to meet own needs.	112
T42. Maintain practice procedures that provide for consistent care in the event therapeutic services must be interrupted or discontinued.	K95. Knowledge of ethical considerations and conditions for interrupting or terminating therapeutic services.	112
	K96. Knowledge of referrals/resources to provide consistent care in the event therapeutic services must be interrupted or discontinued.	113
	K97. Knowledge of methods to facilitate transfer when referrals to other professionals are made.	114
T43. Terminate therapeutic services when no longer required or no longer benefits the client.	K98. Knowledge of factors and/or conditions that indicate client is ready for termination of therapeutic services.	114
	K99. Knowledge of factors and/or conditions that indicate client is not benefiting from treatment.	115
	K100. Knowledge of methods for managing the termination process.	115
	K101. Knowledge of methods to prevent client abandonment and/or client neglect.	115

IIC. Business Practices and Policies (15%)

Task Statement	*Knowledge Statement*	*Page*
T44. Advertise services by adhering to ethical guidelines regarding the use of accurate representations and information to promote services and/or expand practice.	K102. Knowledge of ethical guidelines regarding the use of accurate representation of qualifications and credentials in advertisements and/or solicitation of clients.	121
	K103. Knowledge of ethical guidelines pertaining to the solicitation of testimonials or statements from clients or others.	121
	K104. Knowledge of ethical guidelines regarding the recruitment of clients through employment and/or professional associations.	122
T45. Maintain client records by adhering to ethical guidelines to document services and/or protect the client's confidentiality.	K105. Knowledge of ethical guidelines regarding the documentation of therapeutic services consistent with sound clinical practice.	122
	K106. Knowledge of methods for providing reasonable protection of the confidentiality of client records.	123
	K107. Knowledge of ethical guidelines for releasing client records upon request.	123
	K108. Knowledge of methods to assist client understand/interpret information contained in therapeutic records.	124
T46. Clarify role(s) when acting in a professional capacity other than licensed clinical social worker to avoid confusion and/or inaccurate representation of qualifications.	K109. Knowledge of the ethical responsibility to clarify roles when acting in a professional capacity other than licensed clinical social worker.	124
	K110. Knowledge of ethical guidelines regarding engaging in conflicting and/or dual roles.	125

Task Statement	*Knowledge Statement*	*Page*
T47. Implement policies/procedures that address ethical issues associated with the use of electronic media and technology in the course of providing services.	K111. Knowledge of the potential for harm to the client or therapeutic relationship with the use of electronic media in the therapeutic process.	125
	K112. Knowledge of ethical standards for implementing electronic media in the therapeutic process.	126
	K113. Knowledge of the limits and risks associated with electronic means of service delivery.	126
T48. Maintain fee/payment policies that are commensurate with services provided and protect the therapeutic relationship.	K114. Knowledge of methods and conditions for determining fees commensurate with professional services.	127
	K115. Knowledge of prohibited business practices/forms of remuneration for making/accepting client referrals.	127
	K116. Knowledge of the potential for client exploitation or harm that may result from bartering/exchanges for services.	127
	K117. Knowledge of ethical standards pertaining to the collection of unpaid balances.	128
	K118. Knowledge of ethical obligations regarding providing for continuation of treatment to the client.	128
	K119. Knowledge of ethical guidelines regarding the provision of therapeutic services when interacting with third-party payers.	129
	K47. Knowledge of referrals and resources to assist in meeting the needs of clients.	84

Task Statement	*Knowledge Statement*	*Page*
T49. Adhere to ethical guidelines regarding the acceptance of gifts and/or tokens of appreciation from clients.	K120. Knowledge of conditions/situations that may interfere with professional judgment or have a detrimental effect on the provision of therapeutic services.	129
	K121. Knowledge of ethical standards regarding the acceptance of gifts from clients.	129
T50. Adhere to ethical guidelines for protecting the welfare and dignity of research participants when conducting research related to the provision of therapeutic services.	K122. Knowledge of procedures to safeguard participants when conducting research projects.	130
	K123. Knowledge of disclosures required to inform participants of the nature and role of research projects.	130
	K124. Knowledge of client's rights regarding participation in research projects.	130
	K125. Knowledge of methods for protecting client confidentiality and data when conducting research projects.	131
T51. Address unethical or incompetent conduct of colleague by taking action to promote the welfare and interests of clients.	K126. Knowledge of conditions/situations that may impair the integrity or efficacy of the therapeutic process.	131
	K127. Knowledge of guidelines for addressing unethical or incompetent conduct of colleagues.	131
T52. Adhere to ethical guidelines for engaging in the supervisor/ prelicensure practitioner relationship.	K128. Knowledge of the ethical guidelines governing the supervisor/ prelicensure practitioner relationship and responsibilities.	132